GLOBALIZING CONFEDERATION

Canada and the World in 1867

Edited by Jacqueline D. Krikorian, Marcel Martel, and Adrian Shubert

Globalizing Confederation brings together original research from 17 scholars to provide an international perspective on Canada's Confederation in 1867. In seeking to ascertain how others understood, constructed, or considered the changes taking place in British North America, *Globalizing Confederation* unpacks a range of viewpoints, including those from foreign governments, British colonies, and Indigenous peoples.

Exploring perspectives from the Austro-Hungarian Empire, France, Latin America, New Zealand, and the Vatican, among others, as well as considering the impact of Confederation on the rights of Indigenous peoples during this period, the contributors to this collection present how Canada's Confederation captured the imaginations of people around the world in the 1860s. *Globalizing Confederation* reveals how some viewed the 1867 changes to Canada as part of a reorganization of the British Empire, while others contextualized it in the literature on colonization more broadly, while still others framed the event as part of a realignment or power shift among the Spanish, French, and British empires. While many states showed interest in the Confederation debates, others, such as South Africa and the West Indies, expressed little interest in the establishment of Canada until it had profound effects on their corners of the global political landscape.

JACQUELINE D. KRIKORIAN is an associate professor in the Department of Political Science at York University.

MARCEL MARTEL is a professor of Canadian History at York University and Avie Bennett Historica Canada Chair in Canadian History.

ADRIAN SHUBERT is a professor in the Department of History at York University.

Globalizing Confederation

Canada and the World in 1867

EDITED BY JACQUELINE D. KRIKORIAN,
MARCEL MARTEL, AND ADRIAN SHUBERT

UNIVERSITY OF TORONTO PRESS
Toronto Buffalo London

© University of Toronto Press 2017
Toronto Buffalo London
www.utorontopress.com

ISBN 978-1-4875-0229-4 (cloth)   ISBN 978-1-4875-2190-5 (paper)

___

Library and Archives Canada Cataloguing in Publication

Globalizing confederation : Canada and the world in 1867 /
edited by Jacqueline D. Krikorian, Marcel Martel, and Adrian Shubert.

Includes bibliographical references and index.
ISBN 978-1-4875-0229-4 (cloth). – ISBN 978-1-4875-2190-5 (paper)

1. Canada – History – 1867–. 2. Canada – Foreign public opinion.
I. Krikorian, Jacqueline, 1965–, editor II. Martel, Marcel, 1965–, editor
III. Shubert, Adrian, 1953–, editor

FC500.G56 2017   971.05   C2017-905006-0

___

University of Toronto Press acknowledges the financial assistance to its
publishing program of the Canada Council for the Arts and the Ontario
Arts Council, an agency of the Government of Ontario.

 Canada Council   Conseil des Arts
for the Arts   du Canada

Funded by the   Financé par le
Government   gouvernement
of Canada   du Canada

Contents

Introduction: Canada and the World in 1867 3
JACQUELINE D. KRIKORIAN, MARCEL MARTEL,
AND ADRIAN SHUBERT

Part One: Perspectives from the Americas

1 Confederation Unknown? Latin American Views on
   the Emergence of Canada in 1867 27
   CARSTEN-ANDREAS SCHULZ

2 The 1867 Union of the British North American Colonies:
   A View from the United States 47
   JACQUELINE D. KRIKORIAN AND DAVID R. CAMERON

3 "Such Bastard Despotism": Fenian Views of Canadian
   Confederation 61
   WILLIAM JENKINS

4 Confederation Comes at a Cost: Indigenous Peoples and the
   Ongoing Reality of Colonialism in Canada 79
   GABRIELLE SLOWEY

Part Two: Perspectives from Europe

5 The View from the Quirinal: The Holy See and
  Confederation 97
  ROBERTO PERIN

6 Model and Anomaly: The Canadian Confederation Seen from
  France, 1864–1871 110
  ALBAN BARGAIN-VILLÉGER

7 *War Was?* Habsburg Perspectives on Canadian Federation 127
  BENNO GAMMERL

8 Canadian Lessons, Roads Not Taken: Spanish Views on
  Confederation 143
  JOSEP MARÍA FRADERA

Part Three: Perspectives from Britain and the Empire

9 British Views of Canada at the Time of Confederation 161
  EDWARD BEASLEY

10 The Impact of Canadian Confederation in Ireland 178
   THOMAS MOHR

11 Distant Relations: Australian Perspectives on
   Canadian Federation 194
   ANN CURTHOYS

12 The Delinquent Colony: The New Zealand Press and Canadian
   Confederation 210
   KENTON STOREY

13 "The Word Is Steeped in Blood and Violence": Canadian-Style
   Federation in Southern Africa 226
   TIMOTHY STAPLETON

14 The Federation Idea in the British West Indies and Canadian Confederation   242
FRANKLIN W. KNIGHT

Contributors   257

Index   261

GLOBALIZING CONFEDERATION

Canada and the World in 1867

Introduction: Canada and the World in 1867

JACQUELINE D. KRIKORIAN,
MARCEL MARTEL, AND ADRIAN SHUBERT

On 1 July 1867, in the window of his residence, the Archbishop of Halifax left a short note for Nova Scotians. The road to Confederation had been a bruising one, as many of them were opposed to the unification of the British North American colonies. Archbishop Thomas-Louis Connolly wanted to assure not only his parishioners but also the local residents that the 1867 project was a worthy one. The placard's message, however, was unusual in the sense that it framed the Confederation debate – which had focused on local issues to the exclusion of almost all others – in a larger global context: "To-day UNION MAKES A DOMINION OF A PROVINCE; DIGNIFIES OUR MANHOOD; EXPANDS OUR SYMPATHY; LINKS US WITH THIRTY-FIVE HUNDRED THOUSAND FELLOW-SUBJECTS IN OUR OWN LAND; AND FIFTY MILLIONS OF HUMAN BEINGS NORTH OF PANAMA. GOD SAVE THE QUEEN."[1]

Connolly was appealing to residents, particularly those who had opposed the new arrangements, to move away from narrowly thinking about what Nova Scotia had won or lost in the agreement. He was calling on them to envision Confederation in broader terms, as part of a larger shift in governance that would affect human relations in a continental, if not a global, sense. Progress required change, and he wanted Nova Scotians to think about the benefits of the 1867 project on a grander scale than they had previously envisaged.

Connolly's message was unusual, not only for 1867 but also for Confederation scholars. Traditionally, those interested in the establishment of Canada as a formative political event focus on the people, ideas, and issues that underpinned the union. Studies tend to emphasize matters and concerns specific to the Canadian experience or British North America in general. Several reoccurring themes are inherent in this body of work, including the attitudes of French Canada, the ideational underpinnings of the agreement, the perception of external threats to British North America, the influence of the political economy, and the role of political elites and colonial governments.

The exception to what some might view as a relatively introspective approach to studying the 1867 arrangements comes from scholars who focus on the Canada–United Kingdom relationship. These scholars ask why authorities in London agreed to changes between the imperial government and its North American colonies. For example, P.B. Waite[2] and Chester Martin[3] examined Confederation from the perspective of the Colonial Office; Ged Martin looked at it from the broader viewpoint of the British government;[4] and C.P. Stacey emphasized the perspective of the British military.[5]

In undertaking this project, we also were cognizant that as the colonies of Nova Scotia, New Brunswick, and Canada moved towards union in 1867, Indigenous peoples were being displaced and dispossessed of their lands. Principles pertaining to sovereignty and responsible government were recognized as significant for colonists but not for Indigenous peoples. They were not consulted, and their rights were not even considered. As Gabrielle Slowey demonstrates in her research included in this volume, "the Confederation project came at a cost for Indigenous peoples and their descendants" that has not been addressed even today.

Given that the 150th anniversary of Canada's Confederation is taking place in the twenty-first century – when our traditional approach to the study of history is being influenced and re-conceptualized by the forces of globalization – we began to wonder if anyone else noticed or was affected by the changes that took place on the North American continent in the 1860s. Did British colonists in other parts of the Empire monitor or even care about the transformative events in Nova Scotia, New Brunswick, Canada East, or Canada West? How did governments in Europe understand the reconfiguration of British North America? What was the view from the rest of the Americas? Were there any peoples or communities that were interested in the proposed Canadian project? In other words, did any nation or government other than the one in London care about what was happening in our little corner of the world?

This collection explores Confederation from the perspective of those "outside" the British North American colonies. It includes the viewpoints of foreign governments and other British colonies, as well as from London. It seeks to ascertain how others understood, constructed, or used the 1867 project as a model to be adapted or avoided. It looks at which ideas and events captured their imagination and which they tossed into the tired bin of history. The chapters presented here examine not only how others considered or ignored the transpiring events, but also how these events impacted them over the long term.

This book began as a series of papers that were delivered at a conference in September 2016 at York University. The conference was sponsored by the Avie Bennett Historica Canada Chair in Canadian History and was part of a larger initiative of interdisciplinary projects undertaken by the 150Canada@York committee in recognition of the country's sesquicentennial. Conference participants were invited because of their expertise on a range of foreign governments, colonial administrations, and imperial issues during the 1860s. We also invited experts on two communities significant to the 1867 project: North American Indigenous peoples, whose omission from the Confederation talks in the 1860s has had long-lasting implications for them, and Fenians, who, based in the United States, made invading the British North American colonies practically a sport in the 1860s. Not everyone we invited was able to accept our invitation, and, consequently, there were some perspectives, such as the Russian perspective on Confederation, which we hope will one day be addressed even if it cannot be included in this collection.

As a community of scholars, we found that some governments and colonies viewed the 1867 changes to Canada as part of a reorganization of the British Empire, some contextualized it in the literature on colonization more broadly, while still others framed the event as part of a realignment or power shift among the Spanish, French, and British empires. Others explained that there was little interest in the establishment of Canada in, for example, South Africa or the West Indies, but went on to demonstrate that it had profound effects on them at a later date. We expected countries such as France and the United States to be very engaged in the proposed Confederation project, and yet were surprised that it was of little significance to them. We also learned that some issues not usually explored in the Confederation debates (for example, slavery) are relevant to the lens of analysis others use. We also found some humour in noting that the global citizens of the 1860s enjoyed the same kind of media sensationalism that we do today. As one conference participant explained in his presentation, the Fenian invasions and the comings and goings of Maximilian's wife, the empress of Mexico, captured the imagination of Austro-Hungarians thinking about North America in the 1860s in a way that the 1867 Confederation project never did. Newspapers allowed people outside British North America to learn about the emergence of the Dominion of Canada, to imagine and re-envision its true nature, and to use this event as part of their local political landscape.

To provide some context to our collection, this introduction is divided into four sections. The first provides a short introduction to the ins and outs of the 1864–1867 process that led to the Confederation agreement: who were the main players and what were their concerns and perspectives? Next, we highlight how Indigenous peoples were excluded in the discussions leading up to the 1867 project. The establishment of Canada had tremendous implications for Indigenous peoples, but they were not consulted by either the local or imperial political elites. The third section examines how those politicians involved in the 1867 project were influenced by events, practices, and ideas in other countries. What factors in the international realm influenced the nature of Canada's Confederation? Lastly, we provide a brief explanation of how the chapters in this book are organized.

Confederation, 1867

In 1867, there was considerable enthusiasm for the Confederation project, particularly among the political and commercial elite. The Dominion of Canada was seen as a real achievement that would put past disputes to rest and ensure economic prosperity across all regions and westward to the Pacific. While pockets of opposition existed, especially in Nova Scotia,[6] there was an overall sense of optimism about the new arrangements, which was reflected in the press. *Le Journal de Québec* heralded Confederation as a "magnificent celebration,"[7] while the Montreal *Gazette* said it marked not only "an epoch in the political history of America" but also "of mankind."[8] The *Halifax Evening Express* echoed this enthusiasm, explaining that the new Dominion "must fill the heart of every true man with feelings of the deepest gratitude and pride."[9] The *New Brunswick Reporter* noted that "with bright prospects, commercial and political, we can look forward to a good time coming," despite some of the earlier disagreements that existed about the new arrangements.[10] The *Saint John Globe* of New Brunswick, on the other hand, was relatively sanguine and highlighted the opposition in more candid terms. It expressed its "most sincere wishes for the success of the new form of Government in which so many of our people are dragged to-day against their judgment," and it promised "to check the extravagance and recklessness now so prevalent, and which have so closely attended the progress of Confederation up to this date."[11]

Discussions pertaining to Confederation began in earnest in September 1864 when the delegates from the province of Canada (made up of Canada East and Canada West) arrived in Charlottetown to meet with leading Maritime politicians already considering a union of Nova Scotia, Prince Edward Island, and New Brunswick. John A. Macdonald (Attorney General Canada West), George-Étienne Cartier (Attorney General Canada East), and their Canadian political brethren met with Premier Samuel Leonard Tilley (New Brunswick), Premier Charles Tupper (Nova Scotia), Premier John Hamilton Gray (Prince Edward Island), and their respective delegations to consider unifying the colonies across British North America. An agreement was reached to continue the talks in Quebec City in October 1864. Representatives from Newfoundland who were not able to attend the Charlottetown Conference were also invited to join in at that time.

The Quebec Conference produced seventy-two resolutions that provided an agreed-upon set of priorities, principles, and procedures to unite British North America. With the support of the imperial government in London, these resolutions eventually formed the basis of the *British North America Act, 1867*,[12] which merged three British North American colonies – Nova Scotia, New Brunswick, and Canada – into one political system. Manitoba (1870), British Columbia (1871), and Prince Edward Island (1873) joined shortly thereafter. Newfoundland would delay until 1949.

The political leadership in Nova Scotia and New Brunswick supported the unification of the British North American colonies. Commerce and defence was their song. Tilley emphasized the importance of securing "intercolonial free trade" and the establishment of a railroad linking their markets.[13] He also emphasized the need for an arrangement that would be "equitable" for each of these provinces.[14] Key to the equity issue was the payment of provincial debts by the general government.

Defence was an equally important consideration for the two Maritime provinces. Both Tilley and Tupper repeatedly highlighted the American threat. With the end of the Civil War, there was a real fear the Union forces would retaliate against British North America for "sympathies" expressed by Great Britain for the South. As Tupper explained in the fall of 1864, the British colonies were in a "disunited state.

They were weak and defenceless, living at the threshold, and it might be, at the mercy of a great military nation."[15] For both Maritime leaders, Confederation would remedy this problem and facilitate "the maintenance of peaceful relations."[16]

In Canada, debates on Confederation also involved general concerns about defence, the economy, and the railroad. But a significant focus was placed on the protection of linguistic and religious minorities. To address this issue, the seventy-two resolutions accorded the provincial governments exclusive legislative jurisdiction in matters affecting the rights of the French majority in Quebec, the English minority in Quebec, and the French minority in Ontario. Accordingly, the provincial governments would have autonomy in the areas of "property and civil rights,"[17] "all matters of a private or local nature,"[18] hospitals and asylums,[19] and education, "saving the rights and privileges which the Protestant or Catholic minority in both Canadas may possess as to their Denominational Schools, at the time when the Union goes into operation."[20]

Cartier referred to the proposed Confederation as a "momentous occasion"[21] and emphasized there "could be no danger to the rights and privileges of either French Canadians, Scotchmen, Englishmen or Irishmen." As the federal parliament was tasked with issues of general interest such as commerce, "no one could apprehend that anything could be enacted which would harm or do injustice to persons of any nationality."[22]

At the same time, Macdonald, representing Canada West, highlighted the establishment of a great nation emerging across the continent. He pointed out that the power of government would be concentrated at the centre. For him, centralization was important because it would be in contradistinction to the 1776 union of the "thirteen individual sovereignties" south of the border and would ensure "a strong and lasting government under which we can work out constitutional liberty as opposed to democracy."[23]

However, neither the newspapers nor the leading statesmen recognized the rights or interests outside the anglophone and francophone communities in any meaningful way. Immigrants who didn't speak French or English as a first language, communities of non-Christian faiths, and Indigenous peoples were rarely, if ever, considered during this process. As David Koffman has observed, "The Fathers protected just two of the three groups we now consider to be the 'founding peoples' of this country, Protestants and Roman Catholics, each in the other's domain." Indigenous peoples "were entirely elided."[24] Even on those rare occasions when "others" were recognized in the Confederation discussion, it was often in less than favourable terms.[25]

Canada's Confederation and Indigenous Peoples

Although British North American colonists were not directly consulted about the move towards Confederation except in New Brunswick, the elected members of their respective colonial legislatures represented them. Granted there were limitations on who had the vote, but British North Americans at least had some input – even indirectly – into the 1867 project.

Indigenous peoples, however, were completely shut out of the process. Their representatives were not invited to participate in the debates on Confederation. Although the 1857 *Act to Encourage the Gradual Civilization of the Indian Tribes in this Province* [Canada] was designed to give Indigenous men "of good moral character" land, the right to vote, and "Indian status," it was rejected by Indigenous peoples as they "correctly saw the measure as an attempt to destroy First Nations communities and their way of life."[26] Even consultation indirectly through representation in the legislature was not available to them.

Following the successful passage of the *British North America Act, 1867* by the imperial parliament in London, the federal government received exclusive jurisdiction over "Indians, and Lands reserved for the Indians."[27] But Indigenous peoples continued to be framed as "savages" who needed to be "civilized" in order for society to advance through commerce, industry, and agricultural. As John MacMullen explained in his 1868 *The History of Canada*, "Canada must ere long attain to a high position in the scale of nations, and thus leave little room for regret that the possession of her soil has been transferred to the Anglo-Saxon race, and that the rule of the fierce Indian has for ever passed away."[28]

In its pursuit of assimilation, the federal government signed eleven treaties with Indigenous peoples between 1871 and 1921, facilitating the settlement of the west and moving Indigenous peoples to clearly delineated reserves. In 1876, Canada introduced the *Indian Act*, a legal framework that limited Indigenous capacity for self-government by granting federal appointees called Indian agents "broad powers to shape individual lives, exert political control over Aboriginal affairs, and apply sanctions to those who dared to defy their authority."[29] Indigenous children were compelled to attend residential schools, institutions run by Catholic and Protestant religious groups, which were mandated to further the assimilation project by destroying Indigenous cultures and languages. This policy and the federal paternalism embodied in the *Indian Act* are prime examples of an active policy of cultural genocide, as recently documented by the Truth and Reconciliation Commission of Canada.

Consideration of Global Issues and Events

Relatively few records were kept concerning the Confederation debates that took place at the Charlottetown and Quebec City conferences. However New Zealand and the United States were on the minds of the Fathers of Confederation. Although the future constitution of Canada was influenced by the *New Zealand Constitutional Act* of 1853–4, the Fathers of Confederation attributed the general power of "peace, order and good government" only to the federal government. Unlike New Zealand, the federal government in Canada would have greater powers than the provinces, and the governor-general-in-council would have the power to disallow and reserve provincial legislation. In terms of the United States, several Fathers of Confederation agreed that it would not be wise to follow the US example, as they judged the American federal government to be too weak.[30]

The legislatures of Canada, New Brunswick, Nova Scotia, and Prince Edward Island, comprised of both an assembly and a legislative council, kept detailed records of their debates on Confederation. These records show that both supporters and opponents of the Confederation project devoted considerable time to a range of difficult political issues, such as the creation of an economic union, the composition of the Senate and the House of Commons, and the division of legislative powers between the provinces and the federal government. Politicians from Quebec and the east coast colonies ruled out a legislative union. They also were divided over the potential benefits that the new Dominion of Canada would offer. For example, there was uncertainty as to whether the acquisition of the Northwest Territories (which was then under the control of the Hudson's Bay Company) would be of real value, as it would be open to both immigrant and native-born settlers alike.

For Nova Scotia, the fear of becoming "dependent" on Canada in a new colonial order dominated the debates, and several politicians challenged the government to submit their constitutional package to the people. William Annand wondered what good this deal would have for Nova Scotia since "we are asked to be united to a country which is frozen up five months in the year, which has no trade to offer us of which we cannot avail ourselves now."³¹ For their part, politicians in New Brunswick questioned the merits of developing economic and political ties with Canada, a colony that was far away and would dominate the new political institutions because of its demographic might. Politicians in Prince Edward Island worried that their political voice would be lost in the new constitutional arrangement and believed that the new Dominion offered no economic benefits for the island and did not resolve the land issue. If some members of the Canadian legislative assembly congratulated their peers for resolving their differences at the Charlottetown and Quebec conferences and for setting the new Dominion on a new and promising path, others questioned the overall merits of the constitutional deal. At the same time, they cast the world as a witness to what was being accomplished.

The Confederation process took place at the same time as a number of important developments elsewhere in the world. In Europe, two major new states, Italy and Germany, were created between 1860 and 1871. The Kingdom of Piedmont swallowed up the Habsburg domains in northern Italy, the Kingdom of the Two Sicilies, and the Papal States (the extensive territorial domains of the Pope in central Italy). Then, in 1870, this new Kingdom of Italy took control of the city of Rome. In response, Pope Pius IX declared himself to be the "prisoner of the Vatican."³²

Turning the Kingdom of Prussia into the heart of a new German Empire required three wars: against Denmark in 1864, the Habsburg Empire in 1866, and France in 1870. Shortly before Canada's Confederation, the Austro-Hungarian Compromise (*Ausgleich*) converted the venerable Habsburg Empire into the Dual Monarchy of Austria and Hungary. Shortly thereafter, Spain was shaken by a revolution that toppled its Queen and by an uprising in its valuable Cuban colony, which would result in ten years of unrest. Closer to home, between 1861 and 1865, the United States was engulfed in its bloody Civil War, while in Mexico, Maximilian, the brother of Franz Joseph of Austria-Hungary, who had been made emperor with the backing of Napoleon III, was executed on 19 June 1867 after a three-year war. In 1870, the Franco-Prussian War would bring down the French emperor, trigger a revolution in Paris – the Commune – and lead to the creation of the Third Republic.

While debating the merits of Confederation, politicians made occasional references to these and other world events. In the parliamentary debates in Canada, New Brunswick, Nova Scotia, and Prince Edward Island, the United States was often cited as a reference. Some New Brunswick and Canadian politicians saw it as an example of an overly decentralized federal system. They urged elected officials to vote for a new constitutional arrangement with a stronger federal power.[33] On the other hand, for some New Brunswick and Prince Edward Island politicians, the United States' constitution was an inspiration, especially because it allocated two Senate seats to each state regardless of the size of their population.[34]

Notwithstanding their views on Confederation, many politicians believed that their southern neighbour was a military threat with considerable territorial ambitions. The Fenian invasions were viewed as evidence that Americans would support future military action against British North America. George Brown put the issue of defending the new Dominion in a larger context. For him, the colonists had to take on "a share of the burden of defence," as the imperial government now expected its colonies to assume at least some of the costs of defending the British Empire.[35] There were those politicians in Nova Scotia, however, who viewed the "threat of an invasion" as part of a plot to force Confederation down their throats. Others believed the United States would not annex the British North American colonies as long as they remained part of the British Empire.[36]

Unlike their counterparts in New Brunswick, Nova Scotia, and Prince Edward Island, politicians in the Canadian parliament debating the merits and weaknesses of Confederation focused on parallels and contrasts to European societies in the Old World and the Americas.[37] They contextualized the emergence of their new nation within the larger global arena. Their arguments can be assembled under three broad topics: achieving an internal reorganization of the British North American colonies without bloodshed, debating the merits of Confederation as the most suitable form of governance for humankind, and engaging in discussions regarding the importance and role of democracy in the new federal institutions.

Proponents of Confederation insisted that the most astonishing aspect of Confederation was that not one single drop of blood was being shed in its accomplishment. British North Americans did not have to wage war to achieve political unity. Certainly, George Brown, a Father of Confederation himself, was not modest in assessing what he and his colleagues were able to accomplish in 1864. Although the British North American colonies were diverse in terms of ethnicity, language, and religion, he argued, politicians were able to reconcile these realities through peaceful means while other parts of the world, confronted with similar challenges, resorted to revolution and armed conflict.

> We are striving to do peacefully and satisfactorily what Holland and Belgium, after years of strife, were unable to accomplish. We are seeking by calm discussion to settle questions that Austria and Hungary, that Denmark and Germany, that Russia and Poland, could only crush by the iron heel of armed force. We are seeking to do without foreign intervention that which deluged in blood the sunny plains of Italy. We are striving to settle forever issues hardly less momentous than those that have rent the neighboring republic and are now exposing it to all the horrors of civil war. (Hear, hear.) Have we not then, Mr. SPEAKER, great cause of thankfulness that we have found a better way for the solution of our troubles than that which has entailed on other countries such deplorable results?[38]

George-Étienne Cartier, leader of the Bleu or conservative forces in Quebec, reminded his counterparts that colonists were able to double the size of their population without strife, in distinct contrast to bellicose France. Although Napoleon III, argued Cartier, had become a major player on the European scene, he did it only "after great expenditure of blood and treasure," which led to the incorporation of Savoy and Nice and "an addition of nearly one million inhabitants to France."[39]

Supporters of the unification of the British North American colonies believed that a united Dominion of Canada could almost stand shoulder to shoulder with other world powers. To quote a proponent, Fergusson Blair, Confederation "would also improve our position in the eyes of our neighbors in France and other nations."[40] For some, the economic potential of the new Dominion was unquestionable. The size of its commercial navy ranked Canada among the top three or four world powers, behind Britain, the United States, and France.[41] As another intervener in the debate pointed out, taxation would be lower than in England or France.[42] Some even predicted that as a result of Confederation, trade would resume where it had ceased to exist in past decades, as in the case of the Maritimes and the West Indies.[43]

Because of its land mass, supporters argued that the new Dominion would compete with major imperial powers: "as the Russian Empire extends its powerful sway from the Black Sea to the polar regions, so may the people of British North America aspire to raise up a great Northern Power upon this continent."[44] Through the acquisition of the Northwest Territories, the Dominion would triple in size, prompting Henri-Gustave Joly de Lotbinière, an opponent from Quebec who belonged to the moderate liberal group, to respond. Joly de Lotbinière spoke for an entire day on the Confederation issue, and his remarks were reprinted in a pamphlet. He compared Canada to a child forced to grow before its time:

> [T]he vastness of territory in which [so many] take so much pride is precisely what inspires me with uneasiness; we shall have the outward form of a giant, with the strength of a child; we shall be unable to stand up. Hasty and premature growth is as fatal to states as it is to men; a state should extend its limits only in proportion as its strength increases.[45]

Several supporters argued that Confederation as a political system was a natural outcome, since most people were living under some sort of federated structure of government, often quite loosely defined. Without hesitation, Thomas D'Arcy McGee observed – incorrectly – that Spain and the British Isles operated with federal systems, and even "the old French dukedoms were confederated in the States General."[46] For his part, Joseph-Godéric Blanchet described federalism as a transitional political structure, since it allowed different "races of people" to cohabit and over time become united, as in the case of Belgium, France, Spain, and other European countries.[47] Surprisingly, these advocates of federalism did not mention the one existing federal state in Europe: Switzerland.

If opponents of Confederation were silent on the issue of achieving constitutional reform without bloodshed, they nonetheless challenged proponents of the idea that federalism was the most suitable form of government. They also disputed the idea that federalism was a natural or ideal system of government. Why, asked Antoine-Aimé Dorion, the leader of the Rouges, impose on French Canada a political structure that it does not want? Referring to the Belgian revolution against the Kingdom of Holland in 1830, this resolute opponent of Confederation reminded legislators that the people of Belgium "rose *en masse* to protest against that union, and to assert their separate nationality."[48] But it was Joly de Lotbinière who lectured on the "disastrous fate awaiting all Confederations."[49] According to historian Jack Little, Joly de Lotbinière offered a "distinctive" speech because of his "erudition, with copious references to political philosophy and history."[50] For example, he gave a long list of failed experiments, including Greece, the Seven

United Provinces of the Netherlands, and even Switzerland, the latter held together only because France, Prussia, and Austria were "deeply interested in maintaining [its] existence."⁵¹ Turning his attention to the Americas, Joly de Lotbinière argued that the New World experiments with Confederation had also failed, and he gave the example of the Republic of Guatemala and its former constituent countries, which were now the independent nations of Costa Rica, Guatemala, Honduras, Nicaragua, and San Salvador. A new attempt, the Confederation of the United States of South America, which included New Grenada, Venezuela, and Ecuador, was also doomed to fail since, according to his source – the recent annual political journal *Annuaire des Deux Mondes* – the general condition in Venezuela in 1853–4 was "insurrection," and a state of "civil war" prevailed in New Grenada.⁵²

To emphasize his point, Joly de Lotbinière referred to the United States, portraying the republic as the prime example of political instability since "civil war" had prevailed in recent years.⁵³ In his view, attempts at Confederation had failed everywhere because the central power was too weak to counter centrifugal forces. Strengthening the central power would make Confederation function more smoothly, but that would mean the effective creation of a legislative union, which was unacceptable. Joly de Lotbinière's prediction that the Canadian Confederation was doomed triggered strong reactions. Blanchet accused his opponent of fabricating conclusions drawn "from a table of contents" of a book. He even stated that "no constitution suits every people equally well; constitutions are made for the people, and not the people for the constitution."⁵⁴ Consequently, Blanchet argued that Greece entered a period of "decadence" because it had abandoned federalism.⁵⁵

The Canadian politicians also debated the form of the democratic institutions to be established in the new colony. Among opponents, Dorion denounced the anti-democratic nature of the proposed appointed Senate. Why could Canadians not have an elected Senate as in Belgium, a country without "an aristocracy" but whose constitution was inspired by Britain?⁵⁶ Just as several Nova Scotian politicians had suggested, Alexander Vidal pleaded for the constitutional package to be put before the people as France and Mexico had done.⁵⁷

The issue of democracy and the role of the electorate in constitutional change triggered a number of exchanges that focused on the small but politically complex Belgium. Alexander Mackenzie, a future prime minister of Canada in the 1870s, supported Confederation and argued that Belgium was "one of the most democratic countries in Europe."⁵⁸

Mackenzie also sought to end the practice of an unelected Senate. But he reminded his colleagues that what was at stake was not the best form of government, or the extent to which the institutions should be democratic, but rather "what is best that can be framed for a community holding different views on the subject."[59] For prominent Quebec Bleu and ardent advocate of Confederation, Joseph-Édouard Cauchon, Dorion offered too rosy a picture of democracy in Belgium and its Senate. He reminded his fellow members that only "men powerful and rich in titles and fortune can enter"[60] the Belgian Senate: although it seemed meritocratic, the reality was that an elite controlled it. For François Évanturel, an elected Senate was not a model to follow since limits on the exercise of democracy must be imposed on the new Dominion of Canada: "I am quite of [the] opinion that the conservative element ought, of necessity, to be the basis of the Legislative Council, to counterbalance the popular element."[61] In his response, Dorion argued that Belgium had a federal system, and the provinces had a governor and a parliament with more power than in New Zealand. These exchanges on Belgium, which was a unified state at the time, demonstrate that members of the Legislative Assembly, far from being constitutional experts, had an incomplete knowledge of the world and political institutions, which shaped their understanding of federalism and the federal system of government.

Organization of the Book

Politicians invoked political developments and examples from around the world to bolster their arguments and counter those of their opponents. But what did the world have to say about the Dominion of Canada? This collection of articles attempts to answer that question by offering views of Confederation from around the globe, assembled in three groupings.

The first section, "Perspectives from the Americas," has four chapters. Chapter one takes a broad look at Latin America. Carsten-Andreas Schulz argues that the newly independent nations of the southern Americas did not have much in common with the British North American colonies. Economic relations and cultural and linguistic links caused them to look to Europe, with the notable exception of Cuba. However, some newspapers paid attention to Confederation by focusing on what they considered crucial issues: the threat of US expansionism and the relatively peaceful process of achieving self-governance despite the Fenian attacks and in contrast to conflicts that characterized the nation-building process in Latin America.

At the time of Confederation, British North American politicians believed that the United States wanted to invade or absorb their territories. In chapter two, Jacqueline D. Krikorian and David R. Cameron demonstrate, however, that the United States was more focused on domestic politics and external threats than on changes to the governance structures of their northern neighbours. Americans assumed that Canada would be annexed at some point, but that the Canadians themselves would seek such an arrangement. In chapter three, William Jenkins traces the origins and impact of the Fenians in North America, the one group in the United States that did pay close attention to Confederation. Perceived threats from the Union army and the very real crossborder invasions of the Fenians in 1866 made British North American colonists feel insecure and vulnerable. In fact, the whole world was paying attention to the Fenian marauders, as they received international acclaim in the Austro-Hungarian Empire, Australia, and Latin America.

Chapter four by Gabrielle Slowey, the last chapter of this section, underscores how the Fathers of Confederation excluded Indigenous communities from the discussions on proposed governance changes to British North America. She also highlights the importance of reconciliation and the impact of colonialism.

The second section of the book, "Perspectives from Europe," focuses on how Europeans viewed the Confederation process. Rather than seeing Confederation as the birth of an important new nation, Europeans essentially looked on it as an internal issue within the British Empire that had few consequences for world politics. It was widely understood that Confederation was taking place because the British authorities agreed to reorganize their colonies in the northern part of the Americas in response to pressure from local political and economic elites.

For Europeans, far more pressing issues were taking place on the world scene in the 1860s than what was happening in British North America. In Italy, the Papal States were on the verge of being eradicated and subsumed into the newly created Kingdom of Italy. As Roberto Perin's chapter five demonstrates, the Pope and his advisors perceived North America as a continent where the English language would prevail. But as long as the rights of Catholics were protected in the new Canadian constitution, this reorganization was acceptable. The Pope was far more preoccupied with the survival of his Papal States, which were under threat by Italian unification. Despite sharing a similar cultural heritage, the Dominion of Canada was not on the radar screen of most French newspapers and politicians. At the time, Napoleon III had more pressing issues to deal with in Europe and abroad, not the least of which was the fate of his ally, Emperor Maximilian, in Mexico. As Alban Bargain-Villéger argues in chapter six on France, some French diplomats thought that Confederation would benefit French Canadians and prevent a possible annexation by the United States. If Catholic newspapers were paying more attention to the fate of Papal States, the few other French newspapers that did consider Canada welcomed Confederation and assessed it in terms of increasing trade between France and British North America.

Two empires may have been able to draw some lessons from Canada, but did not follow the process of Confederation to any meaningful extent. In the case of Austria-Hungary, we would have expected that the issue of implementing a governing structure to manage the cultural, religious, and linguistic diversity of British North Americans would trigger some interest. Benno Gammerl, however, argues in chapter seven that the lack of economic and cultural ties with Canada made Confederation an afterthought. Instead, the attention of Austro-Hungarian politicians and elites was captured by the Fenians and their active support for republicanism and by the fate of the emperor's brother Maximilian in Mexico. In chapter eight, Josep María Fradera addresses the issue of Spain and its empire. In the 1830s, the Spanish Empire was reduced to Cuba, Puerto Rico, and the Philippines. Although tobacco and sugar were lucrative staples for the metropolis, colonists were denied any form of self-governance. For liberal-minded reformers in Spain, slavery in Cuba prevented granting any form of self-governance. In this context, Cubans were particularly interested in the Dominion of Canada. It provided them with an example they could use to press Spain to change its relatively authoritarian practices.

The third and final section, "Perspectives from Britain and the Empire," looks at views from Great Britain and some of its colonies. Edward Beasley's chapter nine offers an original take on Confederation from a British perspective. Because the views of British politicians on Confederation have already been studied extensively elsewhere, Beasley focuses on the place of Canada in the British imagination. He looks at the international fairs by which the British North American colonies made themselves known in the metropolis and at the writings of some British intellectuals who had travelled and published accounts of their exploration of British North America. These first-hand narratives reinforced the concept of an "empty" land in need of development. Beasley reminds us that the political elite favoured the Confederation project highly since Canada would remain a desirable destination for British "destitute" and other subjects looking for a welcoming land and a new start. He also links the debates on extending the franchise in Great Britain to the move towards Confederation in British North America.

For his part, Thomas Mohr in chapter ten argues that Irish nationalists – and in particular those who promoted a free Irish state – believed that the Dominion of Canada was doomed to fail since the United States would absorb the British North American colonies. That attitude changed over time, partly because dominion status meant greater autonomy for Canadians, and was therefore viewed as a potential model for Ireland. In chapter eleven on the Australian colonies, Ann Curthoys demonstrates that the Australians were paying attention to what was happening in Canada. Despite a lack of direct communications between the colonies in British North America and Australia, Australians monitored the Confederation process and the Fenian attacks through the press. These attacks made them ask if they, too, would have to assume a greater role in the defence of their territory. Australians were also inspired by the Canadian constitutional process and, like the Irish, wondered if it could be a model for them. Kenton Storey's chapter twelve focuses on what New Zealanders learned through the press about the formation of the Dominion of Canada, as it occurred during a troubled time for the island colony. Lengthy armed conflicts were taking place with Maori peoples over control of the land. Since Britain opted to withdraw most of its troops from its colony, New Zealanders interpreted the formation of Canada as part of a policy of "abandonment" by Britain.

The last two chapters in this section look at Confederation as a blueprint for emerging British colonies. Timothy Stapleton argues in chapter thirteen that the Canadian federal model as a system of governance had profoundly negative consequences in South Africa. With the discovery of diamonds and gold, British authorities believed that a federation in South Africa was a blueprint for the way forward. But it led to several wars and conflicts with Africans and Boers, including the Boer War from 1899 to 1902. Stapleton's contribution forces us to pause and reflect on governance and how an ill-conceived structure can result in armed conflicts. Finally, Franklin W. Knight's chapter fourteen on the British West Indies explains why the Canadian form of federalism was not a solution for these colonies. While colonial authorities were looking for better governance structures to manage cultural diversity in the Caribbean, the Canadian model was not a workable solution because of the challenges of geography and the legacies of slavery.

Around the world, the press, legislators, and diplomats considered different aspects of the British North American Confederation process. The Fenian raids seemed to dominate most of this coverage, albeit other issues were discussed to a lesser extent. Although British North American politicians debated the merits of governance models in Belgium and the United States in great detail, officials in Washington and Brussels paid relatively little attention to them. The Confederation debates reveal what the colonial legislators knew of the world at the time, and media coverage shows us that the world knew relatively little about British North America. In fact, there was minimal direct dialogue between British North America and its global observers. However, British North Americans and people around the world did share one common approach to governance: they all ignored the rights and needs of the Indigenous populations.

NOTES

1 "The New Dominion," *Halifax Evening Express*, 3 July 1867, 2.
2 P.B. Waite, "Edward Cardwell and Confederation," *Canadian Historical Review* 43, no. 1 (March 1962): 17–41.
3 Chester Martin, "British Policy in Canadian Confederation," *Canadian Historical Review* 13, no. 1 (March 1932): 3–19.
4 Ged Martin, *Britain and the Origins of Canadian Confederation, 1837–67* (Vancouver: UBC Press, 1995).
5 C.P. Stacey, "Britain's Withdrawal from North America, 1864–1871," *Canadian Historical Review* 36, no. 3 (September 1955): 185–98.
6 Opposition to Confederation in Nova Scotia is detailed in a number of publications, including J. Murray Beck, *Joseph Howe*, vol. 2, *The Briton Becomes a Canadian, 1848–1873* (Montreal & Kingston: McGill-Queen's University Press, 1983), 167–218; Kenneth G. Pryke, *Nova Scotia and Confederation, 1864–74* (Toronto: University of Toronto Press, 1979); P.B. Waite, *The Life and Times of Confederation, 1864–1867* (Toronto: Bass, 2001), 209–47; and *Letter Addressed to the Earl of Carnarvon by Mr. Joseph Howe, Mr. William Annand, and Mr. Hugh McDonald Stating Their Objections to the Proposed Scheme of Union of the British North American Provinces*, Presented to both Houses of Parliament, 8th February 1867 (London: Eyre and Spottiswoode, 1867).

7 The quote in French reads, "La Confédération a été inaugurée hier dans toute l'étendue de la souveraineté du Canada par des réjouissances magnifiques." "Canada," *Le Journal de Québec*, 2 July 1867, 2.
8 *The Gazette*, Montreal, 1 July 1867, 2. The editors' enthusiasm was clearly on display when it toasted Canada by saying, "May the new Dominion maintain a separate and independent status – may it live for ever!"
9 "The New Dominion," *The Halifax Evening Express*, 3 July 1867, 2.
10 "The New Dominion," *The New Brunswick Reporter*, 5 July 1867, 2.
11 *The Saint John Globe*, 1 July 1867, 2.
12 *British North America Act, 1867*, 30–1 Victoria, c. 3. (UK). The legislation was renamed the *Constitution Act, 1867* in 1982, but its original name will be used in this collection.
13 S.L. Tilley, a speech delivered at the Halifax Hotel, Halifax, Nova Scotia, 12 September 1864, in *A Brief Account of the Several Conferences Held in the Maritime Provinces and in Canada, in September and October 1864, on the Proposed Confederation of the Provinces, Together with a Report of the Speeches Delivered by the Delegates*, ed. Edward Whelan (1865; repr., Summerside, PEI: Pioneer, 1949), 38, 39.
14 Tilley, in *A Brief Account*, ed. Whelan, 37.
15 Charles Tupper, MPP, a speech delivered at a public dinner at St Stubb's Hotel in Saint John, New Brunswick, 14 September 1864, in *A Brief Account*, ed. Whelan, 54.
16 Ibid., 38.
17 Section 43.15, "Report of Resolutions Adopted at a Conference of Delegates from the Provinces of Canada, Nova Scotia and New Brunswick and the Colonies of Newfoundland and Prince Edward Island, Held at the City of Quebec, 10th October 1864, as the Basis of a Proposed Confederation of the Provinces," in *Confederation Being a Series of Hitherto Unpublished Documents Bearing on the British North America Act*, ed. Joseph Pope (Toronto: Carswell, 1895), 47.
18 Section 43.18, "Report of Resolutions."
19 Section 43.10, "Report of Resolutions."
20 Section 43.6, "Report of Resolutions."
21 George-Étienne Cartier, Attorney General, Canada East, Legislative Assembly, *Parliamentary Debates on the Subject of the Confederation of the British North American Provinces*, 3rd Session, 8th Provincial Parliament (Quebec: Hunter, Rose & Co., Parliamentary Printers, 1865), 53.
22 Ibid., 55.
23 John A. Macdonald, speech on the first substantive motion at the Discussion in Conference of the Delegates from the Provinces of British

North America in the Conference Chamber, Parliament House, Quebec, 11 October 1864, in *Confederation Documents Hitherto Unpublished*, ed. Joseph Pope, 54, 55.

24 David Koffman, "Confederation as an Intra-Christian Pact," *Canada Watch* (Spring, 2016): 10.

25 David R. Cameron, Jacqueline D. Krikorian, and Robert C. Vipond, "Revisiting the 1865 Canadian Debates on Confederation: Rights and the Constitution," *Canada Watch* (Spring, 2016): 13–15.

26 Olive Patricia Dickason and William Newbigging, "Towards Confederation for Canada, Towards Wardship for First Peoples," in *A Concise History of Canada's First Nations*, 3rd ed. (Toronto: Oxford University Press, 2015), 163.

27 *British North America Act, 1867*, s. 91(24).

28 John MacMullen, *The History of Canada, from Discovery to the Present Time* (Brockville: McMullen, 1868), xxxi.

29 Robin Jarvis Brownlie, *A Fatherly Eye: Indian Agents, Government Power, and Aboriginal Resistance in Ontario, 1918–1939* (Toronto: Oxford University Press, 2003), 34.

30 Rachel Chagnon, "Les Pères de la Confédération et *l'Acte de l'Amérique du Nord britannique, 1867*: leurs visions du constitutionalisme et leurs modèles," in *La conférence de Québec de 1864: 150 ans plus tard*, ed. Eugénie Brouillet, Alain-G. Gagnon et Guy Laforest (Québec: Les Presses de l'Université Laval, 2016), 27–47.

31 Speech of Mr William Annand, *Debates and Procedures of the House of Assembly of Nova Scotia*, 19 March 1867, http://theconfederationdebates.

32 David Kertzer, *Prisoner of the Vatican: The Popes, the Kings, and Garibaldi's Rebels in the Struggle to Rule Modern Italy* (Boston: Houghton Mifflin, 2004), 20.

33 John Mercer Johnson, *New Brunswick Debates of the House of Assembly*, 1866, http://theconfederationdebates.ca.

34 Charles Fisher, *New Brunswick Debates of the House of Assembly*, 1866; George William Howlan, *Debates and Proceedings of the House of Assembly of Prince Edward Island for the Year 1865*, http://theconfederationdebates.ca.

35 George Brown, *Canadian Legislative Assembly Debates*, in *Parliamentary Debates on the Subject of the Confederation of the British North American Provinces, 3rd Session, 8th Provincial Parliament* (Quebec: Hunter, Rose & Co., Parliamentary Printers, 1865), 107; William Miller, 3 April 1866, Charles Tupper, 10 April 1866, Adams George Archibald, 10 April 1866, Hiram Blanchard, 16 April 1866, *Debates and Procedures of the House of Assembly of Nova Scotia*, http://theconfederationdebates.ca.

36 Stewart Campbell, *Debates and Procedures of the House of Assembly of Nova Scotia*, 17 April 1866; John Longworth, *Debates and Proceedings of the House*

of Assembly of Prince Edward Island for the Year 1866, http://theconfederationdebates.ca.
37 There were no references to Asia, the Middle East, or Africa.
38 Brown, *Canadian Legislative Assembly Debates*, 8 February 1865, 85.
39 Cartier, *Canadian Legislative Assembly Debates*, 60.
40 Fergusson Blair, *Canadian Legislative Assembly Debates*, 11.
41 John Ross, *Canadian Legislative Council Debates*, in *Parliamentary Debates on the Subject of the Confederation of the British North American Provinces, 3rd Session, 8th Provincial Parliament* (Quebec: Hunter, Rose & Co., Parliamentary Printers, 1865), 73; Brown, *Canadian Legislative Assembly Debates*, 101–2.
42 Brown, *Canadian Legislative Assembly Debates*, 98.
43 Alexander Morris, *Canadian Legislative Assembly Debates*, 443.
44 George Alexander, *Canadian Legislative Council Debates*, 82; Brown, *Canadian Legislative Assembly Debates*, 86.
45 Henri-Gustave Joly de Lotbinière, *Canadian Legislative Assembly Debates*, 353.
46 Thomas D'Arcy-McGee, *Canadian Legislative Assembly Debates*, 145.
47 Joseph-Godéric Blanchet, *Canadian Legislative Assembly Debates*, 548.
48 Antoine-Aimé Dorion, *Canadian Legislative Assembly Debates*, 264.
49 Joly de Lotbinière, *Canadian Legislative Assembly Debates*, 347
50 Jack I. Little, *Patrician Liberal: The Public and Private Life of Sir Henri-Gustave Joly de Lotbinière, 1829–1908* (Toronto, University of Toronto Press, 2013), 103.
51 Joly de Lotbinière, *Canadian Legislative Assembly Debates*, 348.
52 Ibid.
53 Ibid., 349.
54 Blanchet, *Canadian Legislative Assembly Debates*, 549.
55 Ibid., 548.
56 Dorion, *Canadian Legislative Assembly Debates*, 256
57 Alexander Vidal, *Canadian Legislative Council Debates*, 304.
58 Alexander Mackenzie, *Canadian Legislative Assembly Debates*, 426.
59 Ibid., 427.
60 Joseph-Édouard Cauchon, *Canadian Legislative Assembly Debates*, 569.
61 François Évanturel, *Canadian Legislative Assembly Debates*, 569.

PART ONE

Perspectives from the Americas

1 Confederation Unknown? Latin American Views on the Emergence of Canada in 1867

CARSTEN-ANDREAS SCHULZ

The constitution of the Dominion of Canada in 1867 did not provoke much commentary among Latin American observers. But while Canadian Confederation did not spark lively interest among elites south of the Rio Grande, it did not pass unnoticed. What explains Latin America's disengagement with Canadian Confederation? Although there has been relatively little written on the history of Canada–Latin America relations, existing accounts emphasize the lack of direct contacts between Canada and Latin American societies that persisted despite a shared geographic location in the Western Hemisphere.[1] At first glance, the paucity of direct political or cultural links suggests that Canadian Confederation was simply not seen as important enough to warrant attention. Yet this proposition, while plausible, does not adequately account for Latin American perceptions of Confederation. Taking a synoptic view that draws on secondary accounts and primary source material, in particular contemporary newspaper articles from the region,[2] the essay posits that Latin American observers were indeed interested in Canadian affairs, but they saw events in the British North American colonies primarily through the lens of their own experience with emancipation from colonial rule and state-building. Latin America's road to independence was highly disruptive and fraught with conflict. Its experience stands in stark contrast with the gradualism that characterizes Canada's path to self-rule and independence. This focus explains why insurgencies and foreign incursions, such as the Fenian raids of the late 1860s, caught the attention of Latin American observers, whereas Canadian Confederation itself did not.

The remainder of this essay proceeds as follows: Section two contextualizes Latin American perceptions of Confederation. Section three focuses on the origins of Canada–Latin America relations. Section four discusses the sparse treatment of Canadian Confederation in Chilean, Brazilian, and Mexican newspapers, and evaluates this coverage in light of earlier and alternative instances of news coverage on Canada. The essay concludes that far from being disinterested in the British North American colonies, Latin Americans interpreted Canadian affairs on the basis of their own experience of independence from colonial rule and state formation.

Two Diverging Paths to Statehood

As a cultural and political region south of the United States, Latin America emerged in the early nineteenth century from the disintegration of the Spanish, Portuguese, and French empires in the Americas. Starting in the late eighteenth century, the "Atlantic Revolution" rocked the status quo in the colonies and ushered in decades of civil war. With the exception of Haiti, which was born out of a successful slave revolt (1781–1804), independence began with the French invasion of the Iberian Peninsula by Napoleon in 1808.[3] In Spain, the royal family was forced to abdicate and was replaced by Napoleon's brother, Joseph Bonaparte, whereas the Portuguese Braganza dynasty sought to avoid a similar fate by evacuating the entire court to Brazil. Throughout the Spanish realm, self-governing *juntas* were formed in the name of Ferdinand VII. However, once Ferdinand was reinstated, Spain denounced the autonomy of the colonies, provoking the local Creole elites to proclaim their independence from the metropolis. Because self-government in the Spanish colonies came in response to a legitimacy crisis "from without," independence was fraught with conflict and rapidly escalated into civil war. By contrast, Brazil was elevated to a kingdom equal with Portugal in 1815. Then, in the early 1820s, constitutionalists demanded the return of John VI to Europe, who left his son Pedro back in Rio de Janeiro. Facing the threat that the Portuguese Cortes would revert Brazil back to its former status, independence was declared in 1822, and Pedro I was proclaimed emperor of Brazil. Unlike in Canada, where self-rule was gradually devolved in response to political demands, responsible government came as the result of an external crisis in Latin America.

More generally, in North America the "Atlantic Revolution" had very different effects. Instead of pitting warring factions within the colonies against each other, and against the colonial metropole, loyalists and revolutionaries were able to redistribute themselves between British North America and the United States. Although the process was not free of conflict, after 1814 the ideological boundaries seemed largely settled – despite the continuing threat of annexation.

By the 1830s, most Latin American states had gained de facto independence from the former metropolis and international recognition by the major powers of the time. Yet independence was achieved at a high cost, as years of internecine war left Spanish American economies in shambles with large parts of the countryside militarized, and the resultant regimes were seen as lacking legitimacy even within their own boundaries.[4] Compounding these struggles, and despite having received international recognition from major European powers and the United States, nascent Latin American states remained fragmented polities. There was also considerable ambiguity about their place within the Europe-dominated international order of the time. Much of the literature stresses the economic dependency of these new states, and Argentina, in particular, is often regarded as Britain's "Sixth Dominion" or part of its "informal Empire."[5] Equally important is the unequal treatment that Latin American states received in the first decades of independence. Britain, for instance, installed a limited form of extraterritorial jurisdiction in Brazil that excluded British subjects from local jurisdiction after the Royal Navy escorted the Portuguese court to Rio de Janeiro in 1808. The "office of the judge conservator" only expired in 1844. Furthermore, examples of naval blockades and diplomatic interventions abound, suggesting that these states were seen as being more akin to polities like the Ottoman Empire or the ancient states of East Asia, which were recognized diplomatically but not treated as equal members of the international order of the time.[6] At the heart of this ambiguity was distrust in Europe and the United States about the ability of the local elite to self-rule, as the political unrest of the post-independence period frequently harmed the life and property of foreigners.

Latin American independence was far more disruptive than the gradual emergence of a unified Canada. From the achievement of responsible government in 1848 to equality with Britain in 1926, and the *Statute of Westminster* five years later, the creation of Confederation in 1867 was but one step towards fully fledged independence. As such, it was neither inevitable nor apparent to foreign observers.

The silence on Confederation in Latin American newspapers is especially noteworthy, given the often-observed outward orientation of nineteenth century Latin American elites. Although a highly heterogeneous region that defies easy generalizations, Latin American societies at the time of Confederation were (and continue to be) greatly stratified along socio-economic and ethnic lines, and governed by elites who were predominantly of European descent and conventionally trained in law.[7] This "lettered" oligarchy was closely connected to the Atlantic world. Fixated on the most recent trends and events in London and Paris, they have been frequently criticized, if not ridiculed, for being ignorant of their own societies and oblivious to local realities in Latin America.[8] By contrast, the interpretation advanced here emphasizes the selective appropriation of foreign sources by Latin America's elites in the pursuit of their own political agendas. By the second half of the nineteenth century, this agenda was often geared towards state formation, the centralization of political power, state modernization, and economic liberalization after decades of political strife over the political constitution of the new states and, importantly, the role of the Church.[9]

Foreign affairs, broadly defined, were of great public interest in nineteenth century Latin America, and news from abroad garnered considerable newspaper coverage, even if it was not necessarily of immediate local relevance. Newspaper coverage is selective and reflects public debates only imperfectly. Yet it provides an insightful window to issues of public concern. Its bias reflects both the nature of contemporary communication and communication technology, as well as editorial choices. Because the creation of Canadian Confederation preceded Latin America's connection to the emerging global telegraph network,[10] news was disseminated to the region in a hub-and-spoke fashion, in which news from the British and French metropolis arrived only after considerable delay. The nineteenth century Latin American public was well informed about happenings in other parts of the world.[11] But, being subject to the discretion of editors in Europe (and, increasingly, the United States), Latin Americans received the news that Europeans regarded as important, and which local editors subsequently deemed relevant.

If Latin American elites were interested in other parts of the world, including those with which they had little direct contact, what explains the disengagement with Canadian Confederation? As Ged Martin recounts, British North America consisted of a few relatively unimportant colonies whose confederation was quietly approved by Westminster in March 1867.[12] Unlike the extension of the franchise by the *Reform Act of 1867*, which was hotly debated, discussed, and enacted by the British parliament at that time, the *British North America Act, 1867* did not provoke much public debate in Britain.[13] It is therefore not surprising that Latin American newspapers would be relatively silent on the issue. But perhaps even more telling is what *was* reported from Canada. This essay argues that two points require closer consideration in order to understand Latin American views on Confederation: the international and, in particular, hemispheric context, and the absence of significant direct contacts between Canada and Latin American societies.

For one, the renegotiation of Canada's constitutional status within the British Empire took place during a time of significant international turmoil. In North America, it was no accident that the first conferences on the political future of Canada coincided with the American Civil War (1861–5), an important watershed event that reverberated throughout the region. Just as the authors of Canadian Confederation were spurred to action by the horrors south of the border, so too were their efforts overshadowed by this conflict. It is also important to consider that the *British North America Act, 1867* entered into force only a fortnight after the execution of Habsburg prince Maximilian I dealt the final blow to the French occupation of Mexico (1862–7), an event that captivated the interest of foreign observers, especially in Latin America. At the same time, Spain, in a last attempt to regain control over parts of its former colonies, had just ended its conflict with Chile and Peru in the so-called Chincha Islands War (1864–6), which had seen the Spanish fleet burn down Valparaiso and Callao in 1866. Just as concerning for Latin Americans was the fact that the Triple Alliance of Argentina, Brazil, and Uruguay was still engaged in a bitter fight against Paraguay in what would come to be considered the bloodiest conflict in South American history (1864–70). There certainly were a great many events that caught the attention of the Latin American public, but Confederation was not among them. This "noise" is important for two reasons: first, it captivated the attention of the Latin America public, dominating headlines and marginalizing the less dramatic developments in Canada; second, the violent conflicts in Latin America were dramatically juxtaposed to the relative quietness with which Confederation was achieved.

For another, the central argument of this paper contends that whenever Latin Americans were interested in Canadian affairs, their interest was generally focused on news about insurgencies and armed conflict: in other words, events that were relatable to their own violent struggles for independence and the subsequent challenges of state formation and consolidation. Seen through the lens of their experience, Canada's path to independence was simply too different from their own to be intelligible as such to Latin American elites. This is evident not only in the relative scarcity of coverage about Confederation by the Latin American press, but also becomes apparent when viewed alongside other instances in which Canadian affairs had warranted significant commentary, such as the rebellions of 1837–8, the Fenian raids of the 1860s, and reportage on Canada's strained relations with the United States. Notably, Cuba was an exception to this trend, where autonomists, wedged between revolutionary separatists and reactionary *peninsulares*, looked to Canada as a possible model for self-government within the auspices of the Spanish Empire, as Josep María Fradera demonstrates in chapter eight of this volume.[14] In this sense, even the Cuban exception illustrates how Confederation was understood in terms of Latin Americans' own experiences with emancipation from colonial rule.

Late Encounters

Historiographical accounts of Canada–Latin America relations are scarce. For J.C.M. Ogelsby, whose *Gringos from the Far North* continues to form the basis of most subsequent studies,[15] this scarcity is a reflection of the lack of intellectual exchange, which is symptomatic of the absence of direct political or, in fact, commercial contacts. There is a long-standing view that the potential of Canada–Latin America relations has never been fully realized. The strengthening of commercial ties had been discussed at the Confederate Council of Trade in 1865. In response, a mission was dispatched to explore the possibilities of diversifying Canada's trade relations and reducing its dependency on the United States, a particularly pressing concern once it became known that Congress was in favour of abrogating the Reciprocity Treaty of 1854.[16] Although the mission, as Norman McL. Rogers maintains, "appears as a distinct landmark in the gradual development of colonial participation in external affairs," the commissioners were not authorized to negotiate independently with foreign powers and produced few tangible results.[17] Moreover, and despite its mandate and name, the mission – comprised of delegations from the Canadas, Nova Scotia, New Brunswick, and Prince Edward Island – abstained from going to Mexico, given the "disturbed state of that Empire" stymied by the ongoing conflict between imperial and republican forces.[18]

This is not the place to elaborate on the complicated history of nineteenth century Mexico. However, two points should be noted. First, political instability in the post-independence period and the inability of the local elite to consolidate political authority throughout the territory of the former viceroyalty of New Spain led to tensions with the settlers who emigrated to Texas from the United States, ultimately escalating into war with its northern neighbour. As a result of the Mexican-American War (1846–8), Mexico lost approximately half its territory to the United States. The war was viewed with ambiguity in other parts of Latin America: for one, it spurred a first wave of anti-American sentiment that coalesced into calls for *Latin* solidarity; for another, the United States was envied and admired for its dynamism and rapid development.[19] As becomes clear further on, Latin American observers expected that Canada, in the end, would succumb to a similar fate of annexation. Second, Mexico illustrates how political instability undermined the international standing of Latin American states in the international order of the nineteenth century.[20] After all, the French invasion and the installation of a Habsburg monarchy in 1864 were precipitated by Mexico's suspension of debt payments to Britain, France, and Spain in 1861 – international obligations that had been incurred during the Reform Wars (1857–60). Interestingly, conservative Québécois supported the French intervention as part of a wider struggle of Latin Catholicism against anticlerical forces.[21] In the end, the wariness of the Canadian trade commission proved right: the imperial regime collapsed shortly after France withdrew its troops from Mexico. Maximilian was captured, court-martialled, and finally executed on 19 June 1867. The victorious Benito Juárez suspended all diplomatic relations with those powers that had recognized the Empire. In fact, in 1867, Britain withdrew all diplomatic representatives including consular officers.[22] Although Britain re-established its political ties with Mexico in 1884, it was not until the 1890s that the first Canadian trade commission would visit Mexico.[23]

The trade commission found a more hospitable environment in Brazil. Three commissioners arrived in Rio de Janeiro in March 1866 at a time when the War of the Triple Alliance had shifted to Paraguayan soil in a bloody campaign for which Brazil bore the brunt of the fighting. Importantly, Brazil and Britain had only recently re-established diplomatic relations after a short blockade of Rio de Janeiro in 1862–3, instigated by Britain's minister to Brazil, William Dougal Christie, which had led to the suspension of formal diplomatic ties.[24] The moment of the visit was anything but propitious, and it seems reasonable that Brazil wished not to slight the British government and its representatives from the North American colonies. The Canadians established contact through British representatives, and consequently met with high dignitaries of the imperial government, including the ministers of finance and foreign affairs, and, importantly, Brazil's Emperor Pedro II.[25] Overall, it seems that the Brazilians were keen to display their interest in the mission's concerns, but were reluctant to commit to any concrete steps concerning reciprocal free trade, as is evident in Foreign Minister José Antônio Saraiva's guarded response to the mission's propositions.[26] Furthermore, and despite the high-level contacts that took place, it is noteworthy that neither the government's *Diario Oficial do Imperio do Brasil* nor the capital's principal newspaper *Jornal do Commercio* mention the Canadian visit at all.[27] This lack of coverage supports the conclusion of Andrew Smith and Kirsten Greer that, rather than being genuinely interested in expanding trade with the North American colonies, the warm reception the commission received may have had more to do with Brazil's general interest in improving relations with Britain and Pedro II's personal aspiration for membership in the Order of the Garter.[28]

More generally, two conclusions can be drawn from the historiography of Canada–Latin American relations. First, at the time of Confederation in 1867, there had been little direct contact between British North America and the countries south of the United States. Neither were there necessarily converging political agendas. Ogelsby, for instance, argues that Canadian decision makers have historically only shown interest in Latin America when relations with the United States were strained or when they were concerned about Canada's over-reliance on trade with the United States.[29]

Differences in priorities also shed light on how Latin Americans saw Canadian Confederation. For Canadians, Latin America offered an opportunity to diversify commercial relations, but Canadians were wary of getting "tied to the wheels of Washington's foreign policy" in the region.[30] Nor was the United States particularly keen on Canadian participation in the incipient inter-American system, on the grounds that Canada could offer a foothold to Britain for gaining influence in the region. This reticence was compounded by the fact that, apparently, for much of the inter-war period, "there was still little comprehension, even in State Department circles, of Canada's constitutional status."[31] There is reason to believe that Latin Americans, too, (mis)understood Canada's place in the region in similar terms.[32] Whereas Canadians were principally interested in trade diversification, Latin Americans pursued a more openly political agenda with the aim of counteracting the growing influence of the United States.³³ Although it lies beyond the scope of this paper, this debate suggests that Latin Americans did not understand Canada to be a fully independent political actor, but instead saw it as an important link to and integral part of the British Empire – and this even after the *Statute of Westminster* formally recognized Canada's autonomy in foreign policy matters.

Lastly, it is important to keep in mind that Canada's interests were represented in Latin America by the British diplomatic service until the 1940s.³⁴ Canada only opened its first permanent representations in Washington, Paris, and Tokyo in 1928. Latin America, however, was not a priority, especially given the budgetary constraints of the time.³⁵ Despite the overtures of Latin American governments, it was only during the Second World War that Canada's focus shifted, leading to the opening of the first Canadian embassy in Brazil in 1944.³⁶ Canada's formal equality with Britain was recognized in the Balfour Declaration of 1926, and was subsequently reaffirmed by the *Statute of Westminster, 1931*. Sovereign equality, however, has historically been understood by Latin Americans as the hallmark of independence and statehood.³⁷ The point is not of minor importance: the Canadian path to independence looked unfamiliar to Latin Americans. Viewed from "down south," Canadian Confederation looked more like an administrative reorganization within the British Empire than the end of colonial rule.

Confederation Unknown?

Thus far, the essay has focused primarily on the multiple reasons why we should expect Latin Americans to be disinterested in Canadian affairs and Confederation in particular. For one, Latin Americans maintained few direct contacts with the North American colonies. For another, Confederation took place at a time of great international convulsion in the Western Hemisphere that had the potential of drowning out debates on the changing position of Canada within the British Empire. Adding to this was the "low-key approach" through which the *British North America Act, 1867* was moved through parliament in Westminster, which made it even less likely that news about Confederation would make it to the New World. However, it would be misleading to assume that Confederation happened unnoticed, because news from Canada did frequently appear in Latin American newspapers. The more interesting question, then, is not whether Confederation was known or unknown by Latin Americans, but rather what type of events from British North America were reported and how these were presented to the readership. The selection is necessarily incomplete and suggestive, but it provides plausible evidence for the thesis that Latin Americans understood Confederation largely in terms of their own experience with independence and state formation.

What kind of picture emerges from this analysis? First, if the proposition were true that Latin Americans lacked an interest in Confederation because of the absence of direct political or cultural contacts, we would expect to find little coverage on British North America at large. However, in fact, when focusing on key events prior to the Charlottetown Conference of 1864, it is noteworthy that the rebellions of 1837 and 1838 did receive a considerable amount of commentary in Brazilian and Chilean newspapers, as did Lord Durham's mission to the colonies responsible for dealing with the revolt. Yet it was the rebellion and its repression that caught the attention of Latin American observers. Durham's report and his recommendations for political reform, including the union of the two Canadas and some degree of responsible government, by contrast, did not; or, if it did, it appears to have been of secondary concern.[38] The episode is illustrative for two reasons: first, it demonstrates the way in which metropolitan sources were disseminated and consumed in Latin America. For instance, the *Mercurio de Valparaíso*, Chile's oldest and most outward-looking newspaper of the time, clearly adopted a French perspective on the matter, citing the historical injustice done by Britain to Canadians of French descent as the reason for the "struggle between Canada's settlers [*colonos*] and the metropolis" (apparently drawing from the French *Le Globe*).[39] Similarly, the same newspaper's report on "Canadian affairs" from September 1838 was based on French sources (*Le Temps*), although the conclusion presented here on Lord John Russell's objections to responsible government struck a definitive "postcolonial" tone: if Britain regarded colonial self-rule as incompatible with Canada's colonial status, then the only logical consequence "for any colony is to seek emancipation, given that a colony cannot enjoy the constitutional liberties that the metropolis reserves for herself."[40] More generally, liberal views in Chile reflected the "Western Hemisphere idea," according to which the political institutions of the Old World could not prosper in the Americas, where deep-rooted republican sentiments would eventually lead to the independence of the remaining European colonies.[41] Unsurprisingly, the same could not be said for newspapers in imperial Brazil, even though the *Jornal do Commercio* frequently informed its readers about the rebellions. While generally focusing more on the military aspects of these uprisings than its Chilean counterpart, here, too, Britain's reluctance to concede self-rule was criticized at the same time as the newspaper lauded "the spirit of independence" among Canada's inhabitants.[42]

The mid-nineteenth century offers a similar picture: events in Canada were reported through the perspective of Latin American's own experience. The growing wariness of US expansionism is evident in these reports. In Chile, for instance, the annexation movement in Canada was heralded as inevitable, given the "manifest destiny" of the United States to expand across the North American continent: "The Colossus, then, wants to expand, to which the annexation of Canada will greatly contribute, and which, at this moment, appears to be a certainty [*cosa segura*]."[43] Similarly, Mexican newspapers frequently pointed to the apparent parallels between the events in British North America and their own experience with US expansionism, although, unsurprisingly, reports here adopted a much more critical tone.[44] By contrast, the onset of responsible government in Nova Scotia in 1848 does not appear in Brazilian, Chilean, or Mexican newspapers.

The idea that the colonies would eventually be absorbed by the North American "Colossus" is a recurrent theme that did not dissipate in the 1850s. Quite the contrary, the victory of the Union over the Confederacy in 1865 made annexation appear all the more certain,[45] as tensions rose over Britain's interest in trading with the rebellious South. This apprehension also explains, in part, the interest that the Fenian raids provoked in Latin America. It is well recognized that the raids had a galvanizing effect on the political union of the colonies, especially in New Brunswick, where the "Fenian scare" undermined opposition to Confederation.[46] Brazilian and Chilean newspapers reported frequently on these Irish-American schemes (but little coverage on British North America could be found in Mexican newspapers during the French occupation). As Stacey observes, US newspapers almost certainly exaggerated the threat that the Fenians posed to either British control or the incipient Confederation. Yet they did play into the argument that political union was required to strengthen the defence of the Empire, a justification that was also prominent in debates on the necessity of Confederation in Britain.[47] These debates resonated among Latin American elites. Taking up the *Times* on the issue, the *Journal do Commercio* equated the raids with the filibustering by US citizens that, while not instigated, was certainly tolerated by the government in Washington.[48] Although the filibusters targeted primarily the more politically volatile republics of Mexico and Central America, there was also a long-standing concern among Brazilian elites that the United States would employ similar means to gain control over the Amazon.[49] For Latin Americans, then, Confederation was primarily about strengthening Britain's imperial defence against US encroachment. It is telling that the *Journal do Commercio*'s annual review of the 1867 political year extensively discusses European balance of power politics, the Eastern Question that arose from the disintegration of the Ottoman Empire, and United States expansionism. In this regard, Canada is mentioned, but only in the context of the Fenian raids, whereas Confederation did not receive any comment at all.[50]

There were a few instances where Confederation was discussed in constitutional terms. Brazilian news reported on the conferences that led to the creation of the Dominion of Canada. For instance, in a report from May 1865, the *Journal do Commercio* voiced scepticism over the possibility of a "federation," given the reluctance of the Maritime colonies to put their faith into the hands of the much larger (and more protectionist) Canadas. This rejection, however, and the threat that prominent calls for "representation by population" in Upper Canada would undermine the political compact that held the two Canadas together, once more raised the spectre of annexation by the United States.[51] It is therefore no surprise, and very much in line with the emphasis on the Fenian threat during that period, that reports on the abrogation of the Reciprocity Treaty by the United States were common.[52] The episode was read as retaliation by the United States against Britain's not-quite-so-neutral stance during the Civil War. Growing tensions between the two powers raised the threat of war and the necessity of imperial defence, despite the slim chances of holding Canada against an eventual attack by the United States. As the Canadian conferences progressed, reports in Brazil became more optimistic. In a note from early January 1867, the *Journal do Commercio* pointed to the overall enthusiasm about Confederation in the Canadas (and the lack thereof in the smaller Maritime colonies). Given the largely favourable public opinion, it now fell upon the government in London "to complete one of the most important steps ever proposed for the consolidation of British power [in North America]."[53]

The most detailed commentary, however, came from the liberal *Diário do Rio de Janeiro*. Once more, the "metropolitan bias" comes through strongly: whereas the Reform Bill provoked much public resistance in Britain, "the project for the Confederation of the British North American colonies, by contrast, would enjoy general approval." The tone was unusually optimistic for a Latin America newspaper of the time:

> While remaining bound to the metropole, the colonies that will be part of this union shall enjoy the most complete autonomy and the widest prerogatives. The governor-general and the commanders of the armed and naval forces will continue to be appointed by the Queen, but the Confederation will have in all other points, the character of a great independent State.[54]

The article then goes on to describe the constitutional features of the new Confederation called Canada, whose creation would be important not because of the "application of the principles of colonial independence" but due to its geographic location and sheer size. It received widespread political support in the House of Commons, because only such union within the Empire can ensure that the North American colonies remained British by "imposing an obstacle to the peaceful [*pacificia*] expansion of the United States." It continues optimistically:

> The English colonies located north of the Saint Lawrence have a contagious aspect, that of liberty, and under the risk that they would be pushed to voluntarily seek annexation by their neighbour, it was imperative to concede them liberal concessions. [Then noting not so optimistically] What remains to be seen is whether this union in the same state of the descendants of Norman energy with the English of new Scotland [*sic*] will consolidate a cohesion that is sufficient to form a great state.[55]

Such optimism on Confederation mixed with scepticism about the Dominion's future can also be found in the Chilean press. In Chile, there was much less coverage of Confederation than in Brazil (but more than in Mexico).[56] Again, this coverage was overlain with the expectation that a breakup would ultimately lead to US annexation, for instance, when reporting on the repeal movement and the House of Commons debate on the (defeated) motion, introduced by John Bright, to investigate Nova Scotia's discontent over the union that, if unaddressed, might push it into the arms of the United States.[57]

These news reports are evidence of the way in which Latin Americans "read" Confederation. It was strongly influenced by their own political history of emancipation and state formation. The concern about US expansionism was part of this history. While there were reports on Confederation, emphasis was laid on insurgencies and revolt, an experience that was very relatable to Latin Americans of the time, as was the fact that these revolts jeopardized the viability of the new states and often precipitated foreign intervention if not annexation, as in the case of Mexico. Constitutional questions that discussed the changing position of Canada within the British Empire were scarce.[58]

Conclusion

As Donald Wright remarks in the introduction to Creighton's classic on the origins of Canada as an independent state, "Confederation happened for a variety of reasons and it meant different things to different people in different places."[59] Although intended as a comment on historiographical controversy within Canada, the quote is suggestive of the different ways in which Confederation could be conceived abroad. Taking this statement as a starting point, this essay sheds light on the question of how Confederation was perceived by Latin America. Drawing on secondary sources and newspaper reports from the region, this study argues that Latin Americans saw Confederation primarily through the prism of their own history of emancipation from colonial rule and state formation. There are good reasons to believe that news from Canada would simply be unknown. For one, Canada maintained few political, cultural, or political ties with Latin America; for another, Confederation took place at a time of great international upheaval. Despite these adverse conditions, Latin Americans were indeed sensitive to events in British North America. Yet the gradualism with which Confederation was achieved stood in stark contrast to Latin American's own experience, which was fraught with conflict and civil war.

News on British North America came primarily from sources in Britain, France, and, increasingly, the United States. The nature of news dissemination is important for understanding the way in which news arrived in Latin America. What was reported in Latin American newspapers not only reflected editorial choices in the region, but, importantly, reflected what publishers in Europe (and the United States) regarded as relevant. However, far from merely copying metropolitan debates, news coverage was selective, and this selection provides an insightful window for understanding the way in which Confederation was "read" at the time. By the 1860s, Latin America had achieved a considerable degree of political stability compared with the calamitous post-independence period. But news from Canada was interpreted against the backdrop of civil unrest. Adding insult to injury, political instability in nineteenth century Latin American frequently precipitated foreign interventions and, as Mexico's history forcefully illustrates, provided a pretext for annexation. This is why Latin Americans, in general, paid close attention to events that resembled their own experience, whereas the gradual evolution of Canada's independent statehood passed largely unnoticed. Raids and revolts, the events that make revolutions, attracted Latin American commentary; constitutional designs leading to greater autonomy within the British Empire did not.

On a concluding note, it is striking that the implication of Confederation for Canada's Indigenous communities is entirely absent from Latin American news coverage. And this, despite the obvious parallels of integrating autonomous Indigenous polities within incipient nation states.

NOTES

The author would like to thank Kim Richard Nossal for his helpful suggestions and Leonardo Zapata Vargas for the research assistance provided.

1 For overviews, see J.C.M. Ogelsby, *Gringos from the Far North: Essays in the History of Canadian-Latin American Relations, 1866–1968* (Toronto: Macmillan of Canada, 1976); James Francis Rochlin, *Discovering the Americas: The Evolution of Canadian Foreign Policy towards Latin America* (Vancouver: UBC Press, 1994); Stefano Tijerina, "One Cinderblock at a Time: Historiography of Canadian-Latin American and Canadian-Colombian Relations," *Desafíos* 24, no. 1 (2011): 275–92; Salimah Valiani, "The Articulation of an Independent Foreign Policy: Canada and Latin America in the Early Twentieth Century," *Latin American Perspectives* 39, no. 6 (2012): 165–80.
2 This essay draws primarily on newspaper articles from Chile, Brazil, and Mexico, accessible through the World Newspaper Archive (http://www.readex.com/content/world-newspaper-archive) and Brazil's National Archive (http://bndigital.bn.br/hemeroteca-digital).
3 Note that Cuba became independent from Spain after the Spanish-American War, but was administered by the United States until 1902. Panama formed part of present-day Colombia until 1903. In what follows, the essay focuses on Brazil and Spanish America. Although Haiti is part of Latin America, it was ostracized within the region until after recognition by the United States in 1862 out of fear that bolstering its legitimacy would promote revolution elsewhere.
4 On the "costs" of independence, see Tulio Halperín Donghi, *The Aftermath of Revolution in Latin America* (New York: Harper & Row, 1973); Miguel A.

Centeno, *Blood and Debt: War and the Nation-State in Latin America* (University Park: Pennsylvania State University Press, 2002); Leandro Prados de la Escosura, "The Economic Consequences of Independence in Latin America," in *The Cambridge Economic History of Latin America*, ed. Victor Bulmer-Thomas and John H. Coatsworth (Cambridge: Cambridge University Press, 2006), 463–504; Jeremy Adelman, "Independence in Latin America," in *The Oxford Handbook of Latin American History*, ed. Jose C. Moya (Oxford: Oxford University Press, 2011), 153–80.

5 John Gallagher and Ronald Robinson, "The Imperialism of Free Trade," *The Economic History Review* 6, no. 1 (1953): 1–15; Matthew Brown, ed., *Informal Empire in Latin America: Culture, Commerce and Capital* (Oxford: Blackwell, 2008); James Belich, *Replenishing the Earth: The Settler Revolution and the Rise of the Anglo-World, 1783–1939* (Oxford: Oxford University Press, 2009), 526.

6 Carsten-Andreas Schulz, "Civilisation, Barbarism and the Making of Latin America's Place in 19th-Century International Society," *Millennium* 42, no. 3 (2014): 837–59.

7 Notable exceptions where members of subaltern groups were raised to positions of influence, such as the case of André Rebouças (1838–1898), a mulatto engineer and advisor to Brazilian Emperor Pedro II, or that of Benito Juárez (1806–1872), a Zapotec lawyer and first Indigenous president of Mexico, were exactly that: exceptional cases. After earlier experiments with open franchise, most Latin American states imposed property and literacy requirements. See Eduardo Posada-Carbó, ed., *Elections before Democracy: The History of Elections in Europe and Latin America* (London: Institute of Latin American Studies, 1996); Paul W. Drake, *Between Tyranny and Anarchy: A History of Democracy in Latin America, 1800–2006* (Stanford: Stanford University Press, 2009).

8 For instance, E. Bradford Burns, *The Poverty of Progress: Latin America in the Nineteenth Century* (Berkeley: University of California Press, 1980); Charles A. Hale, "Political and Social Ideas in Latin America, 1870–1950," in *The Cambridge History of Latin America: c.1870 to 1930*, ed. Leslie Bethell (Cambridge: Cambridge University Press, 1985), 367–441; Walter Mignolo, *The Idea of Latin America* (Oxford: Blackwell, 2005).

9 Laurence Whitehead, *Latin America: A New Interpretation* (Basingstoke: Palgrave Macmillan, 2006); Liliana Obregón, "Between Civilization and Barbarism: Creole Interventions in International Law," *Third World Quarterly* 27, no. 5 (2006): 815–32; Iván Jaksic and Eduardo Posada-Carbó, "Shipwrecks and Survivals: Liberalism in Nineteenth-Century Latin America," *Intellectual History Review* (2013): 1–20; Ori Preuss, *Transnational South America: Experiences, Ideas, and Identities, 1860s–1900s* (New York: Routledge, 2016).

10 The first international telegraph line in South America opened between Buenos Aires and Montevideo in 1866; South America was connected to Europe via the submarine cable between Madeira and Brazil's Pernambuco starting in 1874; the opening of a telegraph line between Galveston in Texas and the Mexican port cities of Tampico and Vera Cruz in 1881 eventually rerouted communications from Europe via the United States. See Anton A. Huurdeman, *The Worldwide History of Telecommunications* (New York: Wiley, 2003), 137–9; Dwayne Roy Winseck and Robert M. Pike, *Communication and Empire: Media, Markets, and Globalization, 1860–1930* (Durham, NC: Duke University Press, 2007); Ori Preuss, *Transnational South America: Experiences, Ideas, and Identities, 1860s–1900s* (New York: Routledge, 2016).

11 For a critique of the notion of "the public" in nineteenth-century Latin America, see Pablo Piccato, "Public Sphere in Latin America: A Map of the Historiography," *Social History* 35, no. 2 (2010): 165–92.

12 Ged Martin, *Britain and the Origins of Canadian Confederation, 1837–67* (Vancouver: UBC Press, 1995), 9, 428–90; Donald Grant Creighton, *The Road to Confederation: The Emergence of Canada, 1863–1867*, rev. ed. (1964; repr., Don Mills, ON: Oxford University Press, 2012), 428–90.

13 See chapter nine by Edward Beasley in this volume.

14 See also J.C.M. Ogelsby, "The Cuban Autonomist Movement's Perception of Canada, 1865–1898: Its Implication," *The Americas* 48, no. 4 (1992): 445–61.

15 Ogelsby, *Gringos from the Far North*. For instance, Rochlin, *Discovering the Americas*; Tijerina, "One Cinderblock at a Time"; Valiani, "The Articulation of an Independent Foreign Policy."

16 Norman McL. Rogers, "The Confederate Council of Trade," *Canadian Historical Review* 7 (1926): 281.

17 Rogers, "The Confederate Council of Trade," 277; Ogelsby, *Gringos from the Far North*, 11; Andrew Smith and Kirsten Greer, "Monarchism, an Emerging Canadian Identity, and the 1866 British North American Trade Mission to the West Indies and Brazil," *The Journal of Imperial and Commonwealth History* 44, no. 2 (2016): 215.

18 Commissioners from British North America Appointed to Enquire into the Trade of the West Indies, Mexico & Brazil, *Report of the Commissioners from British North America Appointed to Inquire into the Trade of the West Indies, Mexico & Brazil: Laid before Both Houses of Parliament by Order of His Excellency the Governor General* (Ottawa: Desbarats, 1866), vii.

19 For a classic statement, see José María Torrés Caicedo, *Unión Latino-Americana, pensamiento de Bolívar para formar una liga americana* (Paris: Rosa y Bouret, 1865); see also, Louise Fawcett, "The Origins and Development of Regional Ideas in the Americas," in *Regionalism and Governance in the*

Americas: Continental Drift, ed. Louise Fawcett and Mónica Serrano (Basingstoke: Palgrave Macmillan, 2005), 27–51; Greg Grandin, "Your Americanism and Mine: Americanism and Anti-Americanism in the Americas," *The American Historical Review* 111, no. 4 (2006): 1042–66.

20 Existing scholarship also emphasizes the importance of cultural and racial prejudices, especially in the case of the United States; see Lars Schoultz, *Beneath the United States: A History of U.S. Policy toward Latin America* (Cambridge, MA: Harvard University Press, 1998); for an account that focuses on European great powers, see Schulz, "Civilisation."

21 A.I. Silver, "Some Quebec Attitudes in an Age of Imperialism and Ideological Conflict," *Canadian Historical Review* 57, no. 4 (1976).

22 Paolo Riguzzi, "México, Estados Unidos y Gran Bretaña, 1867–1910: una difícil relación triangular," *Historia Mexicana* 41, no. 3 (1992): 367.

23 Ogelsby, *Gringos from the Far North*, 67.

24 Christie was censored by Parliament for the incident. On the so-called "Christie affair," see Alan K. Manchester, *British Preeminence in Brazil, Its Rise and Decline: A Study in European Expansion* (Chapel Hill: University of North Carolina Press, 1933), 267–84; Richard Graham, "Os fundamentos da ruptura de relações diplomáticas entre o Brasil e a Grã-Bretanha em 1863: 'A Questão Christie'," *Revista de História* 24, no. 49, 50 (1962): 117–38, 379–402.

25 *Report of the Commissioners from British North America*, 17.

26 Ibid., 15–16.

27 The abrogation of reciprocity, however, was discussed; for instance, *Diário do Rio de Janeiro*, 15 March 1865 and 5 March 1866; *Jornal do Commercio*, 17/18 April 1865, 13 February 1866, 28 March 1866, and 1 May 1866.

28 Smith and Greer, "Monarchism, an Emerging Canadian Identity," 231. The monarch was admitted to the Order of the Garter on 11 July 1871; see *London Gazette*, 18 July 1871. On Pedro II's diplomacy of prestige, see Lilia Moritz Schwarcz, *The Emperor's Beard: Dom Pedro II and the Tropical Monarchy of Brazil*, trans. John Gledson (New York: Hill and Wang, 2004); Amado Luiz Cervo and Clodoaldo Bueno, *História da política exterior do Brasil*, 4 ed. (Brasília: Universidade de Brasília, 2011), 191.

29 J.C.M. Ogelsby, "Relaciones canadiense-latinoamericanas pasadas, presentes y futuras," *Estudios Internacionales* 5, no. 18 (1972): 75; see also Rochlin, *Discovering the Americas*, 4.

30 Rochlin, *Discovering the Americas*, 12; Eugene H. Miller, "Canada and the Pan American Union," *International Journal* 3, no. 1 (1947): 28.

31 Douglas G. Anglin, "United States Opposition to Canadian Membership in the Pan-American Union: A Canadian View," *International Organization* 15, no. 1 (1961): 3.

32 For the reference to Perón's alleged misunderstanding of the *Statute of Westminster, 1931*, see Ogelsby, "Relaciones canadiense-latinoamericanas," 76–7.
33 Ogelsby, *Gringos from the Far North*, 287; Rochlin, *Discovering the Americas*, 13. Québécois nationalists, such as Henri Bourassa, seemed to have shared this outlook with Latin Americans. See Miller, "Canada and the Pan American Union," 30; Iris S. Podea, "Pan American Sentiment in French Canada," *International Journal* 3, no. 4 (1948): 335.
34 See H. Gordon Skilling, *Canadian Representation Abroad* (Toronto: Ryerson, 1945); D.R. Murray, "Canada's First Diplomatic Missions in Latin America," *Journal of Interamerican Studies and World Affairs* 16, no. 2 (1974): 153–72.
35 Ogelsby, *Gringos from the Far North*, 40.
36 Murray, "Canada's First Diplomatic Missions in Latin America," 155.
37 For instance, Louise Fawcett, "Between West and Non-West: Latin American Contributions to International Thought," *The International History Review* 34, no. 4 (2012): 679–704.
38 C.P. Lucas, ed., *Lord Durham's Report on the Affairs of British North America*, vol. 3 (Oxford: Clarendon, 1912). For an exception, see *Mercurio de Valparaíso*, 20 April 1839. For a Mexican example that focuses on the repression of the rebellion, see *La Lima de Vulcano*, 4 April 1838.
39 *Mercurio de Valparaíso*, 1 June 1838.
40 *Mercurio de Valparaíso*, 22 September 1838, mostly likely referring to the House of Commons debate of 16 January 1838: http://hansard.millbanksystems.com/commons/1838/jan/16/affairs-of-canada.
41 *Mercurio de Valparaíso*, 13 September 1838. This researcher found twenty-four articles in this newspaper on the rebellions in the period from 1838 to 1839. On the "Western Hemisphere idea," see Arthur Preston Whitaker, *The Western Hemisphere Idea: Its Rise and Decline* (Ithaca, NY: Cornell University Press, 1954); Juan Pablo Scarfi and Andrew Tillman, eds., *Cooperation and Hegemony in US-Latin American Relations: Revisiting the Western Hemisphere Idea* (Basingstoke: Palgrave Macmillan, 2016). On the long tradition of republicanism in Latin America, see Rafael Rojas and José Antonio Aguilar, eds., *El republicanismo en Hispanoamérica: ensayos de historia intelectual y política* (Mexico City: Fondo de Cultura Económica, 2002); on its contradictions, see Joshua Simon, *The Ideology of Creole Revolution: Imperialism and Independence in American and Latin American Political Thought* (Cambridge: Cambridge University Press, 2017).
42 *Jornal do Commercio*, 25 February 1839.
43 *Mercurio de Valparaíso*, 24 January 1850; see also 9 February 1850 and 11 February 1850.

44 See Teresa Gutiérrez-Haces, "Canadá-México: Vecindad Interferida," *Revista Mexicana de Política Exterior* 51 (1997): 11–12. For instance, *El Siglo Diez y Nueve*, 21 March 1845; 29 March 1845; 1 April 1849; 7 May 1849; 4 November 1849; 11 November 1849; 15 November 1849; 26 November 1849; 7 February 1850; 15 March 1850; *El Universal*, 12 November 1849.
45 For instance, *Diário do Rio de Janeiro*, 9 April 1865.
46 C.P. Stacey, "Fenianism and the Rise of National Feeling in Canada at the Time of Confederation," *The Canadian Historical Review* 12, no. 3 (1931): 238, 249; Creighton, *The Road to Confederation*, 374; Martin, *Britain and the Origins of Canadian Confederation*, 9, 22. See also chapter three by William Jenkins in this volume.
47 See Stacey, "Fenianism and the Rise of National Feeling in Canada at the Time of Confederation"; Martin, *Britain and the Origins of Canadian Confederation*.
48 *Jornal do Commercio*, 16 December 1866.
49 Joseph Smith, *Brazil and the United States: Convergence and Divergence* (Athens, GA: University of Georgia Press, 2010), 28–9.
50 *Jornal do Commercio*, 2 January 1868, and also 5 January 1867; consequently, for the *Diário do Rio de Janeiro*, the acquisition of Alaska by the United States was first and foremost a "coup" [*golpe*] against Confederation.
51 *Journal do Commercio*, 27 May 1865.
52 *Diário do Rio de Janeiro*, 5 March 1865; *Diário do Rio de Janeiro*, 15 March 1865; *Journal do Commercio*, 17/18 April 1865, 13 February 1866, 28 March 1866, 1 May 1866.
53 *Journal do Commercio*, 16 January 1867.
54 *Diário do Rio de Janeiro*, 7 April 1867.
55 Ibid.
56 *Mercurio de Valparaíso*, 14 March 1868, 22 July 1868. The only reference to the recently created Dominion is from the liberal *El Siglo Diez y Nueve*, reporting in a short note on the debate in the Privy Council [*consejo privado*] regarding the schedule for the first elections, 28 August 1867.
57 *Mercurio de Valparaiso*, 14 March 1868; see also 22 July 1868.
58 As noted earlier, an important exception to this trend was Cuba.
59 Donald Wright, introduction to *The Road to Confederation, The Emergence of Canada, 1863–1867*, by Donald Creighton (Toronto: Oxford University Press, 2012), xvii.

2 The 1867 Union of the British North American Colonies: A View from the United States

JACQUELINE D. KRIKORIAN
AND DAVID R. CAMERON

Between September 1864 and March 1867, political leaders in British North America worked with their counterparts in the United Kingdom to develop a constitutional framework for a new federal union. They faced many challenges as they moved towards their goal, but American interference was not one of them. Given the history between these communities, one might have expected the United States to intervene in the Canadian Confederation project in some fashion. For decades, Americans had used both the pen and the sword to try to convince Canadians to break their ties with the British Crown and join the United States.

The Continental Congress had tried unsuccessfully to bring Canada into the fold during its War of Independence. American forces, again, tried unsuccessfully to conquer their northern neighbours during the War of 1812. The issue of annexing Canada was practically a mainstay of American politics by the 1840s, as members of both the House of Representatives and the Senate repeatedly introduced resolutions to bring Canada into their union. In both 1845 and 1853, American legislators looked northward to mirror Southern expansion and to ensure an even number of non-slave and slave states.[1]

For Americans, there was a sense that Canadians would eventually merge with them. Governance of all the lands across North America was their manifest destiny. There was an assumption that the British colonists would, themselves, seek American statehood and reject the British Crown. Indeed, many Canadians believed the same, and several were involved in annexation movements on the northern side of the border.

But when the Canadian Confederation discussions rose to prominence across British North America in the 1860s, Americans were more focused on domestic political matters. Although events to the north were followed with considerable interest, there was a relatively muted response from Congress. President Abraham Lincoln was understandably preoccupied with the Civil War. His successor, President Andrew Johnson, faced a hostile Congress that contested his approach to Southern reconstruction and eventually launched impeachment proceedings against him. Officials in Washington quite naturally were more acutely concerned about the outcome of the Civil War (1861–5) and reconstruction in its aftermath than about the emerging governance structure of their northern neighbours.

In the fall of 1864, as politicians from New Brunswick, Nova Scotia, Prince Edward Island, Newfoundland, and the Province of Canada met in Quebec City to lay the foundation for the unification of the colonies of British North America, the *New York Times* correspondent, reporting from Montreal on 3 October 1864, observed: "It is singular that, at the very time when your plotters are endeavoring to compass a separation of States, which have hitherto been bound together, our leading men should be trying to bring about a confederation of provinces hitherto disjointed."[2]

By the time the Civil War came to an end in April 1865, well over 600,000 were dead. The battlefield, not the negotiating table, set the terms on which the war ended. This outcome left a legacy of mistrust and anger between the North and the South. Governance issues became a difficult and thorny matter for both sides. In December 1865, Congress denied representatives elected from Southern states the right to be seated. In March 1867, the same month that the *British North America Act, 1867* was adopted by the imperial parliament in London, Congress enacted legislation to divide the ten Confederate states into five districts, each to be governed by military authority.[3]

From 1865 to 1867, while the colonies of British North America were peacefully negotiating the framework for their new constitution, the Congress was busy focusing on reconstruction. In January 1865, legislators passed the Thirteenth Amendment to the US Constitution to abolish slavery.[4] In April 1866, they enacted the *Civil Rights Act* a second time to override a presidential veto.[5] In July 1866, Congress passed the Fourteenth Amendment to the US Constitution for citizenship rights and equal protection of the law.[6]

Legislators were bitterly at odds with President Johnson, who was more sympathetic to the rapid reintegration of the Southern states into the Union, and less sympathetic to the progressive accommodation of former slaves. The struggle eventually led to Johnson's impeachment in the House of Representatives in February 1868, although the measure narrowly missed being upheld in the Senate.

In the aftermath of the Civil War, officials in Washington were interested in expanding their territories in the Northern Hemisphere,[7] and in particular, towards the Pacific Ocean. Secretary of State William H. Seward convinced Congress of the value and importance of purchasing Alaska from the Russians. In doing so, "he thought it would help the United States to acquire British Columbia."[8] As the editor of the *Daily British Colonist* explained in May 1867, the Alaskan purchase "places the whole of Her Majesty's possessions on the Pacific in the position of a piece of meat between two slices of bread, where they may be devoured in a single bite."[9]

Like the executive branch of government, members of Congress were more focused on their own domestic political problems. Interest in their northern neighbours was largely based on day-to-day trade and security issues rather than on any new proposed federal system. Though members of Congress did address the issue of Canadian Confederation on two notable occasions, these were the exceptions rather than the rule. Overall legislative interest in changes to the governance structure of the colonies of British North America was limited.

When it came to policy issues involving the colonies, American legislators were primarily interested in commercial relations between the United States and the territories to the north. Problems associated with the 1854 Reciprocity Treaty were debated extensively and, in January 1865, Congress recommended its abrogation.[10] The decision to end the free trade arrangement came in March 1865 when British-American relations were near their lowest. But abrogation of the treaty was also due to "protectionist opinion, especially in the state of New York."[11]

The other major issue addressed by Congressional leaders regarding the colonies of British North America was border security. Until the end of the Civil War, Confederate rebels invaded Northern states from the colonies, most notably during the October 1864 St Albans Raid in Vermont. Legislators in both the Senate and the House of Representatives debated how to protect northern communities from these incursions, with some even arguing for the stationing of an army along the border.[12]

There was no significant discussion of the unification of the British North American colonies in the Congress of the Confederate States. The only mention was in reference to developing a reciprocity treaty between the colonies and the Southern states upon their recognition of independence. A resolution "that a secret agent should be sent to Canada to promote" a free trade arrangement was discussed in the Confederate House of Representatives, though not adopted.[13]

When it came to concerns arising about relations between the United States and the colonies, Congressional leaders in the North were primarily focused on trade and defence. The proposed unification of the colonies received only limited attention. The issue of Canadian Confederation only arose in Congress in three contexts: in reports on the end of the Reciprocity Treaty, in a proposed annexation bill, and in a resolution "concerning the establishment of monarchical institutions in America by the despotic governments of Europe" adopted by the House Foreign Affairs Committee. In none of these instances, however, did legislators recommend active intervention in Canadian affairs without the consent of the inhabitants.

To understand the impact of the abrogation of the Reciprocity Treaty on the country's commerce, both the Senate and the House of Representatives sought reports from Hugh McCulloch, the secretary of the treasury. In both reports, there was a clear understanding that politics and commerce were tied together, particularly in relation to the proposed Confederation agreement.

The *Derby Report* was prepared for the Senate and publicly released as an interim report in 1866 and as a final report in February 1867. It demonstrated that commercial relations between Canada and the United States grew considerably during the time the Reciprocity Treaty was in effect.[14] It also highlighted that by the end of the treaty in 1866, the colonies of British North America traded twice as much with the United States as they did with England.[15] The interim report suggested that the United States annex Britain's colonies on the Pacific as payment for outstanding British war reparations.[16] It also recommended a return to the reciprocity agreement and drafted a bill entitled "An Act to Provide for the Temporary Renewal of the Treaty of Reciprocity with Great Britain and the British Provinces of North America."[17] The final version of the *Derby Report* expressly addressed the proposed Canadian Confederation and emphasized that "the United States cannot be expected to favor a measure tending to build up a monarchy on its borders." It argued that one of the impetuses for the proposed unification of the colonies was to create a political organization "strong enough to confront the United States," and that this development would shift the axis of Canada's trade to the east, rather than through the United States to the south.[18]

The House of Representative's report on the abrogation of the Reciprocity Treaty, prepared by James W. Taylor, also emphasized the commercial value of the treaty.[19] By 1865, the colonies of British North America were the second largest market for the United States[20] and the fourth leading maritime community in the world.[21] The report also addressed the emerging significance of trade with British territories and colonies in the west.[22]

Unlike the *Derby Report*, which urged a renewal of reciprocal trade, the *Taylor Report* recommended that, in consultation with the British government, the American government should make "an overture to the people of the English colonies on this continent ... to unite their fortunes with the people and government of the United States."[23] To facilitate this recommendation and circumvent the proposed Confederation of the British colonies, draft legislation for annexing them was attached to the report.

On 3 July 1866, as British North Americans were preparing for another possible Fenian invasion,[24] Nathaniel Banks submitted the annexation bill from the *Taylor Report* to the House of Representatives. Entitled "For the Admission of the States of Nova Scotia, New Brunswick, Canada East, and Canada West, and for the Organization of the Territories of Selkirk, Saskatchewan, and Columbia," the proposed legislation set out the terms and conditions for the annexation of the British North American colonies.[25]

Banks was an enthusiastic proponent of American expansionism. He was convinced that "the extension of American influence was a natural and irreversible process."[26] He was a strong advocate for the purchase of Alaska from the Russians, and as chair of the Foreign Affairs Committee, he worked with Secretary of State Steward to ensure its eventual success. Banks was also a strong proponent of US expansion in the Caribbean, and sought to buy the West Indies from Denmark and annex both Cuba and Santo Domingo.[27] He believed that a policy of granting statehood to the British colonies would have "wide popular appeal, building as it did on the strong sense of nationalism fostered by the Civil War."[28]

Banks submitted the annexation bill with the unanimous support of the House of Representatives, and it received first and second reading before being referred to the Foreign Affairs Committee.[29] The initiative provided that the British colonies would effectively cede all publicly owned resources including lands, canals, and harbours, as well as railway stocks and debts. In consideration, the American government would assume the debts and liabilities of the "late provinces" up to $85.7 million.[30] The United States would also make specified annual grants to each of the colonies in exchange for the right to levy all import and export duties.[31]

Banks's bill was widely reported in the United States and received support in the Northern states. The Annexation League of Massachusetts endorsed the proposal to unite Canada with the United States,[32] as did the Central Annexation Club of New York.[33] But others were less supportive. The New York correspondent for South Carolina's *Charleston Daily News* regarded the "affair as a tempest in a tea-pot, or as a huge mountain – or rather not a huge one – whose labor will bring forth nothing more terrible than an innocent and ridiculous Lilliputian rodent quadruped."[34] Media commentary from the Southern states was particularly harsh in its condemnation of the proposed bill. Banks, who had been a general in the Union army stationed in Louisiana, was widely viewed with contempt for his role in the Civil War. These newspapers, such as Baton Rouge's *Sugar Planter*, viewed the measure as just another ploy to "plunder" and to expand the power of the North at the expense of the South.[35]

The only suggestion of forcing the issue upon the colonists of British North America came from outside of Congress. In a speech in Sandusky, Ohio, which was widely reported from Vermont to Mississippi, General Sherman announced that in regard to the issue of annexation, "We don't want Canada, but if we should, a campaign of five days would bring it."[36]

The bill never received third reading in the House of Representatives and was not considered by the Senate. Though discussion of the bill in Congress was animated, there was relatively little of it. There was a general sense – in both Congressional discussions and the media coverage of the bill – that the British colonists should be allowed to decide their own fate, and that neither the British nor the Americans should determine the issue for them.

The House of Representatives also introduced a resolution addressing Confederation and underscoring their displeasure with the entrenchment of monarchical institutions on their northern borders. In February 1867, while the *British North America Act, 1867* was being debated in the House of Lords, elected officials in Washington began, once again, to address the issue of Confederation in Congress. Some members of the House of Representatives were not only opposed to the initiative, but at times, outright hostile. Their disdain, however, largely reflected the legislators' anti-British sentiment rather than any specific concerns about the colonists themselves or about the specifics of the proposed Confederation. Others, however, were more sanguine, recognizing the inevitability of the measure and looking towards what might be its positive outcomes.

Banks, the chair of the Foreign Affairs Committee, explained it was not their intention "to present any menace or any threat or to make any protest on this question, not even to determine the character." Rather, he told the House, the committee was "looking to positive results proposed in her colonies by the Government of Great Britain." He said he believed the resolution expressed an opinion on the changed nature of the colonies, that they were now "representing principles hostile to the interests, antagonistic to the Government of this country, [and] that it cannot be regarded with solicitude." The principles are found to be "in contravention of the rights and interests" of the United States. But the committee did not advise further action.[37]

The House Resolution No. 46 was referred to Senate on 28 March 1867, and read twice before being referred to the Senate Committee on Foreign Relations.[38] The Senators, however, did not address it further. It is quite likely that it was dropped from consideration because the *British North America Act, 1867* was enacted by the parliament of the United Kingdom only a few days later, and by that point Confederation was a fait accompli.

While Congress was willing to discuss the proposed Confederation plans taking place north of its border, the White House was not so inclined. Contested issues in the context of foreign affairs, such as border security, were addressed, but matters internal to Canada and the Maritime communities were not discussed. The successive presidential State of the Union addresses during this period do not even mention the emerging political regime of British North America; and on those rare occasions when British North America was publicly considered, it was to comment on border issues, such as the Fenian raids, which attracted a good deal of public attention at the time. Despite serious, ongoing problems with Great Britain, both Lincoln and Johnson showed respect for the colonies of British North America. Had the colonists sought to join the United States, there is little doubt the proposal would have been taken seriously, at least by the American government. But officials in Washington respected the principle of self-determination for their northern neighbours. Although Secretary of State Seward was keen to see all the territories of North America under the government of the

United States – or, at the very least, to obtain British Columbia from the British – his goals never materialized.

While Lincoln and Johnson remained relatively quiet about Confederation, the media had no hesitation in expressing their comments. Close to fifty reports on Confederation appeared in the *New York Times* from September 1864 to August 1867.[39] Most of them dealt with the debates that arose during the passage of the *British North America Act, 1867* by the British parliament; some discussed the larger international context within which the formation of Canada was understood at the time. It is apparent that the American readers of the *Times* were regularly informed about the political and constitutional discussions taking place on their northern border.

In reporting on the constitutional debates taking place in British North America, the pages of the *New York Times* discussed a dynamic, unfolding process whose end point was not clear at the beginning. Would British North America reconstitute itself or not? If it did, could the new structure be expected to survive? What would its relationships with Great Britain and the United States look like? These were open questions for most of the reporting during this period, and, inevitably, they offer a very different angle of vision from the perspective of a Canadian, looking back a century and a half later on the period as "the founding of Canada." Thus, the proclamation of the *British North America Act, 1867* on 1 July 1867 was treated in the *Times* as a significant step in an ongoing process of political development, not as the founding act in the formation of a new political nationality. Indeed, commentators were not at all sure that this new political creation would endure. On 2 July 1867, a substantial report notes that "the occasion was naturally marked by demonstrations of a patriotic character, and the First of July, it is announced, will henceforth be regarded as a sort of national anniversary in the United Provinces."[40]

Some communities in the United States, however, voiced criticism of the proposed Canadian Confederation project. Perhaps the loudest opposition to the Confederation discussions came from the state of Maine, whose longstanding grievances with their northern neighbours dated back to the War of Independence. The cross-border disputes between the British and American communities – involving trade, the fisheries, and the New Brunswick/Maine boundary – were contentious. The greatest concern for Maine residents, however, lay with their defence. Even prior to the Confederation proposal, they felt they were vulnerable to attack not only from marauding Confederate soldiers from the South, but also from Britain itself. A new monarchical power of unified colonies situated on their northern border was viewed as a real threat to their territoriality integrity and safety.

A report on the vulnerability of Maine had been tabled in the House of Representatives in June 1864. It had sought better resources to enhance the defence of the state against an aggressive Great Britain, which had displayed "her hostile character" and had "encouraged" the Confederate states against the North. The report highlighted that, with the outbreak of the Civil War, the British had "sent troops to Canada and to her other North American provinces, and ha[d] kept a huge fleet, in conjunction with the French, in the harbor of Halifax ... or hovering along the northern coast of the United States."[41] Maine residents viewed these measures as hostile, not defensive. This fear of invasion was inflamed with the St Albans, Vermont, raid by twenty Confederate soldiers who used British North America as their base of operations. The issue was taken very seriously, and Congress itself sought to investigate what had "to be done to protect our northern boundary from the arson, robbery and raids of the sneaking scoundrels upon our borders."[42]

In his address to the Maine legislature in January 1867, newly elected Governor Joshua Chamberlain highlighted his concern about the implications of the British "scheme" to consolidate the provinces of British North America. Chamberlain contended that this shift in governance, combined with the emerging French Empire of Mexico, constituted a "great conspiracy against Liberty" and was little more than an attempt "to environ us with Monarchies" and to "take advantage" of the United States while it was preoccupied with the Civil War and reconstruction.[43] One month later, a legislative committee was established to examine the proposed Canadian Confederation arrangements and their implications for Maine. The report effectively viewed British North Americans as pawns in a Confederation scheme concocted by the British government.

Franco-Americans also objected to the proposed Confederation initiative. By the middle of the nineteenth century, there were approximately one quarter of a million native French-speaking inhabitants in the United States.[44] While there were large concentrations of Franco-Americans in Louisiana, vibrant communities also existed across the northern states, many with their roots in British North America. Franco-Americans concerned about the move towards Confederation actively engaged in the American political process to bring attention to the issue and to lobby for its end. Their alternative was annexation of the British North American colonies to the United States. They held conferences in New York in April and December 1866, and in Detroit in 1867, which highlighted the Confederation "problem." Senator Sumner, the powerful chair of the Foreign Relations Committee, was presented with a memorial on behalf of Franco-Americans. He then referred it to his committee for consideration. The memorial argued that the proposed Confederation project constituted a threat to the United States. Emphasis was placed on how the British were building up their military and their fortifications along the border. There also was a discussion about the additional security costs facing Americans that would result if this project were achieved.[45] But if Franco-Americans had expected Congress to act on their request, they were sorely disappointed. The memorial was discharged from the Foreign Affairs Committee a few weeks later and not reported back to the legislature. No further action was taken on the matter in the Senate.

Franco-Americans who closely followed the Confederation debates between 1864 and 1867 passionately believed that a better alternative to unifying the colonies was their annexation to the United States. In part, this view was because they wanted to enhance their American presence to ensure they had better representation in the corridors of power. Having a critical mass of native French speakers would serve this goal well.

Colonists in British North America viewed the United States as a real threat. They feared invasion not only from Fenian marauders but also from members of the Union army returning from the Civil War. One of the factors that clearly moved the British North American colonies towards Confederation was this perceived threat of annexation by the American government.

However, despite a few small pockets of opposition, the American government never seriously considered intervention in the domestic political arrangements of British North America over the issue of Confederation. Although suggestions of annexation were sometimes raised as an alternative to Confederation, they were never meaningfully pursued. There was a strong sense in the United States that it was up to the colonists of British North America to decide for themselves on the form of government under which they would live. There was, in addition, a widespread belief that they would, in due course, choose to join the United States.

NOTES

The authors would like to thank Brianna Guenther, Andrew McDougall, and Geleta McLoughlin for their research expertise, as well as Fulbright Canada and the Wilson Center for their generous support.

1 The 1845 annexation debates focused on Canada and Texas, and the 1853 annexation debates focused on Canada and Cuba.
2 *New York Times* Correspondent, "From Canada: The Proposed Confederation of British North America, Its Advantages and Difficulties," *New York Times*, 10 October 1964, 8.
3 *An Act to Provide for the More Efficient Government of the Rebel States*, 14 Stat. 428 (2 March 1867).
4 The amendment was ratified by enough states to become part of the US Constitution in December 1865.
5 *An Act to Protect All Persons in the United States in Their Civil Rights, and Furnish the Means of their Vindication*, 14 Stat. 27 (9 April 1866).
6 The amendment was ratified by enough states to become part of the US Constitution in July 1868.
7 Theodore Clarke Smith, "Expansion after the Civil War, 1865–1871," *Political Science Quarterly* 16, no. 3 (September 1901): 412–36.
8 Walter Stahr, *Seward, Lincoln's Indispensable Man* (New York: Simon & Schuster, 2013), 498. See also David E. Shi, "Seward's Attempt to Annex British Columbia, 1865–1869," *Pacific Historical Review* 47, no. 2 (May 1978): 217–38 and the *Detroit Free Press*, who explained in May 1867 that the purchase of Alaska would only hasten the annexation of these British North American colonies as "they are entirely dependent upon us." "Annexation Meetings at Vancouver Island," *Detroit Free Press*, Michigan, 28 May 1867.
9 "Editorial," *Daily British Colonist*, 16 May 1867, cited in Richard A. Pierce, "Alaska in 1867 as Viewed from Victoria," *Queen's Quarterly* 74, no. 4 (Winter 1967): 668.
10 Congress adopted a joint resolution to authorize the president to abrogate the treaty on 17 January 1865 in the early stage of the discussions on a proposed Confederation in Canada, and this abrogation went into effect on 17 March 1866.
11 See D.C. Masters, *Reciprocity, 1846–1911*, Canadian Historical Association, Historical Booklet no. 12 (Ottawa, 1965), 11.
12 Senator Chandler, *Journal of the Senate of the United States of America*, 38th Congress, 2nd Session, volume 57 (14 December 1864), 26.

13 Resolution introduced by Mr Boyce, House of Representatives, *Journal of the Congress of the Confederate States of America, 1861–1865*, vol. 6 (6 February 1863), Senate of the United States, 58th Congress, 2d Session, Document no. 234 (Washington, DC: Government Printing Press, 1905), 81.
14 The *Derby Report* found that the average growth rate of trade between the British North American colonies and the United States exceeded 25% per annum. When the treaty was abrogated in 1866, commerce between the two communities was worth $82 million, and it involved arrivals and departures of 36,301 vessels containing approximately 7.3 million tons of goods and products. E.H. Derby, *Information Relative to the Practicability of Establishing Equal Reciprocal Relations between the United States and the BNA provinces, and the Actual Condition of the Question of the Fisheries*, Requested by the Senate on 27 July 1866, Ex. Doc. No. 30 (19 February, 1867), 22, in *Senate Executive Documents*, 39th Congress, 2nd Session (Washington: Government Printing Office, 1867). Hereinafter referred to as the *Derby Report*.
15 *Derby Report*, 11.
16 E.H. Derby, *A Preliminary Report of the Treaty of Reciprocity with Great Britain to Regulate the Trade between the United States and the Provinces of British North America* (Washington, DC: Treasury Department, 1866), 64. Hereinafter referred to as Derby, *Preliminary Report*.
17 Derby, *Preliminary Report*, 69–70.
18 *Derby Report*, 25.
19 During the twelve years it had been in effect, the aggregate commerce between the United States and the colonies of British North America had grown from approximately $16 to $69 million. "Trade with British America," in House of Representatives, *Commercial Relations with British America*, 39th Congress, 1st Session, Ex. Doc. 128 (14 June 1866), 4, in *Executive Documents, Printed by the Order of the House of Representatives during the First Session of the Thirty-Ninth Congress, 1865–1866*, vol. 12 (Washington, DC: Government Printing, 1866), 1, 2. Hereinafter cited as the *Taylor Report*.
20 *Taylor Report*, 2.
21 Ibid., 22.
22 Ibid., 4.
23 Ibid., 32.
24 C.P. Stacey, "Fenianism and the Rise of National Feeling in Canada at the Time of Confederation," *Canadian Historical Review* 12, no. 3 (September 1931): 238–61.
25 H.R. 754, a bill entitled "For the Admission of the States of Nova Scotia, New Brunswick, Canada East, and Canada West, and for the Organization

of the Territories of Selkirk, Saskatchewan, and Columbia," 39th Congress, 1st Session (2 July 1866). Hereinafter referred to as the Annexation Bill.
26 James G. Hollandsworth, Jr., *Pretense of Glory: The Life of General Nathaniel P. Banks* (Baton Rouge, LA: Louisiana State University Press, 1998), 229.
27 Ibid., 231.
28 Ibid., 229.
29 House of Representatives, "Annexation of British America," *The Congressional Globe*, 39th Congress, 1st Session (3 July 1867), 3548. See also Theodore C. Blegen, "A Plan for the Union of British North America and the United States, 1866," *Mississippi Valley Historical Review* 4, no. 4 (March 1918): 470–83.
30 Article I, Annexation Bill. The bulk of payments would go to Canada East ($29 million) and Canada West ($36.5 million).
31 Article II, Annexation Bill.
32 "General Intelligence," *The Sun*, New York, 31 August 1866, 1.
33 "New York Letter, from Our Own Correspondent," *Charleston Daily News*, Charleston, SC, 8 August 1866, 1.
34 Ibid.
35 "Congressional," *Sugar Planter*, West Baton Rouge, LA, 7 July 1866.
36 "Don't Want Canada," *The Daily Clarion and Standard*, Jackson, MS, 20 July 1866 and "News Items," *The Free Press*, Burlington, VT, 27 July 1866.
37 Nathanial Banks, House of Representatives, *Congressional Globe*, 40th Congress, 1st Session (27 March 1867), 392.
38 House of Representatives, *Congressional Globe*, 40th Congress, 1st Session (8 March 1867).
39 Elmer Davis, in his book *A History of the New York Times, 1851–1921* (New York: New York Times, 1921), 46, writes: "So by the opening of the Civil War *The New York Times* ... had already won itself a place as one of the great papers of America. Also, it had prospered. As early as 1855 it claimed the honor of being second only to *The Herald* in circulation, and by the end of the first decade nobody in the *Times* office would admit that it had any superior."
40 "The New Government of Canada," *New York Times*, 2 July 1867, 4.
41 House of Representatives, Select Committee, *Report on Defences of the Northeastern Frontier*, Report no. 119, 38th Congress, 1st Session (20 June 1864), 61, 62.
42 Mr Cox, House of Representatives, *Congressional Globe*, 38th Congress, 2nd Session (15 December 1864), 49. For an excellent overview of the tension between American and British governments in the context of British North America, see Yves Roby, *The United States and Confederation*, Centennial Historical Booklet, no. 4 (Ottawa: The Centennial Commission, 1967), 3–19.

43 Governor Joshua Chamberlain, "Provincial Confederation," Address to the Members of the Senate and House of Representatives (January 1867), in *Acts and Resolves Passed by the Forty-Sixth Legislature of the State of Maine* (Augusta, ME: Stevens & Sayward, 1867), 153.
44 Saint-Pierre, cited by A.I. Silver, *The French-Canadian Idea of Confederation* (Toronto: University of Toronto), 24, fn. 70, explains that by 1870 there were approximately 40,000 native French-speaking people in Michigan, which constituted about 5% of its total population.
45 A Memorial to the Senate of the United States, from the French Canadians of the United States, in Opposition to the Scheme for the Confederation of the British Provinces of North America, RG46, Records of the US Senate, 39th Congress, Box No. 39, Committee on Foreign Relations, SEN 39A-H6.1 (10 December 1866 to 26 February 1867), National Archives, Pennsylvania Ave., Washington, DC.

3 "Such Bastard Despotism": Fenian Views of Canadian Confederation

WILLIAM JENKINS

Fenianism was a revolutionary and largely transatlantic phenomenon dedicated to the violent overthrow of British rule and the establishment of republican government in Ireland. By the mid-1860s, many were prepared and determined to act, not least in the growing American Irish diaspora. This chapter examines the shape of Fenian opinion on the moment of Canadian Confederation from beyond the borders of Canada. As the evidence presented will show, news of the impending British North America (BNA) Act that was to confederate three colonies was not met with a warm welcome by this rebellious cohort, who took pride in undermining what they perceived to be "British interests" whenever and wherever possible. Not only did the rather passionless act's preamble confirm that the Dominion of Canada would be closely modelled on British political and legal structures, it also confirmed Canada's place within the British Empire with Queen Victoria remaining, in the words of the new country's later chief archivist, as "chief executive of the Empire."[1] For American Fenians bullish about advancing the expansionist visions of their republic in the aftermath of a bloody civil war, the BNA Act represented an inconvenience if not a frustrating imposition. Adding further to Fenian irritation, one of the leading promoters of Canadian Confederation, Thomas D'Arcy McGee, had, almost two decades earlier, participated in an Irish movement with similarly radical nationalist goals.

Transatlantic Fenianism and the Canadian Dimension

Previous attempts to forcibly plant the republican "tree of liberty" in Ireland had failed. The United Irishmen rebellion of 1798 touched several regions of the island and ended with more than 10,000 deaths; its leader, Theobald Wolfe Tone, would later become one of the most celebrated martyrs of Irish nationalism. The Young Ireland rebellion in 1848, inspired by events in Europe, was, in contrast, a brief and local affair whose leaders either fled into exile or were transported to Australia. This inglorious revolutionary moment, moreover, occurred in the midst of the Great Famine, and the hundreds of thousands in the process of leaving Ireland included many who continued to believe in physical-force solutions so that Irish statehood might one day align with Young Ireland's concept of a culturally distinctive Irish nationhood.

Chief among the North American destinations of these famine-era emigrants was New York, and it was there that the Fenian Brotherhood (FB) was founded in April 1859, with John O'Mahony as leader or "head centre."[2] O'Mahony had participated in the Young Ireland rebellion and fled to revolutionary Paris in its aftermath. A Gaelic scholar, O'Mahony anglicized the term for the bands of warriors (*Fianna*) defending ancient Ireland from foreign invasion for the naming of the new outfit. In 1858, he and Michael Doheny, a Young Irelander now resident in New York, bankrolled James Stephens, another 1848 survivor who had joined O'Mahony in Paris, to found a new revolutionary organization in Ireland, and on 17 March 1858 (St Patrick's Day), in Dublin, a body subsequently recognized as the Irish Republican Brotherhood (IRB) was born.[3] This latest attempt to organize Irish revolutionary separatism, with poles on either side of the Atlantic, would become known to members, sympathizers, and opponents alike as the "Fenian movement" or "Fenianism."

While IRB head centre Stephens considered Dublin to be the headquarters of this revolutionary operation, the balance of transatlantic power was reversed by late 1865.[4] In the United States, the Fenians could openly proclaim their objectives, unlike in Ireland, where secrecy remained imperative (though elusive) in a tightly policed society and access to arms was restricted. Nonetheless, the determined and dictatorial Stephens directed a nationwide recruitment campaign from 1861, and in 1863 a Dublin-based weekly newspaper, the *Irish People*, was founded, aiding not only the raising of funds but also the popularity of the movement among Irish migrants in England and Scotland. All in all, R.V. Comerford estimates that about 50,000 men, drawn largely from the ranks of the artisanal and lower middle classes, joined the organization.[5] In contrast, news about American FB meetings, picnics, and the progress of local "circle" formations was openly reported in newspapers such as New York's weekly *Irish American*, owned and edited by a member of the FB "senate," or Buffalo's more explicitly titled *Fenian Volunteer*, run by the city's chief Fenian, or "district centre." The *Irish People* never mentioned the IRB, but its rhetoric made its sympathies clear (it also noted the progress of the FB), and as public unease grew over the presence of a shadowy revolutionary movement, a wave of arrests on 15 September 1865 shut down the newspaper and proved debilitating to the IRB.[6] Contrary to James Stephens's hopes, 1865 would not be the "year of action."

Across the Atlantic, American Fenianism was strengthened by the wave of recruitment that followed the Civil War. Months after the cessation of hostilities, the FB was transformed into a formidable organization with weaponry, hardened and experienced military men, and financial resources at the ready. A report submitted at the second FB congress, held in Cincinnati in January 1865, enumerated 247 circles in good standing, most of these being in New York (45), Massachusetts (36), and Illinois (24); by the end of the year, the number of circles was close to seven hundred.[7] David Brundage has recently estimated that the FB comprised approximately 50,000 members at this point, most of whom were drawn from the working classes, which, alongside an estimated 200,000 supporters, made it "the first mass-based Irish nationalist movement in American history."[8]

Veterans among the FB volunteers were particularly convinced that their loyalty to the American Union was now unquestionable given wartime sacrifices. Though the prospects of post-war occupational mobility may have been promising, there were those who believed that participation in the effort to remove an age-old Irish colonial stigma, while simultaneously cultivating their manhood and employment prospects, were reasons enough to enlist as a modern "soldier of Erin." From their vantage point, the sites of potential military engagement would include not only Ireland itself but also the British North American colonies that stretched from the Great Lakes to the Atlantic Coast, and especially the most populous of them, Canada.

The enduring presence of the British Crown on the other side of a long northern frontier thus led to the revival of an idea to invade the territory, disrupt Anglo-American diplomatic relations, and extract concessions from Britain that could pave the way to Irish freedom. Rhetoric about invading Canada was not new since the Anglo-American War of 1812–14, but a plot was hatched in the revolutionary year of 1848 by some radical Irish-Canadian nationalists, with hopes of assistance from the

New York world of Young Ireland exiles as well as from Louis-Joseph Papineau and republican-leaning French Canadian Rouges.[9] Nothing came of this idea, but a return to it in 1865 contributed to the weakening of the FB as internal rancour led to its division into two wings by the end of the year. One wing led by the now-deposed O'Mahony maintained that insurrection should take place in Ireland; the other, known as the "senate wing" or the "Men of Action" and led by the new president, William R. Roberts, countered that the British Navy in the North Atlantic presented too great a challenge, and that striking the British Empire through raids on Canada was a more fruitful course of action.[10] With Irish Fenianism hit by a climate of suppression after September 1865, American Fenians retained hope that another Anglo-American war could work in Ireland's favour. Invading Canada might not only kick-start such a conflict but also claim territory for the United States.

Radical Irish-Canadian nationalism also experienced some rejuvenation in the political climate of these years. Toronto was its epicentre by the mid-1860s, as Fenianism made inroads within the city's lay-controlled Hibernian Benevolent Society.[11] The weekly *Irish Canadian* newspaper commenced publication in 1863, and its editor Patrick Boyle went on to become a persistent critic of British imperialism and anti-Catholic attitudes in Canada West. Not surprisingly, then, the paper dismissed the Confederation proposals as utopian – "a mere fantasy, an empirical trick" – in the face of what it regarded as continued danger from south of the border; its proposed remedy, however, was nothing less than annexation to the American republic![12] The paper also contained commentaries and correspondence on the subject of Fenianism, and all in all, the network of Fenian "lodges" operating in Canada West was believed to have reached a peak of seventeen, with nine in Toronto alone.[13] Not that Boyle could print such news; these figures were rather derived from the efforts of operatives working for Canada West's "embryonic secret police," the Western Frontier Constabulary, established in 1864.[14] These Canadian Fenians, led by outspoken Toronto tavern-keeper Michael Murphy, leaned more towards the O'Mahony wing than that of Roberts, however.

As the American Civil War entered its final months, promotion of the Confederation idea reached an advanced stage north of the border with its approval by the Canadian legislature in March 1865. Challenges remained, however, in the Maritime colonies, where the benefits of a political union were not clear to all who possessed a vote and a public voice. Significantly for Fenians and their supporters, ex–Young

Irelander D'Arcy McGee saw in Confederation the path towards an exciting new northern nationality under the British Crown. McGee had sketched out his vision almost ten years before the BNA Act was passed, and, as his biographer notes, excelled in "his ability to articulate these ideas in a powerful, persuasive, and memorable way," especially when Confederation returned to the political agenda in 1864–5.[15] McGee had participated in the 1848 rebellion and had even approved of the idea to invade Canada when resident in New York. But he grew disillusioned with life in the American republic with its recurrent nativism and limited economic prospects for Irish Catholics, and moved with his family to Montreal in 1857. Irish republicans had been aware of McGee's about-face for years, but a controversial speech presented and published in Ireland in May 1865 brought revulsion for the man to new heights.[16] McGee exalted the advantages of migration to "a quiet British province" and reflected that on the basis of his experience, he "would much rather direct [his] steps to British America than to Republican America."[17] His intemperate words on Fenianism, which he dismissed as made up of "Punch-and-Judy Jacobins" led by a mentally unstable O'Mahony, appeared, however, not in his presented speech but in a written copy sent separately to the *Dublin Evening Mail*.[18] Besides being publicly scorned in the Fenian press for more than a month afterwards, McGee's political sentiments were useful foil for those within the Anglophobic world of Fenianism.

Although the FB was now a fractured organization with separate headquarters in New York, British North Americans, and Canadian Attorney General John A. Macdonald in particular, were under no illusions about the threat they posed to colonial security. As news about Fenian movements was relayed to Macdonald from detectives and secret service men on both sides of the border, public alarms were activated in Canada in the winter of 1865–66 and on St Patrick's Day 1866, creating an almost constant sense of emergency. At the fourth FB congress in Pittsburgh in February 1866, Roberts was effusive about the opportunity that now existed "to free Ireland from a galling bondage, and place her as a brilliant star in the firmament of republicanism."[19] The next moment of public intrigue belonged not, however, to Roberts's wing but to that of O'Mahony, as an attempt was made in April 1866 to capture Campobello Island off the coast of New Brunswick. This action was a desperate pitch to seize the initiative from Roberts, appease impatient comrades, and reverse funding setbacks, but the logic was familiar: claim contested territory for the United States, use the island as a base for a war against Britain, and then provoke the much-desired Anglo-American war. With the Campobello affair ending in ignominious failure, the Men of Action wasted little time in striking at the beginning of June with border raids at Niagara and Vermont. The most sustained engagement with the Canadian militia occurred near the Niagara village of Ridgeway, eight miles west of the border with Buffalo, involving more than 1,000 soldiers of the "Irish Republican Army" led by US Civil War veteran John O'Neill.[20] A combination of intelligence lapses and complacency had provided an all-important window of opportunity for the raiders. A small, but symbolically significant, number of deaths occurred on both sides, with dozens of others wounded. The swift action of the American government to enforce the Neutrality Act and prevent the arrival of reinforcements from Buffalo, coupled with the looming arrival of Toronto cavalry and other units, forced the Fenians to retreat across the border where they were promptly arrested. The episode lasted barely more than two days.

As Peter B. Waite and C.P. Stacey have argued, the Fenian raids, and the alarms that both preceded and succeeded them, went some way to reducing, if not dissolving, the resistance to Confederation that remained in Nova Scotia and New Brunswick.[21] Nonetheless, former Nova Scotia premier Joseph Howe had collected more than 40,000 signatures for an anti-Confederation petition by the end of October 1866. As Waite concludes: "Confederation was not, except in Canada West (Ontario), what is usually referred to as a popular movement. It was imposed on British North America by ingenuity, luck, courage, and sheer force."[22]

Dismissing the Dominion

Waite's words provide a convenient point of departure for mapping the strands of Fenian opinion on Canadian Confederation in the remainder of this chapter. Evidence is taken mostly from the Fenian press on both sides of the Atlantic, but particularly from the United States, where the implications of Confederation to the north were felt most acutely. Moreover, while the intensity of Fenian Anglophobia and their much-rehearsed narratives of British misdeeds in Ireland need to be kept in mind, the passionate, ultra-loyal devotion of FB members to the United States and its republican institutions was also striking. As Timothy G. Lynch writes, these Irish nationalists "held themselves up as the true inheritors of America's republican heritage."[23] This sentiment was, to some degree, informed by an upsurge in American civic nationalism in the era of Reconstruction that, in tandem with Irish-American nationalism, recognized "a republican tradition dating back to the eighteenth century," which emphasized "political liberty and equality and the institutionalization of those ideals in a state."[24] The third FB congress in Philadelphia in October 1865 restructured the organization along the lines of the United States Congress, for example, with the head centre replaced by a president to be elected annually; other highlights included a fifteen-man senate and a new constitution.[25] Elsewhere, the *Fenian Volunteer* encouraged Irish immigrant children to "be taught to love and honor the principles of American freedom," though they were also expected "to regard with abhorrence the name of England, associated as it has always been, with famine, sword and flame, as well the thousand nameless cruelties which have been practiced upon the Irish race from time immemorial."[26] The American republic also provided a role model for a future free Ireland. As Roberts put it at the fourth FB congress in Pittsburgh, their object was "the elevation of our suffering brethren to the dignity and blessings of free manhood, such as is today the birth-right of the people of this Republic."[27] This remark also spoke to the perceived advantages of American citizenship over British subjecthood, a point that will be returned to later.

Fenian-style devotion to the American republic was built upon an unshakeable faith in democracy and strong notions about the rights of "the people," conferred from birth and confirmed in the constitution. To the Fenians, the contrast with Canada could hardly have seemed sharper. As Reginald Whitaker has written, the BNA Act was "almost entirely innocent of any recognition of the people as the object of the constitutional exercise."[28] It was therefore not hard for Fenian editors such as Patrick J. Meehan of the *Irish American* to extract the seemingly undemocratic elements from the proposed jumble of new political arrangements to the north. As with so many others who embraced radical Irish nationalism, Meehan had departed Ireland during the famine era while still a teenager. Growing up in the southwestern port city of Limerick, he could not have failed to comprehend the endless drama of ships laden with the poor and desperate leaving for North America before eventually boarding one alongside his family.[29]

Unsurprisingly, an April 1867 editorial issued a "notice to quit" to "John Bull," who was denounced for his efforts "to plant an embryo Guelphic throne on our Northern border," a sentiment likely encouraged by a resolution adopted in late March in the US House of

Representatives that reacted to Confederation with "extreme solicitude."[30] Less than two months later, a longer editorial, entitled "The Kingdom of Canada," focused its critique on the new Canadian Senate. Although the Province of Canada had conducted elections for its upper house since 1856, this new cohort of senators were to be appointed for life, which for Meehan illustrated that

> the old feudal idea, which even effete Europe is now rejecting ignominiously with every new stride of progress, is about to be reproduced in America ... and the Colonists are to be saddled with the burden of a mushroom aristocracy, embodying all the evils and dangers to liberty which made the system of the old world obnoxious.[31]

The privileging of property holders in the moulding of a Canadian elite/upper class was predicted in turn to "nullify the effect of the elective franchise," a jarring contrast to American traditions of manhood suffrage. While the idea of terming the new entity a "kingdom" was rejected by the British largely to allay American concerns, the components of the machine were nonetheless familiar to radical Irish eyes. As the editorial continued:

> The new Senators, being selected principally by the office-holder politicians who have hatched and fostered the Confederation scheme, and thrust it upon the colonies despite the expressed dissatisfaction of the majority of the population ... will represent not the interests of the community at large, but the selfish desires and corrupt ambition of the clique to which they owe their tenure of power; while the Crown ... will find in them a convenient band of dependents.[32]

The *Irish American* was not alone at the time in ridiculing the Canadian Senate-to-be in this respect, but as Christopher Moore has since argued, the commitment by the makers of Confederation to the principle of responsible government was such that "no competing interest could induce them to create a rival power" to the elected lower House of Commons.[33] While it was true that American senators held office for six years as opposed to for life, they were elected by state legislatures rather than by the voters, a measure that remained until the Seventeenth Amendment to the US Constitution in 1913.[34] Moreover, Article Five of the Constitution, providing equal suffrage of two senators per state, was hardly a model of representation by population.

The tone of Meehan's journal was not less withering when the Dominion of Canada took its place on the world map. Given the multiple levels of government involved in the new apparatus, the *Irish American* scorned the "rejoicing of all the 'loyal' folk who expect office or emolument under its *regime*," an accurate enough prediction of the volume of letters that would soon reach the office of the first prime minister, John A. Macdonald.[35] Meehan was sensitive not only to the cultivation of an entitled political class in the new Dominion, but also to the general top-down nature of the Confederation project.

Abhorrence at this apparent sidestepping of "the people" north of the border was not only a tip of the hat to American political rhetoric but also reflective of the strong strain of anti-elitism that ran through Fenianism generally. Unlike Young Ireland, the Fenians, whether in Ireland or America, were unable to attract strong intellectual personalities to their ranks.[36] Geopolitical relations with Britain were, for instance, conflated into essentialist Manichean categories and presented as timeless struggles between tyranny and freedom, monarchism and republicanism, or despotism and egalitarianism. A proclamation of "The Irish Republic" published in Dublin's weekly *Irishman* by the so-called Provisional Government on 9 March 1867, mere days after an ineffectual IRB uprising in Ireland, denounced the aristocratic "locusts" and "leeches" who had taken Irish land, denied the Irish their "political rights," produced "an existence of utter serfdom," and caused mass emigration.[37] Bereft of sophisticated visionaries, details of what a reformed post-independence Ireland might look like were noticeably lacking.

It is nonetheless helpful to locate Fenian condemnations of a "mushroom aristocracy," propped up by "British gold" and set to spread within post-Confederation Canada, within the context of Ireland since the *Act of Union* of 1800. As the *Irish American* saw it, the process of securing agreement among political elites for Confederation in Canada was comparable to the way in which the "perjured votes" of "wretched hirelings ... consummated the fraudulent 'Union' which has cost Ireland so dear."[38] Indeed, a number of historians have documented the way in which an illegal slush fund was used to bring about the end of the Irish parliament in the aftermath of the 1798 rebellion.[39] But Fenian ire was directed not only at the Chief Secretary, Lord-Lieutenant, and other members of the Irish establishment, but also at those moderate middle-class nationalists whose efforts to repeal the Union ended in frustration and failure. The "address to Ireland" at the FB congress in Cincinnati in January 1865 denounced the constitutional politics of "pseudo-patriots" sent by the Irish electorate "to the Saxon capital to prove themselves traitors to Ireland by sitting in the legislature of England."[40] At Cleveland in September 1867, Repeal was described as "a political faith that taught cowardice to be a virtue, and buncombe to be sublime, and the attainment of office under the piratical government of England as the greatest glory that ambition could attain."[41] From this ideological vantage point, Fenian opinion-shapers needed little reminder of how in Canada the likes of D'Arcy McGee provided a textbook illustration of a one-time rebel lulled into political moderation by the spoils of office.

The *Irishman*, the main outlet for Fenian news in Dublin in the absence of the *Irish People*, was similarly unimpressed with the Confederation scheme. "By a stroke of statesmanship," it stated on 3 August 1867, the peoples of three provinces "have been taken up and flung together into one heap, which operation is termed a recasting of the provinces, and the formation of one confederation ... 'A House divided against itself cannot stand,' says Holy Writ; and the Canadian Confederation most resembles such a house."[42] While the elements of disunity thought to be the most significant were not specified, the paper argued that enduring internal animosities would produce persistent economic stagnation and emigration southward as "the border towns, the town of Toronto, for instance, find their population ebbing away across the river into the States, leaving them high and dry with empty warehouses."[43]

Dismissing the country as "unprogressive," the paper hoped that its "younger men" would "all be annexationists ... by shaking the British dust from their feet and seeking their fortunes under the Stars and Stripes."[44] Commentaries from more mainstream publications about Canada's shaky levels of net migration were not uncommon in these years, however, and in the three decades following Confederation, the Dominion struggled with its sieve-like qualities as hundreds of thousands born within its borders did indeed go on to make lives for themselves in the United States.[45]

Opinions on the changing political shape of Canada were expressed beyond editorial offices and congress platforms, of course. Residing in, or just visiting, border cities and towns could, alongside the sight of flags, focus Fenian thoughts on the political and military challenges that lay ahead. Shortly after the passing of the BNA Act, Fenian senator A.L. Morrison of Missouri clarified to those assembled at a Fenian picnic in Buffalo:

We are not hostile to the people of Canada, our hostility is against the tyrant flag, the hated flag which flies there ... You are nearest to the enemy's territory, within half-a-mile of this ensign, the emblem at once of your degradation and this tyranny. It flaunts in your very face its infamous defiance. Shall it continue there to insult you and to remind us of our wrongs? (Shouts No, No).[46]

Several months before Confederation but in the aftermath of the Ridgeway encounter, J.M, an enthusiastic attender of a Fenian meeting at Niagara Falls, New York, described how in his eyes

the tantalizing sight over the river is an incentive that does not operate in vain. The "sign of slaughter" that waves on Canadian soil under our eyes every day is about the most urgent appeal that can be made in Ireland's behalf. The flag of the old pirate on American soil is an insult. To us the sight is fraught with a thousand harrowing memories.[47]

Dubbing the Union Jack a "sign of slaughter" chimed well with other Fenian descriptions of it as a "blood-stained rag" and such like. This phrase was also used, however, in an older poem wherein an Irish exile, finding himself on the American side of Niagara Falls, has his attention drawn away from the great cataract:

A flag against the northern sky
Alone engaged his eager eye
Upon Canadian soil it stood
Its hue was that of human blood
Its red was crossed with pallid scars –
Pale, steely, stiff as prison bars.
"Oh, cursed flag!" the exile said,
"The hair grows heavy on my head;
My blood leaps wilder than this water,
On seeing thee, thou sign of slaughter.
Oh, may I never meet my death
Till I behold the day of wrath,
When on thy squadrons shall be poured
The vengeance heaven so long has stored."

The poem, entitled "The Red-Cross Flag," was penned more than a decade earlier by none other than Thomas D'Arcy McGee, likely during his time in Buffalo, and at a stage when his revulsion for British imperialism remained intact. In 1863, the poem was republished in the Toronto *Globe* in an effort to embarrass McGee, who was in the process of switching his Canadian party allegiance from Liberal to Tory.[48]

Whether experienced physically or in the imagination, then, border landscapes such as those of Niagara Falls and Buffalo revealed the limits of American continentalism.[49] True, a cartographic representation of the new Dominion circa 1868 would have depicted a rather modest-looking sliver of territory stretching across the northeastern part of the continent. There was still all to play for in the west, as wagon trains continued to cross the Mississippi River, the purchase of Russian Alaska was finalized in March 1867, and the first transcontinental railroad approached completion. At the time of Confederation, Buffalo's *Fenian Volunteer* blasted:

> Of right, "the whole boundless continent is ours." The world admits it, and if we be but true to ourselves, the day is not far distant when the stars and stripes shall float triumphant over every inch of land between Tierra del Fuego and Baffin's Bay. But to succeed, we must first tramp out this conspiracy among us which is fed by British sentiment and gold, and inscribe on our banners: "death to all tyranny and freedom to the world."[50]

The following year, and one week before the Dominion's one-year anniversary, the *Irish American* restated its hopes for the world view of its average (male) reader who "loves the land of his adoption and hopes for the regeneration of that land which gave him birth, and believes that the whole of this continent, from the Atlantic to the Pacific, should be consecrated to freedom, and not desecrated by such bastard despotism as that which England has attempted to set up on our northern frontier."[51]

Confederation did nothing, therefore, to stem Fenian bluster, though its military capabilities were now on the wane with funds dwindling. More generally, the suspension of the writ of habeas corpus and the imprisonment of Irishmen in Canada following the 1866 raids, coupled with similar measures undertaken earlier in Ireland, now presented Fenians with a trans-imperial picture of British injustice towards Irishmen. Fenian congress rhetoric about "bondage" and "unfree manhood" reflected a belief that the Irish were being, in Gerry Kearns's words, "excluded from effective citizenship."[52] Radical nationalist energy was further added to as three Fenians were hanged in Manchester, England, in November 1867 after a prison rescue resulted in the death of a policeman; with the men's bodies buried in quicklime, "ghost funerals" took place in New York and other cities.

Britain was also being held up for denigrating the American citizenship much beloved by Fenians. The doctrine of perpetual allegiance held that "those born under the jurisdiction of the British Crown remained its subjects," and the return of Irish-American citizens to Ireland, armed and ready to aid the IRB, brought the limitations of American naturalization to light.[53] Kearns enumerates 145 Americans among some 1,260 taken into custody following the suspension of habeas corpus in February 1866, with 298 of the prisoners later released without charge "required to depart Britain and Ireland for America."[54] In May 1867, the arrest of the two leaders of a transatlantic filibustering mission on the *Erin's Hope* vessel was followed by their claiming American citizenship. The dismissal of these claims led to a vigorous public letter-writing campaign, and resolutions denouncing Britain's "insulting claim of 'once a subject, forever a subject'" as "odious and obsolete," such as at a Buffalo meeting, were replicated on both sides of the Atlantic.[55]

The ex-rebel D'Arcy McGee was unmoved by such controversies. Indeed, he recommended that those responsible for the Ridgeway affair be hanged for their crimes. For many if not most American Fenians, McGee's name was the only one that stood out from north of the border, and for all the wrong reasons. As one scans through commentaries and speeches on Confederation in the Fenian press, all other Canadian politicians are strikingly anonymous. Personalities such as Macdonald or George Brown were of no evident interest, though the Irish-born Governor-General Lord Monck received a periodic name check. In between the swipes at a faceless colonial elite are scattered references to "Loyalists" and "Orangemen," familiar Fenian bogeymen. Critics of D'Arcy McGee's 1865 Irish speech noted his omission of the Orange presence in Canada, with one regional newspaper dismissing the then-province's "dismal Orangeism" and "gloomy and cheerless soil."[56] A letter to the *Irish People*, moreover, reminded readers of the "religious distinction" that continued to operate in Canadian provincial society and politics, to the detriment of Irish Catholics.[57] Sectarianism also possessed a trans-imperial dimension, and despite provisions made in the BNA Act in the area of education, for instance, it was not to be quickly expunged.

Elected as a member of the first Dominion parliament, D'Arcy McGee was assassinated upon returning to his Ottawa lodgings from the federal chamber in April 1868. As intrigue swirled around the news of a Fenian assassin, and habeas corpus remained suspended, Toronto's *Irish Canadian* was suppressed, and editor Patrick Boyle interned among dozens of others.[58] The *Irish American*, now banned from Canada, reminded its readership that "as Canada is British territory (and, therefore, hostile soil) as well as the prison of good Irishmen – we go in for striking here as heavily, as effectively and as quickly as possible."[59] The Dominion remained a legitimate target, and the Fenians made good on their threats of further attacks in 1870 with brief and unsuccessful incursions into southern Quebec. Canada's secret service, now housed within the newly constituted Dominion Police, proved more efficient than in 1866, with the English-born master infiltrator Thomas Beach/Henri Le Caron climbing so far within the Fenian organization as to assist Ridgeway raid hero John O'Neill with strategy for the next assault![60]

All in all, those Fenians who gave the moment of Canadian Confederation any consideration took a dim view of it. To them, the retention of the British flag on the continent was an unwelcome check on the inevitable realization of American destiny. In addition, the energy behind Confederation, as they saw it, came not so much from within Canada but from the old enemy, Britain. The agency of Canadian politicians was downplayed to the point of them being presented as easily corruptible pawns in a wider imperial game, while the presence of Maritime-based opponents justified Fenian condemnations of Confederation as underhanded and undemocratic.

In the years that followed, constitutional nationalism gained a new impetus in Ireland with the Home Rule movement to restore the Irish parliament lost by the *Act of Union*. In an ironic twist, Canadian Confederation was now hailed as a blueprint of sorts, and Irish-Canadians with Irish nationalist sympathies would, alongside Irish politicians in the British House of Commons, celebrate the new-found freedoms for Canada that Confederation seemingly represented.[61] Canada had remained loyal to monarch and empire, and if only Ireland were let off the imperial leash a little more, so too would the Emerald Isle become loyal. But as the subsequent transatlantic history of Irish nationalism reminds us, there remained those for whom the heroic sacrifice associated with armed rebellion was the only effective means of achieving Irish independence.

NOTES

The author is grateful to the editors, Jerome Devitt, and David A. Wilson for their comments on a previous draft of this chapter.

1 Wilfred I. Smith, "Confederation and the British Connection," *Revista de Historia de América* 65–6 (January–December 1968): 20.
2 David Brundage, *Irish Nationalists in America: The Politics of Exile, 1798–1998* (Oxford: Oxford University Press, 2016), 99.
3 See R.V. Comerford, *The Fenians in Context: Irish Politics and Society, 1848–82* (Dublin: Wolfhound Press, 1985), 47–8. At the outset, the IRB was known variously among its initiates as "the organisation," "the brotherhood," "the movement," and other similar terms.
4 For a recent account of the foundational era, see Patrick Steward and Bryan McGovern, *The Fenians: Irish Rebellion in the North Atlantic World* (Knoxville: University of Tennessee Press, 2013), 1–27.
5 Comerford, *The Fenians in Context*, 124–7.
6 Matthew Kelly, "The *Irish People* and the Disciplining of Dissent," in *The Black Hand of Republicanism: Fenianism in Modern Ireland*, ed. Fearghal McGarry and James McConnel (Dublin and Portland: Irish Academic Press, 2009), 34–52.
7 *Proceedings of the Second National Congress of the Fenian Brotherhood Held in Cincinnati, Ohio, January 1865* (Philadelphia: James Gibbons, 1865), 23; *Proceedings of the Fifth National Congress of the Fenian Brotherhood at Troy, NY, September 1866, with Message of William R. Roberts, President of the F.B.* (Philadelphia: n.p., 1866), 22.
8 Brundage, *Irish Nationalists in America*, 89.
9 Hereward Senior, *The Fenians and Canada* (Toronto: Macmillan Canada, 1978), 27–32; Marta Ramón-García, "Square-Toed Boots and Felt Hats: Irish Revolutionaries and the Invasion of Canada (1848–1871)," *Estudios Irlandeses* 5 (2010): 83, and Shane Lynn, "Before the Fenians: 1848 and the Irish Plot to Invade Canada," *Éire-Ireland* 51, nos. 1 and 2 (Spring/Summer 2016): 61–91.
10 Marta Ramón, *A Provisional Dictator: James Stephens and the Fenian Movement* (Dublin: University College Dublin Press, 2007), 193–9.
11 Peter M. Toner, "The Fanatic Heart of the North," in *Irish Nationalism in Canada*, ed. David A. Wilson (Montreal and Kingston: McGill-Queen's University Press, 2009), 34–51.
12 *Irish Canadian*, 12 April 1865. See also the issues of 29 March and 5 April.

13 Reg Whitaker, Gregory S. Kealey, and Andrew Parnaby, *Secret Service: Political Policing in Canada from the Fenians to Fortress America* (Toronto: University of Toronto Press, 2012), 25.
14 Whitaker, Kealey, and Parnaby, *Secret Service*, 23.
15 David A. Wilson, *Thomas D'Arcy McGee*, vol. 2, *The Extreme Moderate, 1857–1868* (Montreal and Kingston: McGill-Queen's University Press, 2013), 39.
16 See David A. Wilson, "Thomas D'Arcy McGee's Wexford Speech of 1865: Reflections on Revolutionary Republicanism and the Irish in North America," *Canadian Journal of Irish Studies* 26–7, nos. 2 and 1 (Fall 2000 and Spring 2001): 9–24.
17 See *The People* (Wexford), 20 May 1865.
18 *Dublin Evening Mail*, 16 May 1865. The copy of the speech published here contained inserted instances of supposed laughter and cheering, much to McGee's embarrassment.
19 *Proceedings of the Fourth National Congress of the Fenian Brotherhood at Pittsburgh, Pa., February 1866 with the Constitution of the F.B. and Addenda Thereto* (New York: J. Craft, 1866), 20.
20 See W.S. Neidhardt, *Fenianism in North America* (University Park: Pennsylvania State University Press, 1975), 59–75; and Peter Vronsky, *Ridgeway: The American Fenian Invasion and the 1866 Battle That Made Canada* (Toronto: Allen Lane Canada, 2011).
21 C.P. Stacey, "Fenianism and the Rise of National Feeling in Canada at the Time of Confederation," *Canadian Historical Review* 12, no. 3 (1931), 238–61; Peter B. Waite, *The Life and Times of Confederation, 1864–1867: Politics, Newspapers, and the Union of British North America* (Toronto: University of Toronto Press, 1962).
22 Waite, *Life and Times of Confederation*, 323.
23 Timothy G. Lynch, "'A Kindred and Congenial Element': Irish-American Nationalism's Embrace of Republican Rhetoric," *New Hibernia Review* 13, no. 2 (Summer 2009): 88.
24 Mitchell Snay, "The Imagined Republic: The Fenians, Irish American Nationalism, and the Political Culture of Reconstruction," *Proceedings of the American Antiquarian Society* 112, part 2 (2002): 311. See also his *Fenians, Freedmen, and Southern Whites: Race and Nationality in the Era of Reconstruction* (Baton Rouge: Louisiana State University Press, 2007).
25 Ramón, *A Provisional Dictator*, 195.
26 *Fenian Volunteer*, 24 August 1867.
27 *Fourth National Congress*, 18.
28 Reginald Whitaker, "Democracy and the Canadian Constitution," in *And No One Cheered: Federalism, Democracy, and the Constitution Act*, ed. Keith Banting and Richard Simeon (Toronto: Methuen, 1983), 240.

29 Having lost his father in youth, Meehan travelled to New York with his mother and the family of his stepfather, Patrick Lynch. Not long after arrival, Lynch launched the *Irish American*, and upon his death in 1857 Meehan took over as proprietor and editor. See James W. Gavan, "Patrick J. Meehan: The Nestor of Irish-American Journalism," *Donahoe's Magazine* 25 (Boston: Pilot Publishing Co., 1891): 209–15.
30 *Irish American*, 6 April 1867. See chapter two by Krikorian and Cameron in this volume.
31 *Irish American*, 1 June 1867.
32 Ibid.
33 Christopher Moore, *1867: How the Fathers Made a Deal* (Toronto: McClelland & Stewart, 1997), 110.
34 See Sean Wilentz, *The Rise of American Democracy: Jefferson to Lincoln* (New York: W.W. Norton, 2005), 32–4. American voters were, on the other hand, directly engaged in the election of members of the House of Representatives.
35 *Irish American*, 13 July 1867.
36 See James Quinn, "The IRB and Young Ireland: Varieties of Tension," in *The Black Hand of Republicanism: Fenianism in Modern Ireland*, ed. Fearghal McGarry and James McConnel (Dublin and Portland: Irish Academic Press, 2009), 3–17.
37 *Irishman*, 9 March 1867. For the context in which this document was produced, see Comerford, *The Fenians in Context*, 136–7.
38 *Irish American*, 30 April 1867.
39 Patrick Geoghegan, "The Making of the Union," in *Acts of Union: The Causes, Contexts and Consequences of the Act of Union*, ed. Dáire Keogh and Kevin Whelan (Dublin: Four Courts Press, 2001), 34–45.
40 *Second National Congress*, 50.
41 *Proceedings of the Sixth National Congress of the Fenian Brotherhood at Cleveland, Ohio, September 1867* (New York: J. Craft), 21.
42 *Irishman*, 3 August 1867.
43 Ibid.
44 Ibid.
45 See Walter Nugent, *Crossings: The Great Transatlantic Migrations, 1870–1914* (Bloomington: Indiana University Press, 1992), 136–48.
46 *Irishman*, 10 August 1867.
47 *Irish American*, 17 November 1866.
48 *Globe*, 28 August 1863; see also 4 September for additional commentary.
49 For more on this idea, see Patrick McGreevy, "The End of America: The Beginning of Canada," *Canadian Geographer* 32, no. 4 (1989): 307–18; Janet

Baglier, "The End of America: The Beginning of Canada – A Response," *Canadian Geographer* 34, no. 3 (1990): 270–1.
50 As reprinted in the *Irishman*, 13 July 1867. The "conspiracy among us" was a reference to those editors and opinion-shapers in the American press who either supported, or were tolerant of, Canadian Confederation.
51 *Irish American*, 20 June 1868.
52 Gerry Kearns, "Bare Life, Political Violence, and the Territorial Structure of Britain and Ireland," in *Violent Geographies: Fear, Terror, and Political Violence*, ed. Derek Gregory and Allan Pred (New York: Routledge, 2007), 23.
53 David Sim, *A Union Forever: The Irish Question and U.S. Foreign Relations in the Victorian Age* (Ithaca, NY: Cornell University Press, 2013), 98.
54 Kearns, "Bare Life, Political Violence, and the Territorial Structure of Britain and Ireland," 23.
55 *Irish American*, 10 November 1866.
56 *Dundalk Democrat*, reprinted in *Irish People*, 8 June 1865; *Irish American*, 10 June 1865.
57 *Irish People*, 15 July 1865.
58 See *Irishman*, 23 and 30 May, and 6 June 1868; Whitaker, Kealey, and Parnaby, *Secret Service*, 32.
59 *Irish American*, 16 May 1868. Copies of the *Irish American* were found in the possession of Patrick James Whelan, the man found guilty of McGee's murder and hanged on 11 February 1869.
60 Whitaker, Kealey, and Parnaby, *Secret Service*, 33.
61 See chapter ten by Thomas Mohr in this volume.

4 Confederation Comes at a Cost: Indigenous Peoples and the Ongoing Reality of Colonialism in Canada

GABRIELLE SLOWEY

For historian Ken Coates, "one of the founding myths of the nation-state is that Canada has treated Indigenous peoples fairly."[1] Traditionally, the narrative of Canadian Confederation is one of discovery, commerce, settlement, and nationhood. The recent report of the Truth and Reconciliation Commission has demonstrated, in vivid terms, the legacy of settlement on Indigenous communities in North America. Moving forward, it is important to think of Indigenous-settler relations in terms of reconciliation, and for settler society to create meaningful space for Indigenous "resurgence." More concretely, reconciliation means rethinking how to transform Canada and its institutions and norms. As Canada celebrates its 150th year, it is important to recognize that it was – in large part – the Confederation arrangements in 1867 that caused a "break" in the relations between the Canadian state and Indigenous peoples. The Confederation project came at a cost for Indigenous peoples and their descendants. This chapter argues, however, that at the time of Confederation in 1867, Indigenous peoples paid a high price that has not been addressed even 150 years later.

A Land of Many Sovereign Nations

At the time of Confederation, Indigenous peoples of Turtle Island (also known as North America) comprised many sovereign nations, all of which had very different political, economic, and social structures. They were self-governing, with sophisticated land and resource management regimes. They possessed their own constitutions and laws, which were rooted in a deep and reciprocal relationship with the land that prioritized people, place, animals, nature, and respect for the earth.

There were numerous confederacy organizations across the country. A notable example is the Haudenosaunee Confederacy and the Great Law of Peace. It provided a clear system of laws and government, assigning duties and responsibilities to the different nations involved (Mohawk, Onondaga, Oneida, Cayuga, Seneca, and Tuscarora, geographically located in the regions of southwestern Ontario, northern New York state, and southwestern Quebec). Indigenous peoples in the Prairies, much of British Columbia, and the North dominated their local economies to ensure continued maintenance and access to buffalo, fish, and fur-bearing animals.

As early as 1701, the British Crown entered into treaties with Indigenous peoples. Over the next century, in what would become Canada, the Crown continued to engage in treaty-making as a way to define, among other things, "the respective rights" of Indigenous peoples and governments to use and enjoy the lands occupied by Indigenous peoples.[2] In many ways, prior to Confederation, Indigenous peoples were valued and respected for their roles in facilitating resource development (for example, acting as middlemen in the fur trade) and in military engagement. Indigenous peoples were important allies for Europeans, and the more important knowledge transfer was Aboriginal to European, not simply European to Aboriginal.[3] As historian John Leslie explains, "In these traditional functions, Indian people shared, to a degree, in decision-making, devising trade practices, and planning military operations."[4] Cree constitutional scholar Kiera Ladner underscores that "the Mi'kmaq never relinquished their territory nor their rights and responsibilities as a nation; they merely agreed to establish relationships of peace and friendship, and to pursue military, political and economic alliances with the British."[5] This Mi'kmaq experience echoes those of other Indigenous nations across the country. None of these nations believed they were "giving up" sovereignty let alone control over territory through a treaty or any other means such as, in the case of the Métis, scrip.[6]

According to Leslie, as early as 1755, when the Indian Department was founded,[7] Indigenous-state relations began to shift. Leslie explains that the officials of the Indian Department became the custodians of imperial policy in order to "oversee and manage the acquisition of Indian lands required for European settlement."[8] He writes: "Following the end of the War of 1812 [well in advance of Confederation], the traditional roles for Indian people in colonial society declined rapidly. [However,] instead of abandoning Indian people to face the harsh, new political and economic realities, the first principle in Indian policy, that of Indian protection, was reasserted."[9] The job of protecting Indigenous peoples and making policy would fall to the new Canadian state and its leaders, who took up this role on Indigenous peoples' behalf.

To "protect" Indigenous peoples also meant "protecting" their land. It meant "protecting" them from their own "barbarous" ways. In his biography of famed historian Donald Creighton, Donald Wright writes how British North America was seen as a place of "violent contrasts," where European finery was confronted by North American barbarism; where "exquisite *toilettes* and civilized license confronted ... greasy buffalo robes and the barbarous codes of the Indians."[10] Given Indian communal property values and the Crown's need to claim land for settlement, "the first piece of legislation to protect Indian reserves was passed in Upper Canada in 1839, and what it did was basically include Indian lands in with crown lands."[11] With this legislation, the goal of Euro-Canadian settler society was quite clear: bring the Indigenous peoples from their "savage and unproductive state" and force (European-style) civilization upon them, thus confirming Canada's place among European Christian nations. So, at the same time as treaty-making was underway, already it was evident, even prior to Confederation, that the relationship between the state and Indigenous peoples was being set out according to the terms and values of the settlers, with the state claiming control and responsibility for Indigenous peoples without their consultation or consent.

Confederation: A Turning Point?

During the Confederation debates that took place in the legislative assemblies of New Brunswick, Nova Scotia, and Prince Edward Island, politicians debated the merits of the seventy-two resolutions agreed upon at the Quebec Conference. Although proponents argued that the new political arrangement was a necessity, some opponents denounced a deal that would be dominated by the colony of Canada and demanded a vote on the proposed union. In the colony of Canada, only five members of its Legislative Assembly made vague references to "Indians." As historian Donald B. Smith points out, "No obvious evidence exists that First Nation matters occupied John A. Macdonald's attention from 1857 to the Confederation debates."[12] Smith goes on to suggest that there was no actual discussion of the role of Indigenous peoples in the new British North American federation. Upon review of the Confederation debates, what is evident is that the leaders of the day were mired in colonial mindsets and European Christian values; the men in attendance were concerned about matters of race, by which they meant Irish, Scottish, French, and English. The Confederation debates focused on issues of jurisdiction and the division of powers between the new provinces and a central government; the creation of an internal market linked by a railway; language and education rights for Catholics, Protestants, English-speaking, and French-speaking people; and the value and necessity of federalism.

The acquisition of the territories under control of the Hudson's Bay Company helped to fuel the dreams of some of the Fathers of Confederation. During the 1865 debate in the Legislative Assembly of the Province of Canada, George Brown stated that the territory between British Columbia and the future province of Ontario would "be opened up to civilization under the auspices of the British American Confederation."[13] For politicians of the day, these territories, and Indigenous rights to them, were to be claimed for the Crown rather than remain the rightful territories of sovereign Indigenous nations – this, despite the Royal Proclamation of 1763, in which King George III had made clear that all Indigenous territories remained the land of Indigenous peoples unless otherwise ceded, surrendered, or purchased. In theory, the Royal Proclamation was issued to prevent the unlawful theft of Indigenous lands throughout the new empire. In practice, in large parts of Canada, particularly the Maritimes and British Columbia, government officials and legal authorities assumed that European settlement superseded Indigenous rights to territory and used the terms of the Royal Proclamation as a blueprint for "how to" claim Indigenous lands.[14]

Here, Ladner contends that, despite Canadian claims of sovereignty, Indigenous constitutional visions did not simply disappear with Confederation. Rather, the new state acquired lands, rights, and resources through what she terms "magical ways." Even though Indigenous peoples were largely absent from the minds of those who would ultimately lay the foundations for the Canadian nation, Indigenous lands (and the resources contained therein) were central to the Canadian Confederation and colonial project. In the end, Canada's Confederation documents were written in a colonial era in which the "Fathers" of Confederation worked to unite a nation and build a country that was predicated on the displacement and dispossession of Indigenous peoples. This reality is a very different version of the Confederation story from the myth of the fair treatment of Indigenous communities;

however, as Coates cautions, "the reality of the past only rarely conforms to national mythology."[15]

Upon Confederation, the *British North America Act, 1867* assigned exclusive responsibility for Indians to the federal government. Section 91(24) makes the federal government responsible for "Indians, and Lands reserved for the Indians" because, as Leslie also points out, Indian policy was considered "too sensitive a policy field" to fall to the provinces.[16] Hence the *British North America Act, 1867* formalized the role of Indians as wards of the state. It laid out the fiduciary relationship between the federal Crown and Indigenous peoples, and set the tone for future state-Indigenous relations.

Donald B. Smith pleads with scholars to take a closer look at the first prime minister of Canada, John A. Macdonald, and his relationship with Indigenous peoples. Smith argues that "if judged by the standards of his age, not ours, he emerges as a complex and relatively tolerant individual."[17] However, in his edited collection of Macdonald's letters, J.K. Johnson observed that deep within Macdonald lay an "inborn, unbidden, unquestioning assumption of the inherent superiority of all things British, and the consequent inferiority, in however small degree, of every other living human being."[18] According to Smith, throughout his prime ministership, Macdonald believed in the necessity to assimilate Indigenous peoples. He was focused on destroying their social structures and transforming their communal lands into individual family holdings.[19] Smith adds that Macdonald "combined a romantic sentimentalism for First Nations people with a total disregard for their rights to keep their ancestral cultures and religions."[20] While Smith asks us to let Macdonald off the hook, Donald Wright points out the importance of keeping Macdonald on the hook. In his biography of Donald Creighton, Wright recounts how Creighton, in his review of the Riel rebellions, depicted the mounted police as men of honour and fair dealing, but similarly cast Indigenous leaders such as Poundmaker and Big Bear as "terrorists."[21] Indeed, although Smith is correct in maintaining that historical figures like Macdonald are complex, these political figures must also be held accountable for the roles they played in setting the tone for ensuing settler/state-Indigenous relations. Leaders like Macdonald believed firmly in their own benevolence and considered that their actions would best serve Indigenous interests: "Indians" were a problem they were going to help solve. As Coates points out, "Canadians have found considerable solace in the idea that British and Canadian governments looked after their colonial wards."[22] However, this attitude, as Wright indicates, means that there has been significant "silence on the implications of Confederation for Aboriginal peoples."[23] As the authors of the *Report of the Royal Commission on Aboriginal Peoples* remind us:

> At no time, however, were First Nations included in the [Confederation] discussion, nor were they consulted about their concerns. Neither was their future position in the federation given any public acknowledgment or discussion. Nevertheless, the broad outlines of a new constitutional relationship, at least with the First Nations, were determined unilaterally.[24]

These last words point to an ongoing reality in which subsequent federal leaders and governments have consistently failed to consult Indigenous peoples about matters that directly affect them, a legacy that has continued to confront subsequent generations of Indigenous peoples and which remains an ongoing colonial practice.

The *Indian Act*

Shortly after Confederation, the new Dominion government passed the *Indian Act* (1876), consolidating an array of statutes passed by the former Province of Canada. Assuming greater administrative control over Indigenous nations and peoples, this all-encompassing federal legislation not only set out to "remake the Indian" into a European, but also "provided the legal foundation for government authority over indigenous peoples and communities."[25] The legislation was broad and wide-ranging. Most significantly, it defined who was and, by implication, who was not considered to be an "Indian"; established the band council system of government; and set out the criteria by which Indians could be enfranchised (that is, the ways in which they could give up their Indian status and be normalized citizens).

With the responsibility to educate Indians being a federal one, Duncan Campbell Scott, who joined the civil service in 1879, famously stated why he thought the residential school legislation (the system of education whereby Indian children were taken from their families and placed in residential schools) was a good idea. As he put it:

> I want to get rid of the Indian problem. I do not think, as a matter of fact, that the country ought to continuously protect a class of people who are able to stand alone ... Our objective is to continue until there is not a single

Indian in Canada that has not been absorbed into the body politic, and there is no Indian question, and no Indian Department, that is the whole object of this Bill.[26]

An advocate and architect of the residential school system, Scott is often vilified for his approach to dealing with Indigenous peoples and for the adverse outcomes of the policies he constructed. Referencing the work of J.R. Miller (1996), Coates notes that "residential schools, not so long ago hailed as the route to native economic salvation, have been shown to have been oppressive instruments of cultural domination."[27] Similarly, Confederation, which has been hailed as an important step in the nation-building process, was in fact premised on the erasure of Indigenous peoples and cultures.

For his part, Leslie points out how post-Confederation policy "as established in colonial times" – its policy, administrative, and legislative framework – has served as the basic model for the federal government approach and endures today.[28] The *Indian Act* has been amended many times over since 1876, but it remains in existence. It is the only piece of colonial legislation enduring today that specifically aims to assimilate and control a specific group of people in Canadian society. No other group – no settler group, no newcomer to Canada, no refugee, or immigrant – is subject to legislation anywhere close to the same degree of scrutiny and control by the state as are Indigenous peoples. This legislation is one of the reasons there remains an inherently disrespectful and problematic relationship: one that requires reconciliation. It is also one reason why Indigenous peoples are not, and should not be, considered simply another cultural group that makes up the multicultural mosaic of Canada. They are not immigrants to this land; this has been their land since time immemorial. The *Indian Act* is critical evidence that colonialism is alive and well today. It is a constant reminder that the state of Canada is premised on the theft and dispossession of Indigenous lands and colonial control of Indigenous peoples.

Attempts at Reconciliation

Reconciliation remains a contested concept. Indigenous scholars such as Taiaiake Alfred and Jeff Corntassel,[29] and more recently Glen Coulthard,[30] caution that reconciliation is not a gift that can be offered by the state. Rather, it must begin with Indigenous peoples themselves and be rooted in Indigenous concepts, knowledge, and traditions. Indigenous frustration with reconciliation emerges, in part, out of multiple failed efforts by the state to meaningfully address Indigenous concerns to alter the status quo. In their view, these efforts have not been effective at bringing about meaningful change for Indigenous peoples. They have not altered the status quo and/or have occurred at the expense of revitalizing traditional Indigenous institutions and values.

Since Confederation, various national governments have endeavoured to solve the "Indian problem" through legislation. Most notable is Pierre E. Trudeau's first "just society" measure. In 1969, on the first anniversary of his landslide election, Trudeau, along with his minister of Indian Affairs and Northern Development, Jean Chrétien, proposed the now infamous "White Paper," which contained three main proposals: (1) abolish the *Indian Act*; (2) transfer responsibility for Indians to the provinces; and (3) close the doors of the federal Department of Indian Affairs. Indigenous peoples from across the country who had been promised consultation on legislation affecting them were outraged by the terms of the proposal, which had been drafted without their input or consent. As Leslie comments, in many ways "the 1969 white paper went right back to the 19th century. It was straight assimilation."[31] It threatened to eliminate the fiduciary duty owed by the federal government. Consequently, Indigenous peoples mobilized nationally to challenge the legislation, and the Trudeau government ultimately withdrew it.

In 1982, Trudeau's repatriation of the constitution entrenched the term "Aboriginal" to mean the "Indian, Inuit and Métis" peoples in s. 35 of the *Constitution Act, 1982*. It also recognized and affirmed existing treaty rights or those that may be so acquired. The term "Aboriginal" was essentially a catch-all term that was eventually embraced by settler society and lauded as a step towards recognizing Indigenous peoples in Canada. Yet, the term "Aboriginal" essentializes and homogenizes the multiple nations and peoples that exist across Canada under a single umbrella which fails to capture or reflect the reality of diversity that persists.

One might be tempted to point to this constitutional change as a seismic shift in federal policy, especially in comparison to the language of Scott and the 1969 White Paper. However, accommodation and constitutional inclusion must not be mistaken for change or decolonization. As Frantz Fanon[32] famously wrote, beware of the gifts of the oppressor, for they continue to oppress. Indeed, Coulthard and Alfred caution against such state-initiated efforts. In their view, state-offered reconciliation perpetuates state dominance via state institutions and Indigenous inclusion and acceptance. They suggest that the term "reconciliation" remains a ruse to perpetuate the original assimilationist agenda, because the terms of reconciliation are set by the state and negotiated with Indigenous governments, many of which are colonial creations themselves. In this, and in many other important ways, Canada, Canadians, and Confederation continue to fail Indigenous peoples. Settler society offers reconciliation as a new way or word being used to, once again, "solve" the Indian problem without actually reconciling settler society with Indigenous society and engaging with Indigenous knowledge and norms to actually alter settler society, institutions, and norms in a meaningful and transformative way.

Another example of a failed attempt at reconciliation was the Royal Commission on Aboriginal Peoples (RCAP). Launched in 1990 in response to the Oka crisis,[33] the RCAP was a major and costly undertaking that produced a five-volume, 4,000 page report with 440 recommendations on how to renew the state-Indigenous relationship. Ladner suggests that the form of reconciliation recommended in the RCAP report is not about promoting Indigenous governance but rather is tantamount to a relationship based on "negotiated inferiority." She writes: "We need to create a renewed relationship based upon a true partnership in Confederation, which is based upon a realization of a postcolonial vision and not a perpetuation of colonialism through the creation of negotiated inferiority and an unequal partnership."[34] Indigenous legal scholar John Borrows adds: "A faithful application of the rule of law to the Crown's assertion of title [and thus, sovereignty] throughout Canada would suggest Aboriginal peoples possess the very right claimed by the Crown."[35] Therefore, as Ladner concludes, we must begin the process of reconciliation by moving away from colonialism to create a postcolonial future.

Acknowledging Colonialism

Many Canadians simply do not know enough about Indigenous culture and values to appreciate the important contribution they offer to our ways of knowing. Many more continue to believe that Indigenous knowledge and institutions are merely relics of the past or that they are not as sophisticated as those of settler society. They are wrong, but they are not alone. Settler concepts of Canada constructed at Confederation were entirely premised on a lack of understanding, or worse, on the erasure of Indigenous peoples and their institutions. Even the great scholar Harold Innis, whose work on the fur trade was centred on the key role Indigenous communities played during that time, was blind to the contributions of Indigenous people being made during his own lifetime. To that end, he famously confessed that, while the beaver was embodied in the coat of arms and the maple leaf a national symbol, "we have not realized that the Indian and his culture were fundamental to the growth of Canadian institutions."[36] Likewise, Wright, in his writing concludes that other great scholars such as Creighton were "blind to Aboriginal history."[37]

Clearly, Confederation came at a cost. In addition, it was not simply a constitutional compromise between provinces and races. Indigenous peoples whose lands and rights were whittled away as a result of the colonial enterprise were in fact, and remain today, the "biggest losers." As this has been the case since Confederation, much of the Canadian economy is based on the exploration and extraction of resources on Indigenous lands for which Indigenous peoples receive little or no compensation. As Wright put it, the fundamental purpose of Canadian Confederation was the creation of a vast commercial and territorial empire stretching the length of the continent. Consequently, Canadian citizens today continue to enjoy a standard of living that stands in stark contrast to the standard of living experienced by many Indigenous peoples.

While the state has arguably made space for Indigenous peoples to participate in contemporary society, in many more important ways the state remains a barrier to the real inclusion of Indigenous knowledge and an obstacle to real reconciliation. The lack of equal education, the failure to implement treaties and to adequately finance health care, the high rate of youth suicide, the over-incarceration of Indigenous people, the ongoing issue of missing and murdered Indigenous women, and the issues of overcrowded and inadequate housing and lack of clean drinking water in numerous Indigenous communities across the country remind us that settler society fails to treat Indigenous peoples with the same level of respect and in the same manner as settlers (and even refugees) are treated. Coates concurs: "Looking after the needs of [Indigenous] people was simply not a central part of the strategy for settling British North America and Canada."[38] Arguably this trend continues today. Instead, the goal was, and remains, to ensure that Indigenous peoples "did not [and do not] impede settlement or stand in the way of economic [read: resource] development."[39]

In his book, *On Being Here to Stay: Treaties and Aboriginal Rights in Canada*, political anthropologist Michael Asch "encourages settlers to recognize that they have a responsibility to live up to the true spirit and original intent of the treaties made with Indigenous peoples regardless if we arrived yesterday or last year or a century ago or more."[40] Taking up that challenge, I am reminded of Ladner's argument that to fully reconcile, it is necessary to examine both the Canadian and different Indigenous constitutional orders because "both orders provide both nations and their governments with the rights and responsibilities which they seek to exercise."[41] As she points out, it is our ongoing lack of knowledge and understanding of Indigenous constitutional politics that contributes to the current state of relations between Indigenous peoples and Canada, and which perpetuates misunderstanding and the colonization of Indigenous peoples.[42] Therefore, in order to "overcome colonialism," understanding and coming to terms is required, as well as accepting, engaging, and working with "other" Indigenous constitutional orders.

Looking at the international community and global reconciliation efforts, Sheryl Lightfoot, in her book *Global Indigenous Politics: A Subtle Revolution*,[43] points to a global shift occurring in state-Indigenous relations. In her assessment, the United Nations Declaration on the Rights of Indigenous Peoples (UNDRIP) signified an often overlooked and underappreciated accomplishment on the part of Indigenous peoples. She acknowledges that there exists real potential moving forward for Indigenous peoples, as they define and insist on their rights, to transform international norms. This international development can be turned into potential pressure on state and non-state actors to rethink the Westphalian state model that is currently taken for granted. Lightfoot is hopeful that UNDRIP is indicative of a nascent new political world order that will lead to more meaningful and reciprocal relationships based on new norms and a new imagining of the global world order. In short, she is cautiously optimistic that more pressure will come to bear on settler states such as Canada and settler societies to engage in real reconciliation as Indigenous peoples and their rights come more into focus in the international arena.

Conclusion

What the Truth and Reconciliation Committee and its chair, Justice Sinclair, did in 2015 was put up a mirror to Canadian history to reveal

Canada's colonial past as an ongoing reality. It is impossible to celebrate Confederation without also acknowledging that Confederation came at a cost. Inherently, Confederation was a colonial project, claiming territory in the name of the Crown and assuming ownership of it. At no point were Indigenous nations or their rights, laws, or constitutions acknowledged. Implicitly (in the minds of leaders like Macdonald and reinforced by policies introduced by his government and many since), though not in law or in practice, Confederation is based on the principle of *terra nullius* – a term from Roman law meaning "land without people." Yet, Indigenous people were, and are, connected to the land in ways in which the leaders of Confederation did not, and many Canadians still do not, recognize or appreciate. Quoting Harald Prins, Ladner adds that "when Mi'kmaq country was thus 'magically' transformed into Crown land, it was as if a terrible curse had been put on its Indigenous inhabitants."[44] Referencing Patrick Macklem, Ladner concludes that "it was a curse that, despite promises to the contrary and agreements affirming the continued sovereignty of the Mi'kmaw, sought to magically transform the Mi'kmaw into subjects/wards of the Crown through the mythology of *terra nullius* and the magical assertion of Crown sovereignty."[45]

In as much as Indigenous resurgence involves fighting for land, for rights, and for resources, it also requires that settler society reconcile its role in its relationships with Indigenous people. Like Justice Sinclair, scholars such as Asch, Ladner, and Lightfoot appear hopeful and offer ways forward to rebuild relations between Indigenous peoples, nations, and the settler state/society rooted in reconciliation. Clearly, Canada, with its roots in a colonial document, remains a nation entrenched in colonialism, searching for reconciliation. If we are to venture down the path towards real reconciliation, we need to rethink how we govern and how we conceptualize ourselves, our society, our institutions, and our norms to meaningfully and genuinely embrace and make space for Indigenous ideas and institutions that can better shape the journey going forward. As Canada celebrates 150 years of its existing constitutional order, reconciliation requires we embark on a new constitutional order together. As a nation, it is important that we take this opportunity to pause and to confront the reality of the past and the colonial relationship with Indigenous peoples in order to bring into stark focus Canada's journey forward towards real reconciliation.

NOTES

This chapter was originally written for the publication *Canada Watch 2016: Debating the Confederation Debates of 1865*. It has been revised for the purposes of this publication. In terms of positionality, I am a first-generation settler Canadian whose parents emigrated from Ireland. I have been working with and in First Nation communities across/throughout Canada for over twenty years. My main thesis is that reconciliation is primarily the responsibility/job of settler society as Indigenous peoples engage in resurgence.

1. Ken Coates, "The 'Gentle' Occupation: The Settlement of Canada and the Dispossession of the First Nations," in *Indigenous Peoples' Rights in Australia, Canada and New Zealand*, ed. Paul Havemann (Auckland, NZ: Oxford University Press, 1999), 141.
2. Indigenous and Northern Affairs Canada, "Treaties with Aboriginal People in Canada," http://www.aadnc-aandc.gc.ca/eng/1100100032291/1100100032292.
3. Donald Wright, *Donald Creighton: A Life in History* (Toronto: University of Toronto Press, 2015).
4. John F. Leslie, "The Indian Act: An Historical Perspective," *Canadian Parliamentary Review* 25, no. 2 (Summer 2002): 23.
5. Kiera Ladner, "Up the Creek: Fishing for a New Constitutional Order," *Canadian Journal of Political Science* 38, no. 4 (2005): 945.
6. A scrip was a promissory note provided to Métis people in exchange for title to their land. The note was "redeemable" for land or cash value, but neither of these options was ever honoured.
7. Leslie, "The Indian Act: An Historical Perspective," 23.
8. Ibid.
9. Ibid.
10. Wright, *Donald Creighton: A Life in History*.
11. Leslie, "The Indian Act: An Historical Perspective," 23.
12. Donald B. Smith, "John A. Macdonald and Aboriginal Canada," *Historic Kingston* 50 (2002): 14.
13. George Brown, *Parliamentary Debates on the Subject of the Confederation of the British North American Provinces, 3rd Session, 8th Provincial Parliament of Canada* (Quebec: Hunter, Rose & Co., Parliamentary Printers, 1865), 86.
14. See Terry Fenge and Jim Aldridge, eds., *Keeping Promises: The Royal Proclamation of 1763, Aboriginal Rights, and Treaties in Canada* (Montreal & Kingston: McGill-Queen's University Press, 2015).
15. Coates, "The 'Gentle' Occupation," 157.

16 Leslie, "The Indian Act: An Historical Perspective," 23.
17 Smith, "John A. Macdonald and Aboriginal Canada," 21.
18 Cited in Donald B. Smith, "Macdonald's Relationship with Aboriginal Peoples," in *Macdonald at 200: New Reflections and Legacies*, ed. Patrice Dutil and Roger Hall (Toronto: Dundurn, 2014), 65.
19 Smith, "Macdonald's Relationship with Aboriginal Peoples."
20 Ibid., 72.
21 Wright, *Donald Creighton: A Life in History*, 22.
22 Coates, "The 'Gentle' Occupation," 141.
23 Donald Wright, new introduction to *The Road to Confederation: The Emergence of Canada, 1863–1867*, by Donald Creighton (Don Mills, ON: Oxford University Press, 2012), x.
24 Royal Commission on Aboriginal Peoples, *Report of the Royal Commission on Aboriginal Peoples*, vol. 1, *Looking Forward, Looking Back* (Ottawa: Indian and Northern Affairs Canada, 1996), 179.
25 Leslie, "The Indian Act: An Historical Perspective," 23.
26 Duncan Campbell Scott, quoted in E. Brian Titley, *A Narrow Vision: Duncan Campbell Scott and the Administration of Indian Affairs in Canada* (Vancouver: UBC Press, 1986), 50.
27 Coates, "The 'Gentle' Occupation," 141. Citation accredited to J.R. Miller, *Shingwauk's Vision: A History of Native Residential Schools* (Toronto: University of Toronto Press, 1996).
28 Leslie, "The Indian Act: An Historical Perspective," 25.
29 Taiaiake Alfred and Jeff Corntassel, "Being Indigenous: Resurgences against Contemporary Colonialism," *Government and Opposition: An International Journal of Comparative Politics* 40, no. 4 (2005): 597–614.
30 Glen Coulthard, *Red Skin, White Masks: Rejecting the Colonial Politics of Recognition* (Minneapolis: University of Minnesota Press, 2014).
31 Leslie, "The Indian Act: An Historical Perspective," 27.
32 Frantz Fanon, *Wretched of the Earth* (New York: Grove Press, 1963).
33 As the Oka crisis reminds us, colonialism is a violent process, and throughout Canadian history Indigenous peoples have been the victims of violence inflicted on them by the state. For more on the events that took place at Oka, refer to Geoffrey York and Loreen Pindera, *People of the Pines: The Warriors and the Legacy of Oka* (Toronto: McArthur, 1999).
34 Kiera Ladner, "Negotiated Inferiority: The Royal Commission on Aboriginal People's Vision of a Renewed Relationship," *American Review of Canadian Studies* 31, nos. 1–2 (2001): 263.

35 John Borrows, "Questioning Canada's Title to Land: The Rule of Law, Aboriginal Peoples, and Colonialism," in *Recovering Canada: The Resurgence of Indigenous Law* (Toronto: University of Toronto Press, 2002), 113.
36 Harold A. Innis, with a new introductory essay by Arthur J. Ray, *The Fur Trade in Canada: An Introduction to Canadian Economic history* (Toronto: University of Toronto Press, 1999), 392.
37 Wright, *Donald Creighton: A Life in History*, 155.
38 Coates, "The 'Gentle' Occupation," 157.
39 Ibid.
40 Ryan Eyford, "Review: Michael Asch, *On Being Here to Stay: Treaties and Aboriginal Rights in Canada*," Manitoba History 77 (2015): 49–50.
41 Ladner, "Up the Creek," 936.
42 Ibid.
43 Sheryl Lightfoot, *Global Indigenous Politics: A Subtle Revolution* (London: Routledge, 2016).
44 Ladner, "Up the Creek," 945. Citation accredited to Harald Prins, *The Mi'kmaq: Resistance, Accommodation and Cultural Survival* (Toronto: Harcourt Brace, 1996), 154.
45 Ladner, "Up the Creek," 945. Citation accredited to Patrick Macklem, *Indigenous Difference and the Constitution of Canada* (Toronto: University of Toronto Press, 2001).

PART TWO

Perspectives from Europe

5 The View from the Quirinal: The Holy See and Confederation

ROBERTO PERIN

If judged by the sheer volume, variety, and detail of information flowing into its offices, the Holy See was doubtless the most knowledgeable government on world affairs in the nineteenth century. Its information originated from a complex and sophisticated network, which included diplomatic officials to and from the Holy See such as nuncios, ambassadors, legates, and unofficial representatives; members of the hierarchy who were regularly required to visit Rome and provide detailed reports on their areas of jurisdiction; missionaries who operated in the remotest corners of the globe; young clerics from around the world who attended pontifical institutions of higher learning and usually remained in contact with their professors, themselves often consultants to the Curia; and finally the laity of various ethnicities, social classes, and religions who took up the pen to share their thoughts on some subject or other with the Pope.

In the 1860s Roman officials and bureaucrats were particularly concerned about the Papal States' dramatic loss of territory in central Italy to the forces fighting for the unification of the peninsula under the king of Piedmont-Sardinia, Victor Emmanuel II, supported by Emperor Napoleon III of France. The ability of the Pope to be a free agent was linked in the minds of these officials to his position as a divinely ordained temporal ruler. Also of concern were the revolutionary movements that had recently shaken a number of European states, threatening the established order and most notably the legal and social position of the Church in these lands. The siren calls of liberty and an end to privilege had struck a chord with the masses, subverting the very authority exercised by the clergy over their flock. A mood of foreboding hung over the Quirinal Palace, the official residence of the

Pope-king, as it prepared for the last onslaught of Piedmontese forces, which finally breached the walls of the city in September 1870. By then Pope Pius IX had already unsheathed his ultimate weapon, the doctrine of papal infallibility, declared dogma in July by the fathers of the First Vatican Council. This dramatic and bold gesture sought to set the pontiff above the maelstrom of human affairs.

It is little wonder then that during these years Roman officialdom showed relative aloofness regarding the reorganization of the British North American colonies. This attitude was not a factor of distance. Information regarding these territories had been arriving in Rome fairly steadily and with increasing frequency since the seventeenth century. The bishops of Quebec and those heading dioceses carved out of it, the nuncios in Paris, the vicars apostolic of the London district often acting as agents of the Quebec Church vis-à-vis the British government, the archbishops of Dublin, the missionaries working among Indigenous peoples of North America and newly arrived Catholic settlers, the students residing at the Scots, Irish, English, North American, or French colleges in Rome, the rectors of these institutions, and the consultants for Roman congregations were all conduits of news and opinion regarding British North America. Letters, reports, briefs, newspaper articles, statistics, books, and even artefacts ended up in the offices of the Congregation for the Propagation of the Faith, or Propaganda Fide, situated since 1633 in Piazza di Spagna, a short walk from the Quirinal.

The Congregation was headed by a prefect who held the rank of cardinal assisted by a secretary who was a lower-level clerical dignitary. They oversaw the affairs of the Church in non-Catholic parts of the world, lands as diverse as Great Britain, India, the United States, Holland, and British North America. Alessandro Barnabò, described by historian Owen Chadwick as "the most powerful of the Pope's cardinals,"[1] was prefect from 1856 to 1874, while Annibale Capalti was secretary from 1861 to 1868, the year of his accession to the College of Cardinals. The written material arriving at Propaganda Fide, known in Italian as *Scritture riferite in Congressi*, was examined by these two men who were responsible for the day-to-day running of the Congregation. Their formal meetings, called *congressi*, were held once a week to expedite current affairs. The *scritture* were then assembled in large bound volumes organized chronologically by geographical area. Disputes and questions requiring greater attention because of their complexity or sensitivity were handled by the cardinals named to the Congregation who gathered together in *congregazioni generali* fortnightly, often in the presence of the Pope. Clerical functionaries identified as *minutanti* with oversight of specific areas of the globe were responsible for collecting pertinent material into dossiers for the cardinals' perusal. If a given question were a long-standing one, relevant documents going back years, sometimes decades or even centuries, would be transferred to the current dossier. Such dossiers were then collected into volumes referred to as *Scritture originali riferite nelle congregazioni generali*, which also followed a chronological and geographical order. It was not unusual for the cardinals to call upon lay or clerical consultants who might be experts in canon law or some other field to provide an opinion on specific points relating to a particular question.[2]

During the 1860s the cardinals of the Congregation never once gave consideration to Confederation, even though they dealt with other matters of concern to British North America, such as the conflicts between the dioceses of Montreal and Quebec over Laval University, between the bishop of Montreal and the Sulpician Seminary over the division of the parish of Notre Dame, and between the Quebec and Ontario episcopates over whether the newly created ecclesiastical province of Toronto would encompass territory in Ontario belonging to the diocese of Ottawa including the city itself.[3] There is therefore no file on Confederation in the Vatican archives. This lack, however, does not mean that Roman officials were unaware of impending changes to the constitutional status of the British North American colonies. In 1866, Bishop Charles-François Baillargeon, administrator of the archdiocese of Quebec, requested an audience with the Pope for George-Étienne Cartier, Quebec leader of the Conservative Party, his deputy, Hector-Louis Langevin, and Thomas D'Arcy McGee, the Irish Catholic representative in the cabinet.[4] Although Cartier and McGee were Montrealers, it is significant that they turned to Baillargeon for letters of introduction, given their implacable opposition to the division of Montreal's only parish of Notre Dame promoted by Bishop Ignace Bourget.[5] The three statesmen stopped in Rome on their way to the London Conference, which put the finishing touches to the Confederation agreement. Although we do not know what was said between the pontiff and the politicians, there can be no doubt that the latter would have wanted to stress how the civil rights of Catholics would be protected under the new arrangement. From London, Cartier sent Cardinal Barnabò two copies of the *British North America Act, 1867*, which, he noted, had just been adopted by the House of Commons.[6] Before leaving the imperial capital, the Conservative leader thanked the cardinal for the welcome he had received while in Rome.[7] Two other figures closely connected to Cartier, Pierre-Olivier Chauveau, superintendent of public instruction, and Joseph Cauchon, legislator and mayor of Quebec, visited Rome around the same time with letters of introduction signed by Bishop Baillargeon.[8]

Apart from its preoccupation with the Roman Question, how else is one to interpret the Holy See's relative insouciance relating to Confederation? The answer to that question lies in the way Rome viewed the British North American territories. Because of their colonial status on the one hand, and their geographic position on the other, they were observed through a lens that was at once British and American. The Holy See and Great Britain had convergent interests at mid-century, notwithstanding the powerful anti-Catholic reaction unleashed by Pius IX's re-establishment of the Catholic hierarchy in England in 1850.[9] The two states undoubtedly found comfort in the fact that they had a common foe, France, whose continental ambitions were once again extending to Italy. Underlying such tactical considerations was the fact that they shared a common set of values grounded in social hierarchy, religion, social order, and stability, as well as a positive fear of popular unrest. A symbol of the relative goodwill uniting Britain and the Holy See was the appointment of Odo Russell, a skilled and trusted diplomat serving as secretary of the British legation in Florence, as the unofficial British representative in Rome, where he remained for twelve years until 1870 to the apparent satisfaction of the Curia.

Added to these philosophical and diplomatic considerations were issues internal to Great Britain. Rome appreciated the improved condition of Catholics in the wake of the British parliament's adoption in 1829 of the *Roman Catholic Relief Act*. This was especially true of course in Ireland. There the Holy See had a faithful ally in the person of Paul Cullen, archbishop of Dublin from 1854 to 1878 and probably the most powerful man in the English-speaking Catholic world.[10] Having spent thirty years in Rome, almost twenty of them as rector of the Pontifical Irish College, and having witnessed first-hand the Roman Revolution of 1848 that had forced Pius IX into temporary exile, Cullen was unflinching in his support of ultramontanism and his opposition to both liberalism and nationalism. In his mind, the position of the Church and of Catholics in general would be advanced through quiet diplomacy between government and ecclesiastical leaders, not through electoral politics, much less through popular agitation.[11] This stance set him in opposition not only to nationalist Irish politicians, but also to significant segments of the high and low clergy sympathetic to the national movement. Both groups were kept in check during Cullen's incumbency for reasons that at times were unrelated to his actions. Thus, the Holy See was satisfied that the civil rights of British Catholics were secure and could progress, despite the actions of troublemakers such as the anti-papal crusader Alessandro Gavazzi and the passions he and his ilk succeeded in unleashing.[12]

The United States was also prone to sometimes violent expressions of anti-Catholicism, as witnessed in the Know-Nothing movement of the 1850s, which targeted the massive arrival of Catholic immigrants widely perceived as being antithetical to American republican values.[13] Gaetano Bedini was both a witness and a victim of its ferocity.[14] Born, like Pius IX, in Senigallia in the Papal States and named apostolic nuncio to Brazil in 1852, the newly named archbishop was asked to stop off in Britain and the United States before taking up his post in South America. His seven-month stay in the United States coincided with the speaking tour Gavazzi had undertaken there. Bedini became a target of personal abuse in the press, which represented him as reaction incarnate, of public demonstrations, and even of an attempted assassination. The prelate never made it to Brazil, but returned instead to Rome. He was soon appointed secretary of Propaganda Fide (1856–61), where, according to historian Matteo Sanfilippo, he wielded significant influence on American affairs even after his subsequent appointment as bishop of Viterbo and elevation to the College of Cardinals.[15] He was in fact the only member of the Curia to have first-hand knowledge of the United States, which he was determined to disseminate. As secretary of the Propaganda, he strongly supported the establishment in 1858 of the North American College, which would provide American students with a thoroughly Roman education. Until his untimely death in 1864, Bedini clearly had had the ear of Cardinal Barnabò, as well as that of his fellow townsman, Pius IX.

What most had impressed the prelate about the United States was its economic might and technological development. It was clear in his mind that the country would soon become a major player on the international stage.[16] And, notwithstanding popular expressions of hostility towards the papacy and Catholicism, he was enchanted by the goodwill political leaders had shown him. In Washington, for example, he had been received by the secretary of state and by the president himself. What is more, Michigan Senator Lewis Cass, whose son was US diplomatic representative to the Holy See, publicly came to the defence of the prelate in the midst of the bitter newspaper attacks directed against him.[17]

These events were interpreted as signs of the positive effects freedom of religion was producing in the United States, which allowed for the extension of the Church's influence in the public sphere. The United States' bright prospects were also linked to the huge influx of immigrants from Europe, which included an ever-growing number of Catholics. As a result, not only was the proportion of Catholics to the overall American population steadily increasing, but a willingness and readiness to publicly defend Pius IX and the faith was emerging. The prelate especially singled out Irish immigrants for praise. In Montreal, for example, they had not hesitated to take to the streets to express their violent reaction to Gavazzi's invectives, and in New York they had openly expressed their unbounded affection for the Pope at a time when the public discourse was decidedly chilly if not outright hostile.

In the final analysis, influential figures at the Holy See were pinning their hopes for the future of Catholicism on the English-speaking world, especially as forces hostile to the Church were beginning to pick up steam in continental Europe. Despite their Protestant majorities, which at times reacted explosively to Rome's pretensions, Great Britain and North America had developed tolerant regimes where the Church was given a free hand to develop and expand. It was in such a climate that the Oxford Movement took root in England. Composed of a number of figures connected to the eponymous university, the movement was determined to bring Anglicanism back to its architectural, artistic, and liturgical heritage rooted in the Middle Ages. After the public scandal that was caused when a minority of followers, notably John Henry Newman, Robert Wilberforce, and Nicholas Wiseman, converted to Catholicism, the movement recovered and spread well beyond England's borders. In the United States too, the movement had produced conversions leading to the creation of the Missionary Society of St Paul the Apostle (Paulist Fathers), the first male Catholic congregation to be founded in the United States. Dedicated to the conversion of North America, the order was strongly supported in Rome by Bedini.[18] While an elite's sympathy for, if not outright identification with, the Catholic Church was not to be discounted, Rome nurtured even greater hopes for the future because of Irish immigration to England and the United States. Rural migrants from Ireland were pouring into English and Scottish cities in the wake of the catastrophic potato famine.[19] Meanwhile co-religionists were settling in the United States, British North America, and Australia, significantly augmenting the number of Catholics there and giving the Church in these regions a decidedly Irish face.

For these reasons, Confederation did not trigger alarm bells in Rome. The tolerant regimes that had evolved in Great Britain and the United States were also operational in British North America. Dioceses and parishes were being erected; clergymen were being trained locally, recruited from abroad, or sent to Rome for advanced studies; funds were being collected by the Church for various purposes; Catholic institutions in the fields of health, education, and welfare were expanding; and worship was practised without the slightest legislative restriction. Civil rights were guaranteed. Catholic education was firmly implanted in the Canadas and was developing in the Maritime colonies and the North West.

Nor had the bishops collectively expressed any anxieties about Confederation. This is hardly surprising since institutionally the Catholic Church in Canada was fragmented by language, ethnicity, and region, its leaders also falling prey to issues of personality. Repeated efforts by the irrepressible Bishop Bourget to have the Maritime dioceses included in the ecclesiastical province of Quebec, created in 1844, and to have them participate in church councils had met with no success. In contrast, in the United States the first Council of the American Church had been held in 1829. In British North America, Irish-born bishops, as English speakers, considered themselves to be entitled to lead and speak for the Catholic Church. They were therefore wary of French Canadian dominance of the institution. Tensions, however, existed as well between clerics of Scottish and Irish origin. What is more, the archbishop of Halifax, Thomas Louis Connolly, and the bishop of Toronto, John Joseph Lynch, men not known for their modesty or self-effacement, vied with each other over which one should be considered the senior prelate, indeed the Canadian primate.[20] One cannot therefore speak of a "Canadian" Catholic Church in this period.

In the three years that Confederation was publicly debated, the hierarchy neither acted in concert nor with one voice on the issue. On the whole, however, they overwhelmingly supported the measure, some keenly promoting it, as was the case with the archbishop of Halifax[21] and the bishops of Arichat, Chatham, Rimouski, Saint-Hyacinthe, Kingston,[22] Toronto,[23] and Hamilton.[24] In fact the fluently bilingual bishop of Kingston, Edward John Horan, went to New Brunswick after the electoral defeat of pro-Confederation forces there in 1865 to persuade Catholics to support the new arrangement. He was accompanied by the vicar general of the archdiocese of Quebec, their expenses being covered by Cartier.[25] Some bishops were lukewarm in their approval of Confederation: Charles-François Baillargeon simply deferred to the authority and wisdom of the civil power, while Louis-François Laflèche, coadjutor of the diocese of Trois-Rivières, saw it as the only realistic option to annexation to the United States or domination by Ontario.[26]

The backing of English-speaking bishops did not signify that they were entirely satisfied with the new arrangement. The issue of the educational rights of Catholic minorities was especially a cause of unease. Archbishop Connolly of Halifax, for example, followed the Fathers of Confederation to London in 1866 expressly to lobby them and the Colonial Office for the entrenchment of such rights in the constitution. Cartier and Langevin had left him with the distinct but incorrect impression that Catholic minorities in the Maritimes would have the same guarantees as those enjoyed by the religious minorities in Quebec and Ontario.[27] In any event, he did not apprise the Holy See of his concerns or his activities in London, perhaps convinced by the reassurances of senior Canadian politicians. As far as Horan was concerned, the fact that Ontario Catholics were on an equal footing with Protestants when it came to compulsory public education was mitigated by the exclusion of Catholic high schools from government funding.[28] His colleague Lynch worried as well that, by introducing the principle of representation by population in the provincial legislature, Ontario Catholics, who until then had relied on the support of Catholic legislators from Quebec, would find themselves at the mercy of an overwhelming Protestant majority.[29] But these episcopal worries dissipated like an early morning mist when the final draft of the Confederation agreement was submitted to Westminster in early March 1867. The bishops then rallied their support for the measure. In advance of the general elections held in the late summer of that year, their French-speaking colleagues wrote pastoral letters that practically obliged the electorate in conscience to vote for pro-Confederation candidates.[30]

Only two bishops stood apart from the others on Confederation. John Sweeny of Saint John had publicly backed the anti-Confederation forces in New Brunswick for reasons that had nothing to do with religion, but accepted the new constitution once it was adopted.[31] For his part, Bourget had grave concerns, especially over questions relating to divorce and the educational rights of Catholic minorities.[32] Without examining in detail his position on these questions, which I have studied elsewhere, suffice it to say that the bishop reacted against a provision in the new constitution that would make divorce a federal responsibility, subject therefore to the will of a Protestant majority. He feared that

Protestant legislators would open the door to state-sanctioned divorce for Catholics. The bishop preferred having the matter placed under provincial authority. In this way, the substantial majority of Catholics, who in any case lived in Quebec, would be protected against the actions of a possibly hostile majority. It is important here to stress that Bourget, who was respectful of the civil rights of Protestants, was not trying to prevent their access to divorce. Be that as it may, he felt so strongly about this question that he was prepared to oblige Catholic legislators in conscience to vote against the new constitution unless divorce become subject to provincial jurisdiction. But he was outflanked by his clerical opponents at the archdiocese of Quebec who were close allies of Cartier and other French Canadian Conservative leaders. They guilefully obtained opinions favourable to their point of view from two canon lawyers in Rome.[33] With the rug taken out from under him, Bourget was prevented from leading a campaign against the legislation as it then stood.[34] For these and other reasons, he refrained from giving Confederation his explicit support, much to the exasperation of his suffragan, Charles Larocque of Saint-Hyacinthe, a friend of Cartier and ardent campaigner for Confederation.

It might well be asked why Pius IX, whose famous *Syllabus of Errors* published in 1864 rejected any accommodation with progress, liberalism, and modern civilization, did not side with Bourget. The bishop was after all the most Roman of Canadian prelates. It was he who erected a cathedral modelled, although on a reduced scale, on St Peter's; who sent Zouaves to fight in defence of the Papal States; who had the liturgy, popular piety, religious teaching, clerical dress, and architectural styles conform to Roman ways. Bourget travelled to Rome seven times in his lifetime, spending almost two years there in the mid-1850s and making his last trip at the ripe old age of eighty-two. Bishop Horan may have unwittingly supplied the answer to this question. When Cardinal Barnabò asked him for his thoughts on Bourget's position on the Civil Code, the bishop of Kingston replied that his colleague was too rigorous in his judgment. While acknowledging the need to amend the Code, Horan pointed out that two of the three jurists who had worked on revising it were Catholic. He also emphasized that the government was in the hands of a Protestant majority.[35] No further argument was needed.

Although members of the Curia did not commit their thoughts on Canadian affairs to paper, their attitudes were quite apparent. In their eyes, British North America was no daughter of the French Revolution. Rather it matured under the watchful eye of Mother England, where the position of Catholics had steadily improved during the nineteenth century. The freedom that was that country's hallmark and had been exported to North America as well was vastly different from *la liberté*, which proved so constraining and demeaning to the Church in France. Catholics in British North America had succeeded in entrenching their civil rights through patient and persistent negotiation with Protestant rulers. Even when compared to co-religionists in the United States and Great Britain, their position was an enviable one. Of course, there was always room for improvement. The Catholic minorities in the Maritimes were not secure in their access to denominational education. But the largest number of Catholics, those living in Quebec and Ontario, had these rights entrenched in the constitution. The rest would surely follow with patience and goodwill. Cardinal Cullen was living proof of how much could be achieved through quiet diplomacy. Overall, French Canadian politicians had shown their loyalty to the Church, and their English-speaking Protestant counterparts had shown a disposition to accommodate them. Bishop Bourget was considered too rash in his readiness to publicize Catholic grievances in *la bonne presse*, mobilize Catholic voters, and publicly confront the Church's opponents. Too often he seemed to think and act as if Quebec were not part of North America where the Protestant majority had to be courted and sometimes mollified, certainly not provoked. Thus, Pius IX, who regarded himself after 1870 as the prisoner of the Vatican, refusing to have anything to do with the new Italian state and even excommunicating its king, preached a meliorist strategy based on conciliation and forbearance.

For Rome, British North America was not unknown territory. Information from as far afield as Vancouver Island, Lake Athabasca, and Red River can be found for the 1860s in the archives of Propaganda Fide. In the same decade the defence of the Papal States prompted 500 young men to enrol in the Pope's armies: 350 of them actually made it to the Italian peninsula, and two were wounded in action.[36] In 1864 British North America's contribution to Peter's Pence, fast becoming the Holy See's main source of revenue, was just below that of Mexico, Germany, and Ireland, and well above that of the United States.[37] Rome was well informed about impending changes to the British North American colonies, not only through the correspondence of local bishops, but through the visits of leading politicians anxious to flaunt before the electorate the approval at the highest levels of the Church hierarchy for Confederation.

On the whole, the episcopate of British North America was either enthusiastic about or tolerant of the new constitutional order. No bishop, except for Sweeny of Saint John, was publicly opposed, and once the *British North America Act, 1867* became law, all stood behind it. Reservations about this or that aspect of the new constitution were quickly set aside. The Holy See, for its part, was satisfied that the civil rights of Catholics were largely safeguarded. From the vantage point of 1867, it was impossible to predict the rise over the next half century of a strident anti-Catholicism that attempted and often succeeded in curtailing Catholic educational rights in Canada. The strategy of patience and conciliation hit a brick wall when political figures in both parties at the provincial and federal levels showed a willingness to exploit religiously based prejudice for electoral advantage. This did not, however, shake the Holy See's conviction that the future of Catholicism lay with the English-speaking world, a view repeated in 1910 by Francis Bourne, archbishop of Westminster, at the International Eucharistic Congress held that year in Montreal. The Holy See therefore unwittingly undermined the more militant elements within the French Canadian Church and their fight for the civil liberties of Canadian Catholics.[38]

NOTES

1 Owen Chadwick, *A History of the Popes, 1830–1914* (Oxford: Clarendon, 1998), 215.
2 Matteo Sanfilippo et Giovanni Pizzorusso, "Le Canada et le pontificat de Pie IX," in *Le Saint-Siège, le Canada et le Québec. Recherches dans les archives romaines*, ed. Luca Codignola, Giovanni Pizzorusso, et Matteo Sanfilippo (Viterbo: Sette Città, 2011). See also their *Inventaire des documents d'intérêt canadien dans les Archives de la Congrégation 'de Propaganda Fide' sous le pontificat de Pie IX (1846–1878)* (Rome-Ottawa: Centre académique canadien en Italie – Université Saint-Paul, 2001).
3 Archivio Propaganda Fide, Roma (APFR), *Acta*, file 43, file 45–6, vol. 229 (1865), file 64, vol. 235 (1869), file 70, vol. 236 (1870); *Scritture Originali Riferite in Congregazioni generali (SOCG)*, files 35, 37, 38, vol. 992 (1865).
4 Ibid., *Scritture riferite in Congressi* (SC), vol. 9 (1866–67), Baillargeon à Barnabò, 24 oct. 1866, f 187–91.

5 Roberto Perin, *Ignace de Montréal. Artisan d'une identité nationale* (Montréal: Boréal, 2008), chap. 4.
6 APFR, SC, vol. 9, Cartier à Barnabò, 22 mars 1867, f 859–61.
7 APFR, SC, vol. 9, Cartier à Barnabò, 1 mai 1867, f 839–42.
8 APFR, SC, vol. 9, Baillargeon à Barnabò, 8 nov. 1866, f. 244–5, 8 fév. 1867, f. 812–13.
9 Chadwick, *A History of the Popes*, 114–15.
10 Colin Barr, "Imperium in Imperio: Irish Episcopal Imperialism in the Nineteenth Century," *English Historical Review* 123 (2008): 611–50. "From about 1832 he set out with great success to mould the Roman Catholic Church in the English-speaking world to his vision of Catholicism," 650.
11 Emmet Larkin, "Cullen, Paul (1803–1878)," in *Oxford Dictionary of National Biography* (Oxford: Oxford University Press, 2004).
12 Robert Sylvain, *Clerc, garibaldien, prédicant des deux mondes, Alessandro Gavazzi (1809–1889)*, 2 vols. (Québec: Le Centre pédagogique, 1962).
13 The classic study in this regard is Ray Billington, *The Protestant Crusade, 1800–1860: A Study of the Origins of American Nativism* (New York: Rinehart, 1952).
14 James Hennesey, *American Catholics: A History of the Roman Catholic Community in the United States* (Oxford: Oxford University Press, 1981), chap. 10; Matteo Sanfilippo, *L'affermazione del cattolicesimo nel Nord America: elite, immigranti e Chiesa cattolica negli Stati Uniti e in Canada, 1750–1920* (Viterbo: Sette città, 2003), chap. 2.
15 Hennesey, *American Catholics*, 63.
16 Ibid., 75.
17 Ibid., 64, 61.
18 Ibid., 103, 106; Sanfilippo, *L'affermazione del cattolicesimo*, 63.
19 Chadwick, *A History of the Popes*, 109–15.
20 Jacques Grisé, *Les conciles provinciaux de Québec et l'Église canadienne* (Montréal: Fides, 1979), chaps. 1–3. For ethnic conflict in the Church, see Léon Thériault, "The Acadianization of the Catholic Church in Acadia,1763–1953," in *The Acadians of the Maritimes: Thematic Studies*, ed. Jean Daigle (Moncton: Centre d'études acadiennes, 1982), 271–339; Robert Choquette, *L'église catholique dans l'Ontario français du dix-neuvième siècle* (Ottawa: Presses de l'Université d'Ottawa, 1984), chaps. 8 and 9; Roberto Perin and Matteo Sanfilippo, "Les conflits ecclésiastiques ," in *La francophonie nord-américaine*, ed. Yves Frenette, Étienne Rivard, Marc St-Hilaire (Québec: Presses de l'Université Laval, 2012), 199–205.
21 K. Fay Trombley, "Thomas Louis Connolly (1815–1876): The Man and His Place in Secular and Ecclesiastical History" (PhD dissertation [Theology)], Katholieke Universiteit Leuven, 1983), 302–62.

22 J.E. Rea, "Edward John Horan," *Dictionary of Canadian Biography*, vol. X (1871–1880), 394–6.
23 T.G.L. Stortz, "John Joseph Lynch, Archbishop of Toronto: A Biographical Study of Religious, Social and Political Commitment" (PhD dissertation [History], Guelph University, 1980), chap. 4.
24 Colin Mackinnon of Arichat, James Rogers of Chatham, John Joseph Lynch of Toronto, and John Farrell of Hamilton, all publicly expressed their support in letters to newspapers. See Trombley, 310; on Rogers, see Laurie C.C. Stanley, "James Rogers," *Dictionary of Canadian Biography*, vol. XIII (1901–1910), 890–4.
25 Marcel Bellavance, *Le Québec et la Confédération: un choix libre? Le clergé et la constitution de 1867* (Québec: Septentrion, 1992), 76–9.
26 Walter Ullman, "The Quebec Bishops and Confederation," *Canadian Historical Review* 44, no. 3 (September 1963).
27 Trombley, "Thomas Louis Connolly (1815–1876)," 327–37.
28 Ibid., 336.
29 Stortz, "John Joseph Lynch, Archbishop of Toronto," chap. 4.
30 Bellavance, *Le Québec et la Confédération*, 80–9.
31 Terrence Murphy, "John Sweeny," *Dictionary of Canadian Biography*, vol. XIII (1901–1910), 1004–7.
32 Roberto Perin, "Clerics and the Constitution: The Quebec Church and Minority Rights in Canada," in *Constitutions and National Identity*, ed. Thomas J. Barron, Owen Dudley Edwards, and Patricia J. Storey (Edinburgh: Quadriga, 1993), 162–80.
33 Perin, "Clerics and the Constitution," 169–70; Bellavance, *Le Québec et la Confédération*, 73–4.
34 Archives de la Chancellerie de l'Archidiocèse de Montréal (ACAM), 420.005, Truteau à Bourget, 31 mars 1865; Registres de lettres Bourget (RLB), vol. 14, Truteau à Cazeau, 3 avr. 1865.
35 APFR, SC, vol. 8, Horan à Barnabò, 17 mars 1865.
36 Jean-Philippe Warren, ed., *Les soldats du Pape: les Zouaves canadiens entre l'Europe et l'Amérique* (Québec: Presses de l'Université Laval, 2014).
37 John F. Pollard, *Money and the Rise of the Modern Papacy: Financing the Vatican, 1850–1950* (Cambridge: Cambridge University Press, 2005), 33.
38 Roberto Perin, *Rome in Canada: The Vatican and Canadian Affairs in the Late Victorian Age* (Toronto: University of Toronto Press, 1990).

6 Model and Anomaly: The Canadian Confederation Seen from France, 1864–1871

ALBAN BARGAIN-VILLÉGER

The nineteenth century is usually considered a key period in the history of nation-building. In addition, its second and last thirds have been called the "age of capital" and the "age of empire," respectively.[1] This particular era, and especially the years 1848–1914, saw the birth or development of many concepts and ideas that have shaped the twentieth and twenty-first centuries. While the past is sometimes described as "a foreign country," the nation-building processes that speckled the nineteenth century also loomed large in the twentieth century, and still resonate in our day and age.[2] In addition to their longevity, these processes inherently defy the very concept of "national history" – nations usually define themselves as peculiar entities, distinct from others (especially their neighbours). In that regard, the Canadian case is of particular interest, as attempting to historicize the very meaning of "nation" in this country is, at best, multifaceted and slippery, and at worst, a constant headache. Nonetheless, one useful way of approaching the national question in Canada consists of focusing on non-Canadian perspectives on the Confederation period. More specifically, this chapter argues that diplomatic corps and newspapers of the French Second Empire viewed Confederation simultaneously as a foreign, unique phenomenon and as a process related to the European nation-building projects of the era.

Few studies have been made on the views expressed in France on state formation in Canada between 1864 and 1871.[3] The reasons for focusing on these years are quite straightforward. The year 1864 is, of course, the year of the decisive Charlottetown and Quebec conferences, and 1871 marked the geopolitically significant entry of British Columbia, which turned the Dominion into a transcontinental entity.

The period spanning September 1870 to June 1871 marked a major break in French history, with the fall of Napoléon III, the establishment of the Third Republic, and the brutal suppression of the Paris Commune. Finally, these years correspond approximately to the Second Empire's "liberalization" period, during which Napoléon III attempted to combine his authoritarian rule with the promotion of free trade and generally progressive, albeit paternalistic, ideas on the rights of peoples to self-determination and to establish nation-states.

This study focuses on three themes: where Canada fitted in French views on what was then known as the "national question"; geopolitics – in other words, the (real or imagined) place of Confederation in the world according to the French diplomatic corps and media;[4] and trade. In order to do these themes justice, this study is mainly based on two types of primary sources: the diplomatic correspondence between several consulate generals of France in Canada (mainly the one based in Quebec City, officially established in 1858) and the French Foreign Office, as well as the latter's correspondence with the French embassy in London; and mostly liberal (pro-regime or not) and republican newspapers. The socialist, anarchist, and Catholic media are conspicuously absent from this sample, as papers of these political hues rarely tackled the subject of Confederation.[5] Finally, references to miscellaneous travel accounts, memoirs, and reports will also appear, albeit sporadically.

Confederation certainly did not come out of thin air. It was driven by a variety of issues: the annexation threat in the wake of the American Civil War, the Fenian raids (most notably the June 1866 Niagara skirmishes), domestic political issues, and British economic interests. However, this process was by no means parthenogenetic, specific to North America. It stemmed, in part, from the development of ideas that pervaded most of the Western world at the time.[6] Although Ian McKay describes this process of state formation as the result of the hegemonic development of liberal ideology in the Canadian context, this "replacement, often with a kind of revolutionary symbolic or actual violence, of antithetical traditions and forms that had functioned for centuries and even millennia with new conceptions of the human being and society" also took place in Europe.[7] In addition, like most (if not all) other states, Canada had been shaped as a result of conflicts (the American War of Independence was, after all, the reason for being of the future entity north of the United States), population movements, and geopolitical factors. In that regard, the conditions for the creation of Confederation were not that exceptional. Finally, while Canada was undoubtedly not birthed on the barricades, and although the unification process was not as dramatic as that of the Italian and German cases, the European revolutions of 1830 and 1848 also had a certain impact on British North America.[8]

But compared with the national liberation movements that speckled Western Europe at that time, the road to Confederation resulted more from pragmatic considerations than from the will to unite a nation with the creation of an independent state. Most prominently, the coexistence of several ethnolinguistic groups in British North America precluded the use of a rhetoric akin to that of German, Hungarian, or Italian nationalists. Indeed, the latter based their ideas on their beliefs in the alleged common destiny of a cultural entity and on well-rehearsed narratives and age-old, more or less invented, traditions.[9] In the Canadian case, and although the Indigenous peoples were not invited to partake of the creation of Confederation, the various peoples who inhabited the British colonies were certainly too diverse to even consider emulating their counterparts across the Atlantic. The two main groups involved in the project, namely the French- and English-speaking elites, did not see Canada as an ageless, homogeneous entity similar to that of Germany or Italy. In that regard, the French Canadians played a major part in ensuring that Confederation would guarantee the existence of a "distinct society" in Lower Canada. According to A.I Silver, "[i]t was the Lower Canadian ministers who had insisted, at the Quebec Conference, that education, civil and religious institutions should be under provincial jurisdiction, in order that Quebec should have the power to take charge of the French-Canadian national future."[10] Confederation was initially more of a state-shaping endeavour that included two nation-building projects than a straightforward nation-building one. It should therefore not come as a surprise that – to the French at least – the Dominion of Canada might not have fallen in the same category as Risorgimento Italy or Bismarck's North German Confederation.

Many decades after Voltaire's caustic comment on "a few acres of snow in Canada," but still long before Confederation, several French authors published accounts of their travels to British North America.[11] One of the most famous of these was François-René de Chateaubriand's controversial *Travels in America*, which focused on the wilderness of the Great Lakes region and provided romantic, picturesque descriptions of the Indigenous peoples' way of life.[12] Works of this type generally presented North America as a wild, spacious expanse only partially inhabited by Indigenous communities. Not surprisingly, the latter did not fit into contemporary French views of a people endowed with a modern sense of nationhood. Indigenous peoples were often viewed as an exotic bloc, a society that belonged more in classical antiquity than in the present.[13] Thus, the pre-settler society was not invariably seen as nationless, but located in an antiquated, backward universe.

In general, such works rarely addressed the question of nation- or state-building in Canada until the mid-1850s, when travellers became more aware of British North America as a political entity of its own. Until then, this part of the world was usually referred to as a "country" or a "region" – or implicitly treated as an appendage of the United States.[14] Reflections on the "French fact" and more or less explicit opinions as to what French attitudes should be towards British North America became more frequent following the 1855 journey of *La Capricieuse* – the first French battleship to travel up the Saint Lawrence River since the British conquest.[15] To a certain L. Dussieux, for instance, "half a million Indians ... still long for the days of French domination, which was so liberal for their race."[16] Nonetheless, such reminiscences rarely went as far as calls to arms. More than anything, the triumphant passage of *La Capricieuse* embodied the Franco-British détente, which occurred in part as a result of the Crimean War (1853–6) and resulted in the creation of a consulate in Quebec City in 1858.[17]

In the 1864–71 years, most French observers did not consider Canada as a fully fledged member of the concert of nations. This view was in part due to the new state's official denomination, namely that of "Dominion," which confused the consul general Frédéric Gautier himself, as his attempt to explain it to the French Foreign Office demonstrates: "The Confederation was given the name of 'Dominion of Canada,' which can be translated as *'Empire,' 'Puissance,' 'souveraineté,'* or *'Domination'* of Canada. We will not know the exact translation of the word 'Dominion' until the official French version of the English has been published."[18] Three months later, Gautier's incomprehension regarding the new regime was again evident when he remarked that Lord Monck "will assume no higher a position than that of Governor General of Canada," before wondering "what 'Dominion of Canada,' which was translated into French as *'Puissance du Canada,'* actually means."[19] From the start, then, the new state appeared as a novelty, a special case that did not have any counterpart in Europe.

As Pierre Savard has rightly remarked, French consuls in Quebec City rarely commented at length on Canadian political institutions, "except at the time of the establishment of Confederation."[20] More specifically, it was the coexistence of the Anglophones and the Francophones that interested Gautier. Here, as in many other instances, the ethnic/national fault line was seen as being of an exclusively linguistic/religious nature. The Indigenous peoples, the Irish (whether Catholic or Protestant), and the Scots barely featured in the correspondence between 1864 and 1871 – except in the context of the Fenian raids. This approach was also mainly of an elitist nature, as the consul only occasionally reported on the local press or referred to sources other than prominent politicians. One of the best illustrations of this dichotomous perspective is Gautier's detailed account of the tensions caused by the award of a higher class in the Order of the Bath to John A. Macdonald (Knight) than to George-Étienne Cartier (Companion). In that regard, the consul opined that "Mr. Macdonald has not done more ... than Mr. Cartier in founding the new state of affairs, and the Crown Counsel's decision to show preference for an English Canadian has wounded and been deeply felt as a humiliation by the Catholic and French-Canadian race."[21] But despite such tensions, the consul general rarely made a secret of his admiration for what he probably viewed as a commendable exercise in maintaining a balance between two distinct cultures engaged in a common state-building project.[22]

Though not overly enthusiastic, Gautier was rather sympathetic to Confederation. Overall the consul saw Confederation as a coldly calculated, necessary enterprise in state-building that would indirectly be beneficial to French interests. Indeed, the frequently expressed relief that some stability presided over francophone-anglophone relations and the certainty that the status of dominion was the best solution against a future annexation by the United States reflected the French government's current geopolitical interests.[23] Although France and the United States have been portrayed as natural allies ever since the 1770s, the 1860s saw a cooling of Franco-American relations. Given their efforts to contain American territorial expansion and influence in North America, the weakening of British North America was of some concern to the French, who were being defeated in Mexico, where they were engaged in part to counter the United States' growing power in that country.[24] But whether the status of dominion was to become a permanent one or Canada was to achieve complete autonomy, the imperial government certainly did not see Confederation as "the birth of a nation,"²⁵ but more as a pragmatic operation. Indeed, none of the letters in the consular correspondence compared the role played by Ontario and Quebec as decisive unifying forces with that of Prussia or Piedmont, respectively. The analogy would, in any case, have been inaccurate. The federation of the three colonies and, later, the incorporation of what was to become Manitoba and British Columbia were understood as part of a broader rearrangement of the British imperial structure, not the dawn of true national emancipation.

To the consul – and probably to the various foreign secretaries who succeeded each other between 1864 and 1871 – Canada did not really belong in the same league as the European nation-states in the making. This view mirrored Napoléon III's stance on what constituted a nation. According to Éric Anceau, the Emperor considered that "nationalities could not simply be defined by common idioms and racial homogeneity, as geographical structures and ideological unity (which are born from common interests and memories) played as important a role."²⁶ To support his argument, Napoléon mentioned the cantons of Neuchâtel and Vaud, which, though very "French," were nonetheless part of Switzerland. In contrast, Alsace was, in his opinion, unarguably part of France despite Alsatian being a dialect of German.²⁷ This perspective does not shed much light on the Emperor's views on Canada. After all, he might as easily have considered that, by the 1860s, the anglophone and francophone elements had enough memories and interests in common to coexist within the same national entity.

While Napoléon III was interested in federal and confederal projects,²⁸ and expressed some interest in the Acadians and the Quebec Francophones, he never openly supported the independence of French Canada (as others had before him)²⁹ and confined his sympathy to making donations to various projects and institutions (including books to the Université Laval).³⁰ According to Robert Pichette, the Emperor's willingness to sponsor some pro-francophone initiatives originated from his plan to "restore France in its role as naval and commercial power."³¹ In any case, he never seems to have expressed himself regarding the future of Confederation. Unlike his more progressive and turbulent cousin Napoléon-Jérôme, who, in the wake of his 1861 visit to Canada, declared that Canada would inevitably become independent, the Emperor could not risk a diplomatic crisis with Great Britain.³²

Outside of governmental and diplomatic circles, there was no scarcity of references to Canada. For instance, Jules Verne's *Twenty Thousand Leagues under the Sea*, published in 1869–70, clearly replicated the official view that Confederation consisted of the unification of two nations into one state, rather than the emergence of yet another national entity. Thus Verne described the rebellious Ned Land as a hybrid, whose identity was somewhat in-between worlds. In addition to being a talented harpooner, "Ned Land was a Canadian ... and when one hears 'Canadian,' one also hears 'French.' And despite his coyness, I must admit that Ned Land felt some affection towards me. My background undoubtedly attracted him. It gave him the opportunity to speak in (and for me to hear) Rabelais's old idiom, which is still in use in some Canadian provinces."[33] Although the effect of the novel on the readers is hard to gauge, one might surmise, given the commercial success of *Twenty Thousand Leagues under the Sea*, that Verne's portrayal of the "Canadian type" did not go unnoticed.

As for the press, it also emphasized the composite nature of the new state. Here too, it is impossible to paint a complete picture of public opinion on Confederation. Since most of the newspapers did not have permanent correspondents in Canada, they received their material second hand, through telegraphic dispatches from London, Washington, New York City, or (albeit rarely) Halifax. That being said, excerpts from Canadian newspapers (mostly Quebec-based) occasionally made their way into the French press. Overall, few original articles were published on Confederation. Besides, it was very likely that few readers actually cared much about that particular subject. But despite the dearth of original articles on Canada,[34] some recurrent themes – especially in the liberal press – can help understand general perceptions of Canada among French intellectuals and journalists. Not surprisingly, the question of the "French element" loomed large in most articles that dealt with the unification of the four colonies. Some authors confined themselves to reiterating half-serious platitudes about the durability of French language and culture, and what a great empire France would have ruled over had it not forgone its North American possessions.[35] Other journalists preferred to conjecture on the future of the French-speaking population under the new regime. For instance, *L'Année européenne* saw Confederation as a golden opportunity for French Canadians, as, according to the champion of the francophone cause, François-Edme Rameau de Saint-Père, the formation of the new state had enabled the "Lower-Canadian administration ... to become, in a sense, national." Nonetheless, the article expressed the hope that French Canadians would not antagonize the British too much and would fight for their interests with moderation. "When one observes the expansion of the French element in Lower Canada," the author continued, "one realizes that it is not at all impossible that, one hundred years from now, a French national community could play a considerable role in the civilization of the new world."[36] Like the government and the diplomatic corps, then, most newspapers viewed Confederation as a positive development for French Canadians and did not seriously regret the loss of New France one hundred years earlier.[37]

When it came to the economic aspects of the question, both the consuls and the press emphasized the state's enormous potential. Although the prospects of engaging in substantial trade with Canada were slim and developed only marginally in the following years,[38] the consuls regularly informed the Foreign Office of the opportunities offered by the lowering of protective tariffs.[39] After all, the development of lasting trade agreements with British North America had been the main rationale for the creation of permanent consular agencies.[40] With the signing of the January 1860 Franco-British trade agreement – which involved the lowering of tariffs and included a "most-favoured nation" clause – and the liberalization of the Second Empire,[41] it should not come as a surprise that French business circles nurtured the hope of infiltrating new markets in Canada. Even before the process that led to Confederation had actually begun, the 1863 customs agreement had already facilitated the importation of Canadian ships to France and, conversely, substantially lowered the tariffs on French wines and brandy.[42]

Without dwelling much on the opportunities of opening the Canadian market to French entrepreneurs, many of the authors who devoted full-length articles to Confederation marvelled at a territory whose fertile soils ("[d]espite its rough climate")[43] destined it to become "a great country."[44] However, while the government and the consuls showed some interest in the possibility of increasing commercial exchanges with the Dominion (and, in particular, in the effects on the French economy of purchasing cheaper goods abroad),[45] the press preferred to focus on the geopolitical consequences of Confederation. The establishment to the north of the United States of a potentially strong state that retained links with Britain could only reassure the French. Given Britain's role as a useful ally of convenience, Confederation appeared to the French as a welcome development.

This alliance – which was facilitated by the Emperor's admiration for Britain's industrial and technological innovations – could mean a real thorn in the side of the United States, especially after France's failed Mexican campaign. As a *Journal des débats* author noted:

> If, as it is likely to happen, all the colonies of British America unite and form a single Confederation, and if the neighbouring great republic allows them enough time to expand and fortify without bothering them too much – which, I concede, is less likely – there is here the seed of what could undoubtedly become a very powerful nation. The proud satisfaction with which the motherland wallows in envisioning the future might of its offspring while showing it the smoothest way to independence is, in my view, both natural and legitimate.[46]

Nonetheless, Napoléon III was a product of his time, and his anglophilia, which had developed during his years of exile and imprisonment, did not extend to Britain's parliamentarianism. Like many of his contemporaries, he considered that there existed irreconcilable differences between French and English political cultures.[47] Of course, one man's opinion, even that of the Emperor, does not reflect that of French society at the time. However, his power of influence in the realm of foreign affairs cannot be ignored, and the fact that much of the press relayed his own views shows how pervasive imperial world views were in the French media and its readers. That being said, this influence was buttressed by a tight and effective censorship regime.[48]

The Catholic press, surprisingly, rarely voiced its views on the subject of Confederation. *L'Univers*, the main Catholic, ultramontane newspaper, was certainly more concerned with the impact of the ongoing process of Italian unification on the Papal States than with North American affairs in general (except concerning the United States or the tragic death of Maximilian I of Mexico). Although *L'Univers* rarely provided any critical analysis of Confederation, it did express concern over the French Canadians' "national" and religious identity in an 8 July article, which consisted for the most part of excerpts from Canadian newspaper articles on Saint-Jean-Baptiste Day. In that regard a quote from the Quebec City–based *L'Événement* is quite revealing:

> [W]ith the dawn of a new political era, it is more necessary than ever to show ourselves to be united, strong, and valiant. The preservation of our nationality is in great part at that price. May French Canadians thus make it their duty to celebrate this year's national day with a greater enthusiasm, with an even greater show of solidarity than usual; may they put

aside all other concern and may they say to themselves: "Today, let us be French Canadians and nothing else!"[49]

Other Catholic newspapers, such as *Le Croisé* and *Études religieuses, historiques et littéraires,* seldom mentioned Canada – and when they did, it was usually obliquely.[50] This apparent lack of interest was probably due to the Catholics expressing more concern for the crisis faced by the soon-to-be-dissolved Papal States, as well as by the various changes occurring in Europe at the time: the rise of (Protestant-dominated) Prussia and the decline of the (generally Catholic) Austrian Empire.

Liberal opposition newspapers pointed at Confederation as an example of intelligent, efficient colonial reform, and used it as a means to criticize Napoléon's antiparliamentarianism. In a lengthy article, a *Journal des débats* author remarked:

> The act, or perhaps should I say, more correctly, the treaty whereby Upper and Lower Canada, New Brunswick, and Nova Scotia were united in a Confederation bearing the collective name of Canada was approved by the English [sic] parliament. The new United States of British America [sic] were thus established with the approval and under the protection of the motherland. Should it one day demand its independence, this new state should rest assured that this (necessary) protection shall never ... be imposed against its will.[51]

Though subtle, this praise of the relatively peaceful process whereby the four colonies united can also be read as an implicit jab at France's authoritarian government.

Another article, this one published in the moderately liberal *La Presse,* openly criticized the French colonial model. In it, the famous traveller Félix Belly asserted that "Canada, Louisiana, the West Indies, and even Brazil would still be ours had France been governed in the same way as England has, and had the conquests of private enterprise not always been systematically scorned by the powers that be." He then complained that the "traditional system of [France's] administration considers the individual as no more than a taxpayer, only has respect for the civil service and its representatives, unscrupulously immolates the interest of the average citizen to any official theory, believes itself invested – by divine right – of all the credentials to regulate everything, to formalize everything, to subject everything – even the most basic aspects of agricultural life – to its own particular goals." This, in his opinion, was why Algeria had become unmanageable, while settlers in the "United States, Canada, Australia, and even in New Zealand" had met with more success, even though they had "faced more aggressive, more intelligent a [sic] race than the Arabs."[52] Unlike the previous article, Belly does not directly denounce the Empire's democratic deficit, but its colonial administration. While the author was certainly not a supporter of the regime, his views seemed to dovetail with the Emperor's project to grant more autonomy to Algeria.

Overall, the new Canadian state was simultaneously seen as a special case – an anomaly among the British colonies – and as a model. For instance, the liberal *Revue moderne* relayed the view, then popular in Britain and its Empire, that "Canada saw an influx of intelligent, righteous immigrants from England and Scotland, who produced healthy generations [of settlers]. By contrast, in Australia, and primarily in New South Wales, there is bad blood in the population."[53] To many French newspapers, especially the liberal ones, the new state could do no wrong. The few articles that covered the Red River Rebellion tended to minimize the responsibility of the Canadian government. The liberal-Protestant *Le Temps* even used the crisis as a means to vilify the Jesuits, arguing that the latter's "authority is still effective on the descendants of our old settlers. One morning, then, the Red River settlers learned with stupefaction that the Hudson's Bay Company had sold them without asking for their permission; it had sold them to the Canadian government, as if they were a disposable item, for 75,000 pounds sterling."[54] While the author did not openly take sides, he nonetheless blamed the Hudson's Bay Company for its poor handling of the situation and the Jesuits for abusing the "naïve" Métis.[55]

The creation of the Dominion of Canada met with relative indifference from French government circles and did not elicit a massive response from the media. While interest in North America as a whole had definitely increased in the course of the nineteenth century, and especially with the outset of the American Civil War, the French government and society in general certainly had bigger fish to fry than to praise or condemn Confederation. This lack of interest was attributable to several factors. First, due to the détente with Britain, British North America no longer seemed like an extension of the not-so-"perfidious" Albion.[56] As a result, the media probably viewed Confederation as inconsequential as far as France was concerned. Second, the 1860s saw the emergence of several new territorial entities, most notably the kingdom of Italy and the basis of what was to become the Second German Empire. Such developments – among others, like the disastrous intervention in Mexico, the consequences of the 1863 Polish uprising, territorial changes in Greece, the 1866 coup in Romania, the Austro-Prussian War that same year, and the Franco-Prussian War – understandably generated more interest among journalists, intellectuals, and politicians.

However, the articles studied here addressed themes that not only pertained to their own day and age, but also dominated the twentieth century and, to some extent, our own time. Issues relating to (neo-)imperial administration, decolonization, international trade, all aspects of globalization (industrial, technological, political, and so forth), cultural and linguistic matters, and the right of nations to self-determination are still on the table – not just in the Canadian case, but also in that of any other state and/or nation. In France, Confederation was seen as both a familiar sight and a foreign, unique project. On the one hand, Confederation echoed the great independence and unification movements that were unfolding in Europe in those years; on the other, it seemed like a generally appealing, pragmatic, peaceful alternative to these very nation-building projects. The 150th anniversary of Confederation provides an excellent opportunity to reflect on the impermanence and fickleness of borders and national identities. Although 150 years might seem like a long time, Canada (similar, in that regard, to France and probably the rest of the world) has been a work in progress, an entity in a constant quest for legitimacy. As a result, this anniversary should be as much a cause for celebration as a time to step back and look at this century and a half with a modicum of humility.

NOTES

1 See Eric Hobsbawm, *The Age of Capital, 1848–1875* (New York: New American Library, 1979); Eric Hobsbawm, *The Age of Empire* (London: Abacus, 1994).
2 Leslie Poles Hartley, *The Go-Between* (Harlow: Pearson Education, 1999), 1.
3 However, several works have been devoted to Canadian-European interactions and/or transatlantic perspectives. See Jacques Portes, Nicole Fouché, Marie-Jeanne Rossignol, and Cécile Vidal, *Europe/Amérique du Nord: Cinq siècles d'interactions* (Paris: Armand Colin, 2008); Yves-Henri Nouailhat,

"L'histoire du Canada vue de France," *Revue d'histoire moderne et contemporaine* 37, no. 2, L'Histoire de l'Amérique du Nord vue de France (April–June, 1990): 230–8; Sylvain Simard, "Les Français et le Canada, 1850–1914: identité et perception," *Revue d'histoire de l'Amérique française* 29, no. 2 (1975): 209–39.

4 The French government was rather coy on Confederation. In fact, Napoléon III himself seems to have shown more interest in Canadian affairs than did the very weak Legislative Body, the Senate, and the Council of State.

5 Except for some liberals, the republican opposition did not seem to pay much attention to what was happening in Canada. Even *Le Siècle*, which devoted about a quarter of each issue to foreign news, did not show much interest in Confederation.

6 Here "Western" is used for the sake of convenience, as that term does not describe a clearly defined reality.

7 Ian McKay, "The Liberal Order Framework: A Prospectus for a Reconnaissance of Canadian History," *The Canadian Historical Review* 81, no. 4 (December 2000): 632. McKay's use of Gramsci's concept of hegemony is in itself telling of the similarities between state formation (and nation-building) in Canada and some European countries, including France.

8 See Michel Ducharme, "Closing the Last Chapter of the Atlantic Revolution: The 1837–38 Rebellions in Upper and Lower Canada," *Proceedings of the American Antiquarian Society* 116, no. 2 (October 2006): 413–30; Jean-Paul Bernard and Michel Grenon, "La Révolution française et les Rébellions de 1837 et 1838 dans le Bas Canada," in *La Révolution française au Canada français: actes du colloque tenu à l'Université d'Ottawa*, ed. Sylvain Simard (Ottawa: Presses de l'Université d'Ottawa, 1991), 26; Miles Taylor, "The 1848 Revolutions and the British Empire,"*Past & Present* 166 (February 2000): 146–80; Aurélio Ayala and Françoise Le Jeune, *Les rébellions canadiennes de 1837 et 1838 vues de Paris* (Québec: Presses de l'Université de Laval, 2011).

9 See Eric Hobsbawm and Terence Ranger, *The Invention of Tradition* (Cambridge: Cambridge University Press, 1992).

10 A.I. Silver, *The French-Canadian Idea of Confederation: 1864–1900*, 2nd ed. (Toronto: University of Toronto Press, 1997), xi, 42.

11 Voltaire to François Augustin Paradis de Moncrif, 27 March 1757, in *Electronic Enlightenment Project* (Oxford: 2008–). Both Chateaubriand's works on North America and Voltaire's *L'Ingénu* (which has for main character a naïve Huron) are still part of the French high school curriculum and are still considered (rightly so) as major works of French literature.

François-René de Chateaubriand, *Atala* (Paris: Bordas, 1985); Voltaire, *L'Ingénu* (London: Eighteenth Century Collections Online, 1767). Unless otherwise indicated, all translations are my own.

12 François-René de Chateaubriand, *Voyage en Amérique* (1826; repr., Paris: Librairie d'éducation, 1870).

13 François Hartog, *Régimes d'historicité: présentisme et expériences du temps* (Paris: Le Seuil, 2003), 89–90.

14 Xavier Marmier, *Lettres sur l'Amérique, Tome -I-*, (1851; repr., Paris: Plon, 1881), i, 72; Émile Chevalier, *Lettres sur l'Amérique du Nord, Tomes -I- et II*, 4th ed. (Brussels: Wouters, 1844).

15 Pierre Savard, *Le Consulat général de France à Québec et à Montréal de 1859 à 1914* (Paris: Pedone, 1970), 13–14.

16 L. Dussieux, *Le Canada sous la domination française, d'après les archives de la marine et de la guerre* (1856; repr., Paris: Lecoffre, 1862), 4; see also Joseph-Guillaume Barthe, *Le Canada reconquis par la France* (Paris: Ledoyen, 1855).

This implicit nostalgia for the bygone days of New France continues to this day, albeit to a lesser extent, and usually comes from a general confusion as to what constitutes Quebec, francophone-dominated areas in Canada, and Canada proper. See Jean-Louis Remilleux, prod., *Secrets d'histoire, De Gaulle, le dernier des géants*, 26 August 2014, 44:24–47:25, https://www.youtube.com/watch?v=11LxsduVoLE.

I also remember a mid-1990s edition of the acclaimed Larousse dictionary featuring the fleur-de-lis flag alongside independent, UN-recognized states (including Canada). Although I am unsure whether it was the 1993 or 1995 edition, it is interesting to note that that controversial choice was made while the debates which resulted in the 1995 referendum were gaining momentum.

17 Jean-François de Raymond, "*La Capricieuse* dans les archives diplomatiques françaises. L'initiative et la décision," and Patrice Groulx, "*La Capricieuse* en 1855: célébrations et significations," in *La Capricieuse (1855): poupe et proue. Les relations France-Québec (1760-1914)*, ed. Yvan Lamonde and Didier Poton (Québec: Presses de l'Université Laval, 2006), 211–26, 233–58.

18 Centre des Archives diplomatiques de La Courneuve (henceforth "Courneuve"), 2CPC/42, "Angleterre – Correspondance politique des Consuls – 1867 – Québec," Frédéric Gautier to Léonel de Moustier (Foreign Secretary), 2 April 1867. The italics designate words that were kept in the original French.

19 Courneuve, 2CPC/42, Gautier to de Moustier, 10 July 1867. The italics are mine.

20 Savard, *Consulat général*, 43.

21 Courneuve, 2CPC/42, Gautier to de Moustier, 10 July 1867.
22 Ibid.; Courneuve, 2CPC/43, Gautier to de Moustier, 18 April 1868.
23 "Several years might pass until the annexation is fulfilled, but the Provinces of North America [sic] will – unless unforeseen events occur in the process – inevitably follow a path similar to that which the Americans called in the antebellum era *'the impeding destiny of the South'*" [The italicized portion was originally written in English]. Courneuve, 2CPC/44, Gautier to Charles de La Valette (French Foreign Secretary), 10 July 1869.
24 The French Intervention in Mexico was a war that lasted from 1861 to 1867. Officially, the war originated from the president of Mexico Benito Juárez's decision to block interest payments on debts owed several European creditors. However, France, alongside Britain and Spain (the latter two until 1862) and other powers, had other interests in invading Mexico, such as the control of silver mines and other resources, as well as the establishment of a free-trading regime dubbed "Second Empire," with the Austrian Archduke Ferdinand Maximilian as its emperor. The empire did not survive its fifth year, and Maximilian I was eventually executed.
25 S.E. Dawson, *The Northern Kingdom* (Montreal: Dawson, circa 1866), 13.
26 Éric Anceau, *Napoléon III: un Saint-Simon à cheval* (Paris: Tallandier, 2008), 270.
27 Ibid.
28 Ibid., 271.
29 Ayala and Le Jeune, *Les rébellions canadiennes*, 178–81.
30 Robert Pichette, "*La Capricieuse*: élément d'une politique étrangère ou personnelle de Napoléon III à l'égard du Canada?" in *La Capricieuse*, ed. Lamonde and Poton, 193.
31 Robert Pichette, *Napoléon III, l'Acadie et le Canada français* (Moncton: Les Éditions d'Acadie, 1998), 16, 66. According to Pichette, Napoléon became interested in Acadia after two "strong-willed" abbots, Hubert Girroir and Georges-Antoine Belcourt, and the French acadophile Edme Rameau de Saint-Père, asked for his support of the French-speaking community in Canada.
32 Armand Yon, *Le Canada français vu de France (1830–1914)* (Québec: Presses de l'Université Laval, 1975), 54–5.
33 Jules Verne, *Vingt mille lieues sous les mers* (Verviers: Marabout, 1966), 29–31. Verne later wrote a novel entitled *Family without a Name – Famille-Sans-Nom* (Montréal: Québec, 1970), originally published in 1888, which takes place in Lower Canada during the 1837–38 Rebellion.
34 In that regard, a remark in a *Journal amusant* article is quite revealing: "There is an old proverb, which is still popular in some lower-class quarters: 'I care about it as much as I care about Canada!'" J. Lovy, "Menus propos," *Le Journal amusant*, 11 April 1863, 7.

35 "Dix jours dans l'isthme de Suez," *Le Figaro*, 14 May 1868, 3; Félix Belly, "La colonisation en Algérie," *La Presse*, 4 October 1866, 1.
36 Vivien de Saint-Martin, ed., "Le Dominion ou État fédéral du Canada. L'élément français," *L'Année géographique*, 7ième année, 1868 (Paris: Hachette, 1869), 342; for more on Rameau de Saint-Père, see Pierre Trépanier, "Rameau de Saint-Père, la France et la vie intellectuelle en Amérique française," in *La Capricieuse*, ed. Lamonde and Poton, 285–305.
37 There were, of course, exceptions. For instance, the republican politician Ernest Duvergier de Hauranne predicted that Confederation would eventually stifle the influence of French culture and language in Canada. Ernest Duvergier de Hauranne, "Huit mois en Amérique: Lettres et notes de voyage, 1864–1865," *Revue des deux mondes*, tome soixantième (Paris: Bureau de la *Revue des deux mondes*, 1865), 200–1.
38 Bruno Marnot, "Les relations commerciales entre la France et l'Amérique du Nord au XIXe siècle," in *La Capricieuse*, ed. Lamonde and Poton, 1, 5.
39 Courneuve, 2CPC/41, Gautier to Édouard Drouyn de Lhuys (Foreign Secretary), 20 August 1866.
40 Centre des Archives diplomatiques de Nantes (henceforth "Nantes"), Londres, Ambassade – Fonds A, 378PO/A48, George Villiers, Earl of Clarendon (Foreign Secretary) to Unknown, 1 August 1855.
41 Anceau, *Napoléon III*, 375, 393–7.
42 Savard, *Consulat général*, 58.
43 Jules Duval, "Les Colonies anglaises d'Amérique," *Journal des débats politiques et littéraires*, 30 October 1867, 1.
44 F. de la Ponterie, "Un nouvel état en Amérique," *Le Temps*, 24 July 1867, 1. Some accounts published in the report on the 1867 Paris World Fair also tend to reflect this optimism. For instance, the author of the section on fauna predicts that, "based on their economic trajectory thus far, these regions are destined to become similar to the most dynamic parts of Europe – as far as material conditions are concerned. As for the other British colonies, this will be a different story altogether!" A.D. Focillon, "Spécimens et collections d'animaux de toute sorte," in *Exposition Universelle de 1867 à Paris*, Tome sixième, ed. Michel Chevalier (Paris: Imprimerie administrative de Paul Dupont, 1868), 108–9.
45 See the interventions of David Jules Pagézy and Félix Lambrecht, "Corps-Législatif. Compte-rendu analytique de la séance du mercredi 11 avril 1866," *Journal des débats politiques et littéraires*, 13 April 1866, 1–2.
46 H. de Lagardie, "Causerie de quinzaine," *Journal des débats politiques et littéraires*, 31 March 1867, 1; see also Anceau, *Napoléon III*, 61, 264; Don H.

Doyle, *The Cause of All Nations: An International History of the American Civil War* (New York: Basic Books, 2015), 185–209.
47 Anceau, *Napoléon III*, 254; Natalie Isser, *The Second Empire and the Press: A Study of Government-Inspired Brochures on French Foreign Policy in Their Propaganda Milieu* (The Hague: Nijhoff, 1974), 41–8.
48 Jacques Godechot, Pierre Guiral, and Fernand Terrou, *Histoire générale de la presse française, Tome II: De 1815 à 1871* (Paris: Presses universitaires de France, 1969), 313.
49 A. Petit, "La Fête nationale des Canadiens-Français," *L'Univers*, 8 July 1867, 2.
50 H. de Charencey, "Les races primitives de l'Europe," *Le Croisé*, 25 July 1868, 1–2; "Incendie des forêts des tributs [sic] sauvages," *Études religieuses, historiques et littéraires, Tome cinquième* (Paris: Charles Douniol, 1864–1865), 677–8.
51 Lagardie, "Causerie de quinzaine," 1.
52 Félix Belly, "La colonisation en Algérie," *La Presse*, 4 April 1866, 1.
53 "L'Hérédité du vice," translated excerpt from an article originally published in *Christian Work* (Australia), *Revue moderne, Tome quarantième* (Paris: Bureaux de la *Revue moderne*, 1867), 1 January 1867, 204.
54 Ch. Du Bouzet, "Lettres des États-Unis," *Le Temps*, 1 April 1870, 2.
55 Ibid.
56 A common expression in France, *"la perfide Albion,"* referring to Britain's allegedly repeated treacherousness, seems to date back to the medieval period. However, the first use of the phrase is usually attributed to Augustin Louis Ximénès. See "L'Ère républicaine" (1793), in *Poésies révolutionnaires et contre-révolutionnaires, ou Recueil, classé par époques, des hymnes, chants guerriers, chansons républicaines, odes, satires, cantiques des missionnaires, etc., volume 1* (Paris: Librairie historique, 1821), 159–60.

7 *War Was?* Habsburg Perspectives on Canadian Federation

BENNO GAMMERL

Even in a discipline as thoroughly informed by meticulous empirical research as history, it is sometimes rewarding to start with a theoretical or an almost hypothetical question: What would historians of imperial formations – the Habsburg and the British Empires in particular – expect when speculating about Austro-Hungarian perspectives on Canadian Confederation in 1867? Two answers come to mind: First, Canada might have been perceived as a British version of Hungary, as an emerging nation-state within the overarching imperial formation that demands far-reaching legislative and executive autonomy. Second, Canada with its ethnically diverse population – Indigenous peoples, English- and French-speakers, and immigrants from other parts of Europe as well as from Asia – could have served as an example for how ethnocultural differences can be accommodated within a common political framework. This question was of particular interest from an Austrian or Cisleithanian perspective where government and administration faced similar issues.[1]

Sections one and two of this chapter discuss to what extent Canadian Confederation attracted attention within the Habsburg Empire for both these reasons and enquire into the broader implications of such inter-imperial transfers and comparisons. They also attempt to explain why Canadian Confederation – in spite of these similarities and potential linkages – was ultimately not considered a particularly noteworthy event within the Habsburg context. This discussion leads to the general observation that Canada and Austria-Hungary were hardly connected with each other in 1867, which, in turn, provokes the question, How can one write a global history of Confederation when there is at best a very wide-meshed network to study? Section three argues that this scarcity of documented links does not at all diminish the value of such an approach, as it offers the opportunity to enquire into the reasons for dis/connection. This endeavour can yield valuable results and sometimes allows for teasing out unexpected and intricate phenomena. Among these are the indirect ties between the Habsburg Empire and Canada that unfolded around the Fenian movement in the United States and Emperor Maximilian in Mexico. Section four discusses these issues and, by way of conclusion, answers the question, What was at the core of Habsburg perspectives on Canadian Confederation?

Canada as a British Hungary? Nation-States Emerging within Imperial Formations

The historical coincidence that the *British North America Act, 1867* and the Austro-Hungarian compromise both took effect in the same year suggests that contemporaries might have drawn parallels between these reforms that decisively rearranged the political structures of the British and the Habsburg Empires, respectively. In both cases far-reaching legislative and executive autonomy was granted to semi-peripheral territories within overarching imperial formations. This political change spurred nationalizing tendencies in Canada as well as in Hungary. Both countries would ultimately develop into nation-states. As these similarities suggest, the Habsburg government and the public might have looked towards Canada as a sort of British Hungary, a foreign, yet comparable case from which they could learn important lessons about how Hungarian aspirations for national autonomy could be handled.

Yet actors in 1867 did not engage in such comparative considerations. Only much later, and even then only very implicitly, did some publications – especially those discussing tariff reforms and policies – hint at similarities and differences in the economic and political relationships between Austria and Hungary, on the one hand, and Britain and its Dominions, including Canada, on the other.[2] The Hungarian request for autonomy and its accommodation were compared, however, to British attempts at pacifying Irish demands for self-government. In 1867 Count Rudolph von Apponyi, the Austro-Hungarian ambassador in London, reported on a conversation he had had with Edward Henry Stanley, Earl of Derby and then secretary of state for Foreign Affairs. Stanley said that he had observed what had happened to the Habsburg Monarchy with much sympathy. He hoped that the "new system of dualism" would prove a success and added that he was very much aware of the difficulties such a compromise entailed. The British government had, he claimed, tried out similar measures when it considered the potential of a "dualism with an Irish Parliament."[3] Irish nationalists occasionally also referred to Hungarian autonomy as a model for what they requested.[4] Yet such singular remarks do not prove that there were widespread debates likening Hungarian to Irish claims. The conversation between Stanley and Apponyi was ultimately only linked to the Canadian context by the rather coincidental fact that Stanley's brother Frederick was later to be appointed governor general of Canada. But the statement is still noteworthy, as it proves that at least some contemporaries did draw parallels between the constitutional constellation of the Austro-Hungarian compromise and the question of how Britain could reshape her relations with the different constituent parts of the British Empire.[5]

That such attempts at restructuring imperial frameworks and hierarchies were intimately intertwined with the intricate relationship between empire and nation can be inferred from another British government statement that Count Apponyi mentioned in his reports. In this instance the Austro-Hungarian compromise was described as reconciling "the sovereign and the nation."[6] This phrase indicates that dwelling upon comparisons between British and Habsburg constitutional arrangements can shed light on the question of how imperial formations and the concept of the nation interacted in the late nineteenth and early twentieth century, an issue particularly relevant for Canadian history.[7] Historical depictions of the interplay between empire and nation were long dominated by the assumption that both models opposed each other. This view resulted in teleological narratives suggesting that backward imperial structures ultimately had to give way to modern nation-states.[8] In the last couple of years, though, such arguments have been subjected to vigorous critiques. While nation and empire may sometimes have collided as opposites, many researchers hold that they could also coexist in symbiotic ways.[9] In this sense, one could speak of a specific, cooperative brand of intra-imperial nationalism.

Such a change of perspective is facilitated by the integration of Habsburg perspectives into the analysis of Canadian Confederation. This endeavour, furthermore, shows that the path along which the interplay between empire and nation unfolded very much depended on the specific situation of the emerging nation within the overall imperial framework. The trajectories of Hungary and Canada ultimately resembled each other because both countries occupied a semi-peripheral position.

After the compromise and after Confederation, they were neither in a fully fledged colonial relationship with the metropolis, which characterized the position of Bosnia (from 1878 onwards), India, and other territories on the imperial periphery, nor were they incorporated into the imperial core, as were Bohemia and Ireland, respectively. This semi-peripheral position enabled cooperative forms of claiming national autonomy and the emergence of a constellation within which advocates of imperial cohesion were not bound to quell every kind of national aspiration. Although national independence was ultimately completed in both Canada and Hungary, it was not clear to contemporaries if and when such a development might occur. In a certain sense, it can thus be said that the specific positions of Canada and Hungary within their respective imperial contexts fostered nationalization processes in both countries. The earlier quoted statement about reconciling the imperial sovereign and the nation demonstrates that British politicians were aware as early as 1867 of the possibility that empire and nation could, in this sense, symbiotically coexist. An Austrian newspaper related a remark by Charles Adderley, the British under-secretary of state for the colonies in charge of the *British North America Act, 1867*, who described Confederation as the "foundation of a new nation."[10]

Given these similarities, it is all the more surprising that there is no evidence of contemporaries directly linking the Austro-Hungarian compromise with Canadian Confederation and the *British North America Act, 1867*, at least not from a Habsburg perspective. This silence necessitates explanation. Two decisive differences between the Canadian and the Hungarian case kept contemporaries from recognizing their similarities. First, although both countries were in a semi-peripheral position, Canada was arguably still slightly more marginal from a London point of view than Hungary was from a Viennese perspective. This discrepancy is closely associated with the second difference: both emerging nations based their claims for autonomy on very different historical trajectories and current situations. While history and the reassertion of ancient rights played a major role for Hungary – with references dating back to the medieval realms of Árpád and Stephen, and the rather fresh memory of the war of 1848 – similar traditions were irrelevant in Canada. Proponents of Canadian autonomy instead talked about self-government and colonial nationalism, and highlighted questions such as, Who would bear the expenses for Canadian defence? and Who could most efficiently decide on local matters – a government in a distant place or one on the spot? (The last point hints at a further difference, namely that Canada relied internally on a federal structure, while Hungary was a centralized state.) Because of these discrepancies, the Austro-Hungarian compromise was likened to attempts at reshaping the relations between Britain and Ireland rather than to negotiations about the relationship between Canada and the imperial metropolis.

Governing Ethnically Diverse Populations: Politics Forging Identities

If one considers the second topic that could have prompted contemporaries to draw connections between Canada and, in this case, primarily the Austrian or Cisleithanian half of the Habsburg Monarchy – the shared problem of how to govern an ethnically diverse population – the findings are likewise scarce. Though Canadian Confederation, by combining hitherto separate colonies, did create a political entity that comprised a large variety of different ethnocultural and linguistic groups, which thus resembled Cisleithania in several respects, contemporary actors did not comment on these similarities. While, as the Austro-Hungarian ambassador in London noted, an occasional article in the *Times* pointed to the crucial task of creating and maintaining a bond between the "different races that form the population of the Monarchy's Eastern parts" and "Austria," parallels between this constellation and similar ones within the British Empire did not attract any attention in 1867.[11]

Such comparisons and transfers gained importance only about four decades later. In 1909 the Austrian Ministry for Educational and Religious Affairs (*Kultusministerium*) required the embassy in London to collect information on the position of Muslims within the British Empire. This enquiry was linked with deliberations to grant Islam the official status of a religious community in Cisleithania.[12] Publications about Canada that began to appear in Austria in increasing numbers from around 1900 onwards also frequently discussed issues of religious and ethnic diversity, primarily in two respects. First, they mentioned the rather recent arrival of mostly Ukrainian and Greek Catholic immigrants from Austria-Hungary and enquired into whether this community quickly assimilated or maintained its specificities.[13] Second, many reports focused on the relationship between English- and French-speaking Canadians that one Austrian author identified as being of particular interest "for us."[14] They pointed out that a certain number of seats in the Canadian parliament were reserved for members from

Quebec, and they discussed the organization of the school system in great detail.[15] One author even claimed that the Canadian principle of granting denominational autonomy in questions of education was very similar to measures Karl Renner had proposed for Austria.[16] The close connection between denominational and ethnonational identities was a feature that Austrian observers were very familiar with. Therefore one author claimed that the Canadian model of "national autonomy in the educational sector" could usefully be employed in Cisleithania, as such a policy could bring about an "armistice" between "two rivalling peoples."[17]

Highlighting such transfers and similarities between Austrian and Canadian attempts at governing an ethnically diverse population can contribute to debates about how certain administrative measures impacted the emergence of ethnocultural or national differences and accorded them significance in specific ways. While dynamics of identity formation were always also shaped "from below," and intriguing comparisons could certainly be drawn between Austria and Canada in this respect,[18] the present argument concentrates on processes initiated "from above." Such measures include separating out ethnically defined electorates or establishing schools with different languages of instruction. These policies were, for example, implemented in Moravia in 1905. They were intended to pacify nationalist strife between Czechs and Germans, but at the same time one can interpret them as manoeuvres along the lines of "divide and conquer." From this point of view, solidifying the division between Czech and German-speaking populations through administrative interventions also served the government's aim of countering demands for universal (male) suffrage and of strengthening the position of loyal landowning elites. Returning to the Canadian case with this constellation in mind highlights the potentially ambivalent effects of Confederation. It implied a move towards a politics of recognition of ethnic differences (at least as far as Anglo and French Canadian communities were concerned), but at the same time it intentionally created a political entity in which the internal diversity should weaken further reaching demands for democratic participation.

The shared problem of governing an ethnically diverse population actually did inform Habsburg perspectives on Canada. Two characteristics of this discussion are particularly noteworthy. First, the discussion focused exclusively on Anglo-French relations and completely ignored other ethnic groups such as the Indigenous peoples or immigrants from South and East Asia.[19] One could assume that this focus was due to a sharp distinction between the latter's "racial" difference, on the one hand, and ethnolinguistic or ethno-denominational identities on the other, which shaped the Anglo-French divide as well as divergences between German-, Italian-, Czech-, Polish-, and Ukrainian-speaking populations in Austria. Although this argument might seem convincing at first, it is challenged by the fact that the concepts of "race," "ethnicity," and "nationality" were not clearly separated from each other within the discourse at hand. Austrian authors spoke of "racial prejudice" when referring to relations between Anglo and French Canadians, and designated Protestants and Catholics as two distinct "races."[20] This ambiguity concerning the notion of "race" makes the disregard for "non-European" communities all the more conspicuous. The second striking feature of the Austro-Hungarian discussion about how ethnic diversity was handled in Canada is that it only commenced after 1900. In 1867 the problem of governing an ethnically diverse population was not commented upon at all.

Dis/connections? Global History within Very Wide-Meshed Networks

This observation once more illustrates that Canadian Confederation was, in general, hardly noted within the Habsburg Empire at the time.[21] Officials at the Ministry of Foreign Affairs in Vienna read the Queen's speech announcing the British government's legislative projects for 1867 very carefully and highlighted several passages. Yet the section that referred to Canadian Confederation remained unmarked.[22] Newspapers likewise only briefly mentioned the "English colonies in North America" and their unification to "one governorate with a common parliament."[23] British North America was obviously not among the topics that attracted much attention within the Habsburg Empire in 1867. This attitude was mainly due to a lack of direct connections between Austria-Hungary and Canada. On an official level there were hardly any links. While the Habsburg government had appointed an honorary consul for Halifax in 1855 because "Austrian ships" were "passing frequently" there, this agent was almost without any business.[24] The same holds true for Montreal, where the first honorary consul was appointed in 1865. Only in the 1890s when the number of immigrants arriving from Austria-Hungary began to rise did the significance of this post gradually increase. In 1901 a professional diplomat took charge of the consulate. A 1914 decision to appoint an honorary consul in Toronto was ultimately not implemented due to the outbreak of the First World War.[25] The level of economic exchange was also rather modest. One commentator mentioned that the carpet in the plenary hall of the Canadian parliament was fabricated in Austria – "*Ginzkeysches Fabrikat*" – but plans to raise, for example, the export of Hungarian wines to significant levels ultimately failed.[26]

In 1867 Canada was thus, for several reasons, far off or, at most, just on the fringes of the Austrian world map, which explains why contemporary actors hardly noticed the parallels discussed earlier. Furthermore, Austro-Hungarian officials and observers were, in general, unlikely to identify similarities between the Habsburg and the British case because many held the two to represent diametrically opposed varieties of empire: one continental, the other maritime; one based on systematic Roman law, the other relying on the precedence of common law; and one adhering to the Josephine heritage of enlightened absolutism, the other cherishing utilitarian traditions. These differences were mirrored in positive self-perceptions as either well-ordered or liberal, and in pejorative descriptions of the respective counterpart as autocratic or chaotic. For this reason, comparisons between the two cases were, if drawn at all, readily dismissed as "irrelevant or unconvincing."[27]

As far as Habsburg attitudes towards North America were concerned, these were, moreover, influenced by the Austro-Hungarian authorities' reluctance to acknowledge the growing economic and political importance of the United States.[28] Habsburg foreign and other policies continued to focus on Europe and on the established Great Power system. This outlook implied that Canada was even less perceived as a future player to reckon with in the global arena. Correspondingly, popular depictions of the country were long dominated by, as one author put it, the "poetics of the Leatherstocking narrative," that is, by images of a vast and uncivilized wilderness that still awaited adventurous European explorers.[29]

All this elicits the question of how one can meaningfully analyse Habsburg perspectives on Canada when so little evidence for actual nodes and connections exists. The relationship between Austria-Hungary and British North America in 1867 was primarily shaped by disconnection and disinterested distance. Does this finding frustrate attempts at globalizing the history of Canadian Confederation? It does so only for those who adhere to a version of global history that exclusively focuses on increasing connectivity and disregards disruptions or separations. More sophisticated approaches try to avoid the teleological pitfall of assuming that the world was inevitably growing ever more integrated and highlight the dialectics of dis/connection instead.[30] Seen from this point of view, considering strange bedfellows and wide-meshed networks holds a specific potential. Trying to explain why there were few direct links generates valuable insights. And the lack of immediate connections sharpens the analytical gaze for indirect or, at first sight, unlikely correlations.

Fenians in the United States and Maximilian in Mexico: Canadian Federation and the Republican Threat?

If one widens the scope of the analysis accordingly and looks for what most occupied the Habsburg mind when thinking of Canadian affairs in 1867, rumours about Irish republican paramilitary or guerrilla forces planning to invade British North America with the alleged support of the United States government come into view.[31] Officials worried about a "second raid on Canadian territory" and meticulously observed Fenian activities on both sides of the forty-ninth parallel.[32] Newspapers discussed this issue as well.[33] In contrast to the cooperative nationalism that allowed empire and nation to coexist and basically enabled Canadian Confederation, the Fenians adhered to a confrontational version of nationalism and were determined to fight imperial rule. Why did Fenian aggressiveness attract so much attention within the Habsburg Empire, while Canadian cooperation went almost unnoticed?[34] Did this focus echo Habsburg fears about militant nationalist movements at home and the danger that these could also find supporters in foreign countries? Such an interpretation is supported by the proposition that Habsburg authorities could learn crucial lessons about "the theory of nationalities" if they closely studied Irish struggles for home rule.[35] In the Habsburg context, this proposal could have referred to the Hungarian uprising of 1848 as well as to conflicts with the emerging Italian nation-state along the Empire's southern border in the 1860s.[36]

Yet the attention Fenians attracted in Austria-Hungary can be attributed to different reasons if one focuses less on the movement's nationalist aspirations and more on its republican agenda.[37] Seen from this angle, the crux of the matter was not the tension between imperial cohesion and national independence, but rather the opposition between monarchical and republican forms of government. This dispute was emphasized by an 1867 resolution of the US Congress, duly reported back home by Habsburg diplomats: "If one allows a despotic

European government to establish monarchical institutions in America," so the argument ran, then the United States could also claim "the right to stimulate and encourage the development of republican institutions."[38] This reasoning brings the Austrian emperor's brother Maximilian and the attempt to establish him as emperor of Mexico into the picture.[39] The ultimate failure of this endeavour became obvious on 19 June 1867 when Maximilian was executed by republican forces. Until then, the war between "imperialists" and "republicans" in Mexico was the single most prominent topic in Austrian newspaper articles and official reports concerning North America in 1867.[40] These circumstances lent the struggle for or against monarchism key relevance in contemporary eyes and pinpointed the role of the United States as a promoter of republicanism.[41] This constellation decisively impacted the significantly less frequent commentaries on Canadian Confederation as well.

The installation of Maximilian as emperor of Mexico and the foundation of Canada could accordingly both be understood as parts of a more or less concerted effort by monarchical European powers to override US claims for supremacy in North America and to counter the US policy of promoting republican forms of government.[42] Therefore the questions of whether Canada would be called a "kingdom" or a "dominion," whether it should be governed by a viceroy, and whether Queen Victoria's son Prince Arthur would accede to this "throne" were particularly prominent in Habsburg perspectives on Canadian Confederation.[43] Austrian observers attached importance to this issue well into the twentieth century. One of them claimed that Canadians' "republican spirit" disposed them to, at best, tolerate the governor general as the British monarch's representative, while they effectively disregarded his official function as "viceroy," obliged him not to interfere, and expected nothing from him other than "dinner-parties" and "good sports."[44]

Habsburg perspectives on Canadian Confederation were thus not primarily informed by the problem of granting national autonomy to certain parts of an empire, nor by the shared problem of how to govern an ethnically diverse population. Austro-Hungarian observers were instead quintessentially concerned with the following question: Was Canada to serve as a bulwark against the dissemination of US republicanism, or was Canadian Confederation a dangerous experiment that would ultimately promote republican dispositions beneath a thin monarchical icing?

NOTES

The title "War Was?" does not allude to a utopian future where war will finally be relegated to the past, but to a German expression that translates as "Has anything happened?" I am very grateful to Joseph Ben Prestel, the anonymous readers, and the organizers as well as the participants of the "Globalizing Confederation" conference for their comments and helpful suggestions from which this chapter greatly benefitted.

1 Cisleithania is shorthand for the kingdoms and lands represented in the *Reichsrat* in Vienna, that is, the Habsburg territories "on this side of the river Leitha," which marked the boundary between Austria and Hungary. Cisleithania also comprised Bohemia and Moravia, Dalmatia, Carniola, Galicia, and Bukovina.
2 Samuel Altmann, *Kanada. Land, Leute und wirtschaftliche Verhältnisse*, Kommerzielle Berichte hrsg. vom k.k. Österreichischen Handelsmuseum, Bd. 1 (Wien 1907), 10; see also Ludwig Láng, *Hundert Jahre Zollpolitik* (Wien: Fromme, 1906).
3 Haus-, Hof- und Staatsarchiv Wien [henceforth HHStA], Politisches Archiv [henceforth PA] VIII, case 69: England, Berichte [reports], 1867, III–IX, no. 69, 25 September 1867. Correspondence between Austro-Hungarian ambassadors and the Viennese government was at this time primarily conducted in French. All quotes have been translated into English by the author.
4 Arthur Griffith, *The Resurrection of Hungary: A Parallel for Ireland* (Dublin: James Duffy et al., 1904); see also Jennifer Regan-Lefebvre, *Cosmopolitan Nationalism in the Victorian Empire: Ireland, India and the Politics of Alfred Webb* (Basingstoke: Palgrave Macmillan, 2009), 122.
5 On comparisons between Canadian Confederation and the handling of claims for self-government elsewhere in the British Empire or within other imperial formations, see also the chapters in this volume by Carsten-Andreas Schulz on Latin America (chap. 1), Alban Bargain-Villéger on France (and Algeria) (chap. 6), Josep María Fradera on Spain (chap. 8), Franklin W. Knight on the Caribbean (chap. 14), Timothy Stapleton on Southern Africa (chap. 13), and Thomas Mohr on Ireland (chap. 10).
6 HHStA, PA VIII, case 69: no. 50, 18 June 1867.
7 On the problem of how imperial formations could adapt to the rise of nationalism and demands for democratic participation, see Carole McGranahan and Ann Laura Stoler, "Introduction: Refiguring Imperial Terrains," in *Imperial Formations*, ed. Ann Laura Stoler, Carole McGranahan, and Peter C. Perdue (Santa Fe, NM: School for Advanced Research Press, 2007), 3–42, 7;

Dominic Lieven, "Dilemmas of Empire, 1850–1918. Power, Territory, Identity," *Journal of Contemporary History* 34 (1999): 2, 163–200, 165.

8 Empires are in this sense unfavourably contrasted with nation-states by Timothy H. Parsons, *The Rule of Empires: Those Who Built Them, Those Who Endured Them, and Why They Always Fall* (Oxford: Oxford University Press, 2010), 3, 15; see also Charles Taylor, *Reconciling the Solitudes: Essays on Canadian Federalism and Nationalism*, ed. Guy Laforest (Montreal: McGill-Queen's University Press, 1993).

9 See, for example, Ulrike von Hirschhausen and Jörn Leonhard, "Beyond Rise, Decline and Fall. Comparing Multi-Ethnic Empires in the Long Nineteenth Century," in *Comparing Empires: Encounters and Transfers in the Long Nineteenth Century*, ed. Jörn Leonhard and Ulrike von Hirschhausen (Göttingen: Vandenhoeck & Ruprecht, 2011), 9–34, 9; Frederick Cooper, *Citizenship between Empire and Nation: Remaking France and French Africa, 1945–1960* (Princeton: Princeton University Press, 2014); Benno Gammerl, *Subjects, Citizens and Other. Administering Ethnic Heterogeneity in the British and Habsburg Empires, 1867–1918*, trans. Jennifer Walcoff Neuheiser (New York: Berghahn Books, forthcoming); Gary B. Cohen, "Nationalist Politics and the Dynamics of State and Civil Society in the Habsburg Monarchy, 1867–1914," *Central European History* 40 (2007): 2, 241–78; Laurence Cole and Daniel L. Unowsky, eds., *The Limits of Loyalty. Imperial Symbolism, Popular Allegiances, and State Patriotism in the Late Habsburg Monarchy* (New York: Berghahn Books, 2007); Nicholas Canny, foreword to *Ireland and the British Empire*, ed. Kevin Kenny (Oxford: Oxford University Press, 2005), ix–xix. The relationship between nation and empire was central to developments in nineteenth century Spain, and especially in its relationship with Cuba, as Josep María Fradera discusses in chapter eight of this volume.

10 *Die Presse*, 4 März 1867, 3. *Die Presse* was a mainly liberal Austrian newspaper published between 1848 and 1896. From 1867 to 1888 the Austrian government co-owned *Die Presse*.

11 HHStA, PA VIII, case 68: England, Berichte [reports], 1867, I–II, no. 5, 16 January 1867.

12 HHStA, Gesandtschaft London, Administrative Akten, case 159. As far as one can tell from the archival documents, nothing came from this request.

13 Altmann, *Kanada* (1907), 32, 36; Eugen Philippovich von Philippsberg, *Im Westen Kanadas* (Wien: Konegen, 1905), 488–92; see also Rudolf Agstner, *From Halifax to Vancouver: Austria(-Hungary) and Her Consular and Diplomatic Presence in Canada, 1855–2005* (Wien: Landesverteidigungsakademie, 2005), 21f.

14 Michael Hainisch, *Die nationale Autonomie in Kanada* (Graz, AT: Leykam, 1909), 3.

15 Altman, *Kanada* (1907), 5, 22; Hainisch, *Nationale Autonomie* (1909), 3. It is very likely that the fierce debates about schooling issues in New Brunswick in the 1870s and in Manitoba in the 1890s drew the attention of commentators to the handling of denominational and linguistic differences in the Canadian school system. It is certainly no coincidence that observers in the Papal States also highlighted the issue of educational rights, as Roberto Perin claims in chapter five of this volume.

16 Hainisch, *Nationale Autonomie* (1909), 5; Cf. Rudolf Springer [Karl Renner], *Der Kampf der österreichischen Nationen um den Staat. Das nationale Problem als Verfassungs- und Verwaltungsfrage* (Leipzig: Deuticke, 1902). On the handling of ethnonational differences in the Cisleithanian school system, see also Hannelore Burger, *Sprachenrecht und Sprachengerechtigkeit im österreichischen Unterrichtswesen, 1867–1918* (Wien: Verlag der Österreichischen Akademie der Wissenschaften, 1995).

17 Hainisch, *Nationale Autonomie* (1909), 13.

18 On ethnicizing and nationalizing dynamics within Cisleithanian civil society, see Miroslav Hroch, *European Nations: Explaining their Formation* (London: Verso, 2015); Daniel Unowsky, "Peasant Political Mobilization and the 1898 Anti-Jewish Riots in Western Galicia," *European History Quarterly* 40 (2010): 3, 412–35; Nancy M. Wingfield, *Flag Wars and Stone Saints: How the Bohemian Lands Became Czech* (Cambridge, MA: Harvard University Press, 2007); Cohen, "Nationalist Politics" (2007); Pieter M. Judson, *Guardians of the Nation: Activists on the Language Frontiers of Imperial Austria* (Cambridge, MA: Harvard University Press, 2006).

19 On how Indigenous peoples were excluded from contemporary discussions about Confederation and other political issues in different colonial settings, see the chapters by Gabrielle Slowey on Indigenous peoples in Canada (chap. 4) and Ann Curthoys on Australia (chap. 11).

20 Altmann, *Kanada* (1907), 19; Emil Gerhardt, *Kanada selbständig? Die natürlichen Entwicklungsbedingungen Kanadas als Grundlage zur Ausbildung eines selbständigen Staatswesens* (Berlin: Puttkammer & Mühlbrecht, 1910), 127. On the unclear distinction between "race" and "ethnicity" in the early twentieth century, see also Robert J.C. Young, *The Idea of English Ethnicity* (Malden: Blackwell, 2008).

21 Canadian Confederation did not attract much attention in other regions of the world either, as some of the contributions to this volume demonstrate. We could almost describe it as a global non-event.

22 This document is attached to HHStA, PA VIII, case 68: no. 10, 5 February 1867.

23 *Die Presse*, 4 March 1867, 3; see also *Neue Freie Presse*, 30 March 1867, 3. *Neue Freie Presse* was established in 1864 in opposition to *Die Presse*, which

had by then become too conservative in the liberal eyes of the journalists behind the "new" press.
24 Agstner, *From Halifax to Vancouver* (2005), 16.
25 Ibid., 23, 48.
26 Altmann, *Kanada* (1907), 5. On economic aspects, see also Emil Fitger, *Der Zollstreit Canadas mit den Vereinigten Staaten* (Berlin: Verlag von Leonhard Simion Nf., 1910).
27 This quote is from a 1918 constitutional reform proposal by the government of India that mentions Austria and some other examples as ultimately insignificant points of reference. *The Montagu-Chelmsford Reform Proposals*, with a foreword by Annie Besant (Madras: Sons of India, no date [c. 1918]), 35. On British-Habsburg relations in general, see Harry Hanak, "Die Einstellung Großbritanniens und der Vereinigten Staaten zu Österreich(-Ungarn)," in *Die Habsburgermonarchie im System der internationalen Beziehungen, Die Habsburgermonarchie, 1848–1918*, ed. Adam Wandruszka, vol. 6, part 2, (Wien: VÖAW, 1993), 539–85.
28 Nicole M. Phelps, *U.S.-Habsburg Relations from 1815 to the Paris Peace Conference: Sovereignty Transformed* (Cambridge: Cambridge University Press, 2013).
29 Albrecht Penck, *Reisebeobachtungen aus Canada. Vortrag, gehalten den 16. März 1898* (Wien: Selbstverlag des Vereines zur Verbreitung naturwissenschaftlicher Kenntnisse, 1898), 21f. This text (31) also claimed that there was "something sea-like in this landscape."
30 David A. Bell, "This Is What Happens When Historians Overuse the Idea of the Network," 26 October 2013, last accessed 2 November 2016, https://newrepublic.com/article/114709/world-connecting-reviewed-historians-overuse-network-metaphor; Frederick Cooper, *Colonialism in Question: Theory, Knowledge, History* (Berkeley: University of California Press, 2005), 91–111.
31 HHStA, PA VIII, case 68: no. 22B, 9 March 1867. With reference to struggles in Ireland this report speaks of "a veritable guerilla war."
32 HHStA, PA VIII, case 69: no. 28, 2 April 1867; see also HHStA, PA XXXIII, case 120, USA, Gesandtschaft Washington, Berichte, Weisungen, Varia [reports, directives, miscellaneous] 1866–67: no. 24, report of the minister in Washington to the government in Vienna, 15 June 1866. One memorandum contains a newspaper clipping about the arrest of James Lynch and John McMahon for partaking in the 1866 Fenian invasion of Canada. HHStA, PA XXXIII, case 120: no. 36, 30 October 1866. Another report mentions a plan to assassinate Queen Victoria. HHStA, PA VIII, case 70: no. 79B, 20 November 1867.

33 *Die Presse*, 29 March 1867, 4; *Neue Freie Presse*, 30 March 1867, 18; see also Altmann, *Kanada* (1907), 6.
34 A similar focus also characterized the perception of Canadian affairs in other parts of the world; see the chapter by Carsten-Andreas Schulz on Latin America (chap. 1) in this volume.
35 HHStA, PA VIII, case 69: no. 69, 25 September 1867.
36 This corresponds with concerns about the possibility that an "Italian Legion" might be formed in New York. HHStA, PA XXXIII, case 120: no. 27, report from Washington to Vienna, 6 July 1866.
37 William Jenkins's analysis of Fenian perspectives on Canadian Confederation in this volume (chap. 3) demonstrates how crucial anti-monarchical impulses and republican ambitions were for the Fenian mindset.
38 HHStA, PA XXXIII, case 22: no. 12, report from Washington to Vienna, 30 March 1867. Austro-Hungarian diplomats might have overemphasized this conflict. David R. Cameron and Jacqueline D. Krikorian demonstrate in chapter two of this volume that opposition against Canadian Confederation in the United States was hardly voiced, let alone influential.
39 A letter sent by Edward Henry Stanley, Earl of Derby and secretary of state for Foreign Affairs, to Henry Herbert, Earl of Carnarvon and secretary of state for the colonies, on 14 October 1866 likewise connects Fenianism, Mexican republicanism, and Canadian politics. In this message Stanley warns Herbert of the possible involvement of a member of the Canadian government, a certain Mr Dougall, in an attempt to support the Fenians, who in turn intended to support the republicans in Mexico. Public Records Office London, 30/6/138, 115–16. I would like to thank Jacqueline Krikorian for drawing my attention to this document.
40 *Neue Freie Presse*, 30 March 1867, 3; see also HHStA, PA XXXIII, case 120. HHStA, PA VIII, case 69 contains a report about Queen Victoria requesting US President Andrew Johnson to intervene on behalf of Maximilian.
41 The question of whether Canada would ultimately remain under monarchical rule or transform into a republic also concerned British officials, as chapter nine by Edward Beasley in this volume shows.
42 HHStA, PA VIII, case 69: no. 28, 2 April 1867; HHSta, PA XXXIII, case 22: no. 15, 2 and 18 April 1867.
43 On US complaints as the reason for calling Canada a "Dominion" rather than a "Kingdom," see *Neue Freie Presse*, 30 März 1867, 3. On US opposition against the notion of viceroyalty and against the installation of "a prince from the English royal family," see HHStA, PA XXXIII, case 22: no. 12, report from Washington to Vienna, 30 March 1867. See also *Das Vaterland*, 2 March 1867, 3; *Neue Freie Presse*, 4 March 1867, 2. *Innsbrucker Nachrichten*,

18 March 1867, 3, also mentioned the alleged plan to create a Canadian "kingdom under Prince Arthur."

44 Altman, *Kanada* (1907), 5. The words "dinner-parties" and "good sports" are English in the German original. That the earlier mentioned Governor General Frederick Stanley is today primarily remembered for his donating the Stanley Cup in 1892 bears testimony to this assertion.

8 Canadian Lessons, Roads Not Taken: Spanish Views on Confederation

JOSEP MARÍA FRADERA

For Spain and its world in the nineteenth century, there was no Canada other than within the British Empire. From that completely reasonable perspective, British North America and, later, the Canadian federation eventually became either a model to follow or, when considering relations between Spain and its American colonies, something to be avoided. In this paper I shall propose a complicated comparison between two very different societies, and I base the comparison on contemporary texts.

The three monarchic empires of the Atlantic – Spanish, British, and French – survived the revolutions of 1763 to 1815. Their survival in America was very much affected by these decades of the making and unmaking of empires, to paraphrase the title of Peter Marshall's book on the Second British Empire.[1] France paid a heavy price, with defeat in the Seven Years' War, the terrible expulsion of the Acadians, the fall of New France, the crisis of Saint-Domingue, and the sale of Louisiana to the United States in 1803. The French retreat allowed the construction of a British sovereign space in North America separate from the Thirteen Colonies, whose crisis began precisely because of the steep economic cost of war with France and Spain, and Britain's policy of co-opting Indigenous peoples to the disadvantage of the colonies' control of the backcountries by the Royal Proclamation of 1763.[2] The indirect result of this new situation was that Spain expanded its presence in the south, starting with New Orleans and the Mississippi Delta. After 1802, however, Spain lost its footing again and again. First came the transfer of Louisiana to the French, and then the dishonourable Adams-Onís Treaty of 1819, by which Spain gave up Florida and its extended coastline to the United States. At the same time, Spain was negotiating with

Great Britain over giving up a tiny strip of land in the future British Columbia. While the Spanish Empire held on to its posts in the Gulf of Mexico, the British Empire rebuilt on the continent. It did so in the north by allying with Indian nations and establishing relations with communities in Quebec and Ontario as well as with territories belonging to the Hudson's Bay Company, the largest landowner in the world. Britain also held on to posts in the West Indies, where sugar profits were inseparable from large-scale slavery, one of the Empire's most pressing problems until 1833.[3]

It is interesting to compare the stabilization of the British and Spanish Empires in America after the revolutionary decades. British North America had inherited major stability problems, both domestically and with its neighbours. The first was for the Protestant Empire to assimilate the Catholic French Canadians. That was the solution abandoned with the *Quebec Act* of 1774.[4] This politically opportune decision meant that the majority Catholic population in Canada would no longer be excluded as it had been between 1763 and 1774. Not much later, their local clergy, fearful of revolutionary policies emanating from France, were very willing to accept British protection, even if that meant Protestants might stir up political-religious fervour. Indeed, between the Treaty of Paris and "We the People," good New England Protestants found it intolerable that George III would sign pacts with the Catholic population. This ideological impasse is one of the factors that explains northern New Englanders' invasion in September 1775.[5] Later, that same tension would spread throughout the Empire, especially in Ireland, with the collapse of Grattan's Parliament and the Gordon Riots in London in 1782. But the road to imperial reconstruction continued straight ahead. Political restrictions in Quebec, softened after 1774, where Catholics were not allowed to hold public office unless they denied the theory of transubstantiation, influenced imperial politics elsewhere. What in North America was an act of political realism – severely criticized by the Founding Fathers of the United States – was later extended throughout the Empire. With the help of Robert Peel and Richard Wellesley – Lord Lieutenant of Ireland and brother of the Duke of Wellington – Catholic integration led to the *Roman Catholic Relief Act* of 1829, Daniel O'Connell's campaigns for Catholic emancipation, and, at long last, Irish entry into Westminster.

The second series of problems concerned border conflicts between the United States and its own people living in the former French *pays d'en haut*, the old hunting and fishing territories in the Great Lakes region. With the foundation of British North America, Britain gave the new entity territories in Ohio, the New York backcountry, parts of New England, and all the way to Minnesota, which set off conflicts both with the expanding US republic and with Indian nations and the Métis, the world of Louis Riel that had lost a great amount of autonomy since the 1780s.

The Canadian experiment, along with East India Company lands in the subcontinent, constitutes the essence of the Second British Empire. By the time of the 1832 parliamentary reform, when Westminster became a truly imperial parliament – with the elimination of lobbies controlled by West Indies planters and Indian nabobs, a condition for the definitive abolition of slavery – the Empire had completed its reconstruction cycle. What gave coherence to the so-called Second Empire was no longer Old-Regime legislative pluralism – by which spaces were joined together in the tradition of composite monarchies – but rather a new norm that guaranteed representation and citizenship to subjects of European origin and pushed everyone else to the margins. Politics in liberal empires was developed and modulated on that very point, on the definition of who fell under one set of rules and who fell under another, and how those rules would be applied. Colonies with large European populations acquired or maintained the traditional form of government used during the First British Empire, the famous triad: a governor appointed by the Crown representing the government; a co-opted council; plus an elected assembly. While in the West Indies this formula survived until the 1865 Morant Bay Rebellion, in Lower Canada it set off relentless struggles between the majority francophone population and the anglophone minority, which was growing in size and economic power since the political balance established by the *Constitutional Act* of 1791 and the Union Bill of 1822. Fitting both groups into one monarchical sovereignty was not easy. The Lower Canadian crisis up to the rebellions of 1837–8 can thus be seen as a struggle by the British blood compact to impose itself on the francophone majority and follow the rules of popular elections without imperial interference. A conflict in Upper Canada concerning control by elected officials over appointees led to similar rebellions in 1837 and 1838. The balance achieved through the 1840 *Act of Union*, which regarded the Durham Report's ethnic conclusions as impractical, was the beginning of a success story that twenty-five years later would lead to the establishment of the Dominion. The same spirit could be found in the Hudson's Bay Company's immense lands, which from 1870 to 1905 were turned into provinces. This Dominion was built by and conceived for descendants of Europeans, not for anyone else.

The Spanish Empire was also a child of its own time; it was not the anomaly it was often described as being. From Havana to Mexico to Chile to Buenos Aires, events in Boston, Philadelphia, Paris, and Saint-Domingue affected its possessions in different ways. Napoleon's invasion of Spain fuelled the final crisis of the monarchic state, which was already suffering from a huge political and financial crisis.[6] After King Ferdinand VII was "kidnapped" in Bayonne by the French, and after the attempt by France and its Spanish allies to convoke the Cortes (parliament) and allow Spanish-Americans to participate, the Junta Central, which at that point claimed sovereignty, called for the Cortes to assemble with American and Filipino representation. The Cortes met in Cádiz under the protection of the British Navy. From then on, the imperial crisis took two parallel paths: war and independence in America, and reform and representation in Cádiz. But while Britain was able to reassemble many of the pieces of its Empire after defeating France in Europe, Egypt, and Asia, and after reforming its own institutional apparatus, Spain's liberals were defeated in America by Creole armies, and the absolutist monarchy re-established itself twice in Spain, in 1814 and again in 1823. Both times the liberal Constitution of 1812 was abolished, and its champions were harshly persecuted. Spanish liberalism would successfully confront the absolutist coalition only after 1835.

It was during this cycle, from 1810 to the 1830s, that Spain's colonial space was reduced to the three possessions it retained after 1824: Cuba, Puerto Rico, and the Philippines. This nineteenth century imperial project was based on three crucial factors: First was the enormous military might centred in the Antilles and left over from the wars on the mainland. The last generation of Bourbon rulers in America was not surprisingly concerned with fiscal and military matters. The scale of the wars in the continent was spectacular. It is noteworthy that one of the most important groups of liberal Spanish military men, members of the Progressive Party led by Baldomero Espartero, were known as *"ayacuchos,"* named after the place (in present-day Peru) where a decisive battle was fought between the Spanish Royal Army and the troops of Simón Bolívar and José de San Martín.

The second factor underlying the nineteenth century imperial project was the economy. The Spanish Empire pushed export agriculture to its absolute limits, dealing in products that had become important only in the last third of the eighteenth century. Two of these products were especially critical: sugar and tobacco. Sugar was the key to Cuban and Puerto Rican prosperity; tobacco ensured that the Philippines would remain a colony.[7] Demand kept rising, with the profits going to local growers and to the state through customs and excise taxes. This trade created a huge problem for imperial reform, given that sugar relied on large-scale slave labour, and tobacco relied on coerced labour. The latter, in the Philippines (similar to India and Java), meant there was always the possibility of local resistance. But the former, slavery, represented a serious political and moral problem once Britain outlawed the slave trade and, later, banned slavery altogether. France and Holland followed suit in the Antilles and Guyana in 1848. The United States abolished slavery in 1865. That left Spain and Brazil as the only countries with slave labour; Spain abolished slavery in 1886, and Brazil in 1888.[8] Without Cuban sugar, which was unthinkable without slave labour, Spain's colonial power, both private and state, would have been much diminished.

The third factor that helps us understand the new Spanish imperial cycle concerns political relations between the colonies and the metropolis. As with other imperial countries, Spanish liberals called upon loyal territories to join the *peninsulares* in their electoral institutions. People from throughout South America, along with Cuba, Puerto Rico, and the Philippines, were asked to participate in elections to send representatives to the Spanish Cortes. This call was the basis for liberal legitimacy in the face of independence and royal stagnation. But this unifying vision fell apart in 1837 when the liberals in power approved a constitution that separated the colonies from the liberal institutions on the peninsula. From then on, citizens, electors, and political representation would be reserved for inhabitants of the metropolis. And that same constitution said the colonies would be governed by "special laws," an obvious act of plagiarism from Napoleon's 1802 constitution. Colonies would now lie outside the institutional framework of liberalism.

Special Laws and Exclusion

The combination of slavery and the absolute elimination of all liberal possibilities obviously limited reform in the second half of the nineteenth century. Once the 1837 solution had excluded overseas residents from the Cortes, authorities in the colonies had free rein.[9] Soon afterwards, the Cuban writer José Antonio Saco wrote a pamphlet called *"Paralelo entre la Isla de Cuba y algunas colonias inglesas"* ("Parallels between the Island of Cuba and Some English Colonies"). British institutions were much more flexible than the Spanish, he wrote. He argued that it was possible to have shared representative institutions, even with slavery, using the West Indies assemblies as an example.

> They might say that I am favouring the English nation or that I wish for Cuba to become a satellite of that planet. But they are mistaken, and those who speak thusly do not know me. If the Spanish government one day were to cut the political ties uniting Spain and Cuba, I would not be so criminal as to propose hitching my *patria* to the British cart. In my humble opinion, the objective of all good Cubans should be to give it an existence on its own, an independent existence, even if that means being as insular in politics as it is in nature. But if circumstances were to force us to throw ourselves into the arms of strangers, there is nowhere more honourable or glorious than the Confederation of North America. There we could find peace and consolation, strength and protection, justice and liberty. With such solid foundations, soon Cuba could grace the world with the magnificent spectacle of a people who rose from the depths and with the speed of lightning reached the highest peaks.[10]

These are sublime words, but one could object that while Britain had abolished slavery four years earlier, the Spanish island was four decades away from imitating the Mighty Experiment. Meanwhile, liberal politicians and governments in Spain used "heterogeneity" as an argument to justify the colonies' political and parliamentary exclusion. The reason why Spain held on so fiercely to colonial autocracy is not hard to see: unrestricted political and military control allowed the powerful colonial elites to use whatever force they deemed necessary. The Cubans thus were confined to establishing a dense network of lobbies in Madrid, London, Paris, and Philadelphia through which they tried to informally channel their political positions at the same time as the Spanish liberal regime became institutionally centralized and consolidated. The colonies remained excluded until the end of the first Cuban War of Independence and the Zanjón Pact of February 1878. It was only then, with the authorization of political parties and a free press (that was nonetheless not allowed to advocate independence), that the Canadian lessons appeared on the Spanish political horizon.

Spain's treatment of its colonists cannot be understood separately from what was going on throughout the monarchy. The same centralized, unitary political-administrative system was being imposed on the peninsula as well. The difference was that colonists had been excluded from parliament, from the Cortes of Cádiz and the Cortes of 1820–3. The system quickly proved inadequate in the metropolis as well. In 1854, a conservative monarchist newspaper editor in Barcelona named Juan Mañé y Flaquer said that the monarchy had two cancers: one was Catalonia, and the other was Cuba. Both suffered from civil strife, and both were fighting against the political centre. The message was clear: the mechanisms of political representation were far too narrow to allow for the interests and needs of Havana and Barcelona. The dilemma regarding how to organize the state lasted throughout the twentieth century, and, of course, it continues today. After a hypothetical reform effort in the mid-nineteenth century failed, Cubans and Catalans each developed their proto-nationalist political projects, which survived through the end of the century and the Spanish-American War, when Spain lost all three colonies to the United States.

While in Canada the problem was how to balance two large communities in representative spaces and promote self-government through the responsible government scheme, in Spain the problem was that the model of the unitary state and administrative centralization remained intact. It is true that the French model underwent modifications when it moved to Spain. First, we have the three overseas possessions, which were separate from the entire legal apparatus of Spain. Though they were claimed as national territory, they were deemed insufficiently Spanish to be given liberal institutions. Instead, they were the beneficiaries of unrestricted proconsular power and a political-military dictatorship in the person of three captains-general who personified the negation of the liberal constitution. This type of governance is not simply a cliché about Spain being on the margins of nineteenth century development, being that, in fact, it had a liberal-representative regime starting in the 1830s, just like the rest of Europe. Rather, it is something simpler: it was a way of keeping sovereign spaces far away from anything, for example, citizens' rights, elections, and parliamentary representation, which might threaten the colonial order. The main problem was Cuba, which determined what happened elsewhere; again and again the argument was made that liberal reforms could not be implemented in a place where one-third of the population, some 300,000 people, were slaves.[11] The spectre of Haiti was invoked. The alleged Escalera conspiracy in Cuba, a supposed slave revolt nipped in the bud in 1844, was used by Spanish authorities to fan the flames of fear and terror.[12]

Beyond the three colonies, there were other exceptions to the unitary nature of Spanish political life. The Canary Islands, for example, which were close to Africa and situated in the midst of international trade routes, were subject to rules that no other province had. The most glaring examples in the metropolis, however, were the so-called exempt provinces: the three Basque provinces plus Navarre. There, widespread anti-liberalism and two civil wars, the Carlist Wars of the 1830s and 1870s, meant they were allowed to keep their local and provincial institutions and enjoy important tax privileges (an arrangement that survives today). But despite these exceptions, the unitary model that came into existence with the constitutions of 1837 and 1845, which was affirmed with the constitution of 1876, remained in place until the turn of the century.

Alternative projects were proposed, though they would not become politically viable until September 1868, when Queen Isabel II was forced into exile and Cuba revolted. It is interesting that these alternatives came out of different ideological traditions, sometimes moving in opposite directions. The September 1868 Revolution and the proclamation of the Republic in 1873 symbolized the victory of local democracy and popular mobilization.[13] The radical current of liberal discourse, aimed at modifying the nature of the state, grew out of this mobilization and built on coalitions both on the peninsula and in the Antilles, which all communicated through the press, emigration, and troop movements. The liberal project and the federal republican project both faced the same challenge: that of articulating a highly decentralized diversity of social and political reform efforts. Many Spaniards in Cuba, obviously including the wealthy and powerful, saw the 1868 crisis – which involved both the prospect of insurrection and interracial democracy – as a separatist threat. But it is not clear they were right. The ideological direction of federal democracy remained unitary, committed to the construction of the nation-state from below, with the US republic, including the recent abolition of slavery, as the great example. Thus the 1873 republican-federal constitution of Spain, which was never actually implemented, divided the country into equal states with equal rights, including the Canary Islands and the Basque provinces. The progressives of the time, who favoured federal reform in this direction, were sometimes called "Canadians" by their conservative adversaries. They were accused of wanting to give Cuba a status similar to that of the British white settlements.[14]

These radical solutions were put forward in the context of the largest political mobilizations of the era, though not from regional conservative interests. The great economic and social power complexes in Cuba and Catalonia were conservative and highly suspicious of the plebeian world, despite their distance from official institutional models. Indeed, after 1868 the strongest ideological critiques of the unitary model emerged in slaveholding Cuba and industrial Catalonia, both stuck between stagnation and fear of the revolution. This period is when regionalism became a force to be reckoned with. Regionalism required instruments with which to organize society and have influence in the framework of transatlantic sovereignty. It needed respected political concepts such as self-government and solutions such as home rule. One of the best examples was the British Empire, along with the newly created German *Kaiserreich*, with its complex transactions among states and the Hanseatic League. Best of all was the Canadian combination of empire and self-government all in one, which was considered a possible model for domestic reform. In the 1880s, after the Bourbon Restoration in Spain and the revived hegemony of the liberal party of order, regionalist proposals in both Cuba and Catalonia pointed in that direction.

Spain continued being an American and imperial nation facing enormous challenges. In Cuba, the great social challenge was obviously emancipation of the slaves, but the great political challenge was deciding between assimilation into the Spanish liberal framework or separation. At the same time, conservative Spanish nationalism (*españolismo* or *incondicionalismo*) was also growing. It was based in Havana's Casino Español, established in 1868 during the insurgency and quickly spread throughout the island. Its success left little room for liberal reforms. Many volunteer troops from Spain (and those recruited on the island) also joined the *españolista* campaign. So at one and the same moment we have insurrectional separatism, non-separatist liberal reforms, and conservative Spanish nationalism. Each wanted hegemony.[15] It is easy to see why the Canadian example was relevant only to those who supported internal political reforms in Spain. That was the inspiration for the foundation of the Cuban Liberal Party in 1878, which after the war was called the Autonomist Liberal Party. The pro-autonomy (or self-government) movement wanted Cuba to be integrated within the general political framework, which meant abolition, a "whitening" of the population (more emigrants from Galicia, fewer Haitians), and social reform. In other words, it defended the unity of Spain and a moderate reform program. Inspired by the Canadian and Irish examples of the time, the idea was to devise a tripartite representative institutional system *à la británica*: a provincial government in Cuba, a governor general representing Spanish sovereignty, and a council led by the governor in partnership with colonial and metropolitan interests.[16]

But though Cuban liberals' demand for self-government followed the British-Canadian lesson plan, there were also important differences.[17] The main one was their desire to participate in the Spanish legislature and accept a tax burden that was proportional to that of the other provinces. Both those factors clearly differentiated their position from that of the Canadian Dominion during the Victorian Empire. Another strategic difference was their refusal to transfer power to provinces on the island, which they believed would weaken the island's general government and the construction of Cuban identity. Antonio Govín, one of the leading champions of the autonomy movement, articulated this simultaneous interest in and distance from the Canadian example. His position can be found in the prologue he wrote to the Spanish edition of John George Bourinot's book, first published in English in 1884 and translated into Spanish in 1898 with the title "How Canada Is Governed."[18] Cuban liberal autonomists were adamantly opposed to Spanish conservatives' initiative to increase the number of provinces, because this would have atomized Cuban demands and guaranteed Spanish control over provincial political clients, the key to the Spanish spoils system. Rather, the autonomists needed to identify Cuba as a political subject, which would be the only way to construct a solid institutional base for ensuring the island's interests, ending slavery, and attracting Spanish colonists and immigrants.[19] But none of this was possible without agreement by the Spanish government, which explains why the Cubans were so anxious to play an important role in Spanish politics and legislation. There might have been an opportunity through the connection between Cuban autonomists, on the one hand, and Spanish liberals and the so-called Spanish dynastic left, on the other. Hopes for this reformist option were highest in 1885 to 1890, when Práxedes Mateo Sagasta and Segismundo Moret were in the government, and again when the liberals returned to power in late 1892. In June 1893, the minister for Overseas Possessions, Antonio Maura, at long last took up the possibility of just one government for the whole island, which was what the autonomists had been demanding for decades. At the same time, the most brilliant representatives of Cuban liberalism travelled to Madrid to defend their positions in the Athenaeum there. It appeared that this transatlantic dialogue might result in some real reforms. But that was not to be. The last step of political reforms – the Abarzuza's provincial reform of February 1895 – was frozen by the outbreak of the Second War of Independence.[20] The autonomists had very little room to manoeuvre and were entirely dependent upon whatever reforms the Madrid governments managed to undertake. Their position was, furthermore, undermined by the unquestionable unity between the great economic interests of Cuba and the peninsula. This attempt at reform from above, clearly the most receptive to Canadian lessons, went into hibernation after an enormous recruitment drive by the Cuban Revolutionary Party, founded by José Martí in 1891, the return of the conservative government in Spain in 1885, and the outbreak of a new war.

In Cuba, assimilation and autonomism were two sides of the same coin, the only possible way to modify the dynamics of liberal state construction. However, in Catalonia the situation was quite different. Cubans were always well aware of the difference between the two regionalist movements. As the Cuban autonomist newspaper *El Triunfo* said in 1885, Catalans were challenging the very "unifying project under way for centuries," which they (the Cubans) wanted to join.[21] The obvious reason for the difference between the two was that the Catalan ruling class had participated in Spanish politics, though with peculiarities, since the dawn of Spanish liberalism. It also participated in the late colonial and imperial campaigns. The commercial, industrial, and shipping interests of Catalonia were deeply involved in the Cuban-Spanish economic complex and were absolutely opposed to ending slavery or giving up any power to the Cubans. Their unequivocal resistance to any talk of reform in the island was exemplified by the establishment of volunteer forces paid for by the Catalan government to fight against Cuban insurgents. But at the same time, Catalonia – land of industry, colonialism, and class struggle – also gave rise to popular mobilizations in favour of reform and abolition. The governments that emerged from the 1868 Revolution in Spain included a group of radical Catalans, starting with Juan Prim, who was briefly prime minister before being assassinated and who initiated talks regarding the possibility of handing Cuba over to the United States. He was followed by Estanislao Figueras and Francisco Pi y Margall, who both served in the ephemeral First Spanish Republic and were staunch abolitionists and in favour of negotiating Cuban independence if necessary.

Like Cuban autonomism, the regionalist movement in Catalonia grew out of the failure of the so-called Democratic Sexennium, which lasted from 1868 to 1874. The idea was not to articulate a state from below, like the United States, which was the wish of the radicals. Rather, it wanted to increase its state power both in Spain and in Catalonia. Catalan regionalism, like the Cuban version, aspired to singularity, to protecting its social and/or cultural differences in the context of the monarchy. They both wanted the greatest decentralization possible within unity. Thus the strong regionalist and nationalist movements that emerged in Catalonia in the 1880s wanted more power and greater influence over law, language, culture, economics, and taxation. And they wanted it all within the framework of the great imperial nation. Once again, the example of Britain, with its world empire and solid dominions, was relevant.[22] A major 1885 Catalan regionalist document known as the "List of Grievances" stated considerations in the following tone:

> The most opulent nation in the world is the British Empire, country of individualism and self-government. But not in that metropolis, nor in the islands that form the nucleus and centre of this endless Empire, has unification been so extreme. Within [its] national unity, particular and local variations can raise their heads ... The Canadian colonies have general and regional parliaments, and there French is spoken officially alongside English.[23]

This was not an isolated example. The desire for both unity and empire was expressed again and again. In one of the first statements of Catalan proto-nationalism, a document called the "Bases de Manresa" (named after the town where it was approved in 1892), one of the authors was quite eloquent regarding support for national unity:

> No, our inclination is not now nor has it ever been to take the foolish position of wishing Catalonia to be isolated within the national whole of which it forms a glorious part. We have never been and are not and will never be so reckless as to turn our backs on centuries of reality. Must we continually remember the War of Independence [against Napoleon], the War of Africa [in Morocco in 1859], or even the Cuban War in order to assert our nationalism?[24]

But the unitary framework of the imperial nation was like a set of communicating or connected vessels. As a result of the Second Cuban War of Independence, Catalan regionalism had to put its opposition to the state on hold until the start of the twentieth century. By then, Spain's defeat by the United States, the loss of the last colonies, and the rise of anarchism combined to transform the old regionalism into explicit nationalism.

National histories tend to be presented as if they describe a country's whole existence. But the process of national construction can be seen from other angles. In this case, the very late abolition crisis in Cuba and the consequences of intense regional industrialization form the backdrop and the catalyst for many struggles, including for independence. Regional variations in Spanish economic development in the nineteenth century gave rise to huge disparities among both the elites and commoners, creating a variety of conflicts and alliances. Many different social, regional, and national identities took shape and developed along complementary lines. The existence of the Empire favoured these ambiguous and multiple identities, Cuban and Spanish, Basque or Catalan or Spanish. It also favoured regionalism both in the peninsula and in the colonies themselves. That was what happened in Cuba: using Juan Pérez de la Riva's language, Cuba-B was far more receptive to independence than Cuba-A, which lived off sugar and mass slavery, and which was based in the capital city, both Cuban and Spanish.[25] Nation and empire, "region" and "nation" are but two sides of one social complex that can be combined in many ways. And neither term ever quite captures the complexity of reality.

NOTES

1 P.J. Marshall, *The Making and Unmaking of Empires: Britain, India, and America c. 1750–1783* (Oxford: Oxford University Press, 2005).
2 Terry Fenge and Jim Aldridge, eds., *Keeping Promises: The Royal Proclamation of 1763, Aboriginal Rights, and Treaties in Canada* (Montreal: McGill-Queen's University Press, 2015).
3 Robin Winks, *The Blacks in Canada: A History*, 2nd ed. (Montreal: McGill-Queens University Press, 1997), 96–113.
4 Carla Gardina Pestana, *Protestant Empire: Religion and the Making of the British Atlantic World* (Philadelphia: University of Pennsylvania Press, 2009).
5 Gustave Lanctot, *Canada and the American Revolution, 1774–1783* (Toronto: Clarke, Irwin, 1967), 62–75.
6 Barbara and Stanley Stein, *Crisis in an Atlantic Empire: Spain and New Spain, 1808–1810* (Baltimore: Johns Hopkins University Press, 2014).
7 Franklin W. Knight, *Slave Society in Cuba during the Nineteenth Century* (Madison: University of Wisconsin Press, 1970).
8 Rebecca J. Scott, *Slave Emancipation in Cuba: The Transformation to Free Labor, 1860–1899* (Princeton, NJ: Princeton University Press, 1985).

9 Josep M. Fradera, *Colonias para después de un imperio* (Barcelona: Edicions Bellaterra, 2005), 140–82.
10 José Antonio Saco, *Paralelo entre la Isla de Cuba y algunas colonias inglesas*, (Madrid: Imprenta de Tomás Jordán, 1837), 23.
11 Christopher Schmidt-Nowara, *Empire and Antislavery: Spain, Cuba, and Puerto Rico, 1833–1874* (Pittsburgh: Pittsburgh University Press, 1999); Josep M. Fradera and Christopher Schmidt-Nowara, eds., *Slavery and Antislavery in Spain's Atlantic Empire* (New York: Berghahn Books, 2013).
12 Robert L. Paquette, *Sugar Is Made with Blood: The Conspiracy of La Escalera and the Conflict between Empires over Slavery in Cuba* (Middletown, CT: Wesleyan University Press, 1988); Michelle Reid-Vázquez, *The Year of the Lash: Free People of Color in Cuba in the Nineteenth-Century Atlantic World* (Athens, GA: University of Georgia Press, 2011).
13 Albert García-Balañà, "À la recherche du *Sexenio Democrático* (1868–1874) dans l'Espagne contemporaine. Crononymies, politiques de l'histoire et historiographies," *Revue d'histoire du XIXe siècle* 52, no. 1 (2016): 81–101.
14 Juan Pro Ruiz, "La mirada del otro: el progresismo desde el moderantismo," in *La redención del pueblo: La cultura progresista en la España liberal*, ed. Manuel Suárez Cortina (Santander: Universidad de Cantabria, 2006), 286–7.
15 Joan Casanovas, *Bread, or Bullets! Urban Labor and Spanish Colonialism in Cuba, 1850–1898* (Pittsburgh: University of Pittsburg Press, 1998), 105–12.
16 J.M.C. Ogelsby, "The Cuban Autonomist Movement's Perception of Canada, 1865–1898: Its Implications," *The Americas* 48, no. 4 (1992): 445–61.
17 A complete account of the intended reforms can be found in Inés Roldán de Montaud, *La Restauración en Cuba. El fracaso de un proceso reformista* (Madrid: Consejo Superior de Investigaciones Científicas, 2000); Consuelo Naranjo, Miguel Ángel Puig-Samper, y Luis Miguel García Mora, eds., *La Nación Soñada: Cuba, Puerto Rico y Filipinas ante el 98* (Madrid: Doce Calles, 1996).
18 Delphine Sappez, *Ciudadanía y autonomismo en Cuba. Antonio Govín (1847–1914)* (Castelló: Universitat Jaume I, 2016), 227.
19 Marta Bizcarrondo and Antonio Elorza, *Cuba/España. El dilema autonomista, 1878–1898* (Madrid: Editorial Colibrí, 1996); Luis Miguel García Mora, "La fuerza de la palabra. El autonomismo en Cuba en el último tercio del siglo XIX," *Revista de Indias* 41, no. 223 (2001): 715–48.
20 Rafael E. Tarragó, "La guerra de 1895 en Cuba y sus consecuencias," *Arbor* 185 (2009): 215–29.
21 Delphine Sappez, *Ciudadanía y autonomismo en Cuba. Antonio Govín (1847–1914)*, 219.

22 Enric Ucelay-Da Cal, *El imperialismo catalán. Prat de la Riba, Cambó, D'Ors y la conquista moral de España* (Barcelona: Edhasa, 2003), 511–25.
23 *Memoria en defensa dels interessos morals i materials de Catalunya* (Barcelona: Imprempta La Renaixensa, 1885), 86. The translation is that of the author.
24 *Assambleas Catalanistas (Primera). Manresa. Deliberacions i Acorts* (Barcelona: Imprempta La Renaixensa, 1893), 35. The translation is that of the author.
25 Juan Pérez de la Riva, "Una isla con dos historias," in *El barracón. Esclavitud y capitalismo en Cuba* (Barcelona: Editorial Crítica, 1978), 169–81.

PART THREE

Perspectives from Britain and the Empire

9 British Views of Canada at the Time of Confederation

EDWARD BEASLEY

For years, there has been controversy among United Kingdom historians over how much the British Empire meant to the English people. We have had historians and literary scholars accentuating the imperial themes in Jane Austen novels. On the other hand, about ten years ago Andrew Porter in his book *Absent-Minded Imperialists* tried to argue away any mention of empire that he could find in Victorian England as coming from some special interest group or another, and never reflecting any broader English interest in the wider British world.[1]

But how much awareness was there of Canada in particular? What I want to do in the first part of this chapter is to convey a sense of the basic understanding of Canada in Great Britain in the run-up to Confederation. Who paid attention to the place, and what did they think of it?[2] The United Kingdom was a teeming nation, and London was the world's largest city. Accordingly, there were many ideas of Canada. Some observers focused on the land, others on the people. Common themes included the way Canada was a new country and a destination for emigrants. But there was also some appreciation of Canada's urban spaces and its increasing economic and social sophistication. Having looked at the idea of Canada not in the British mind (that would be too much of a reification) but in a range of British minds, the chapter will turn to British perceptions of Canada as a political community when the *British North America Act, 1867* was under consideration. The government ministers who framed Canada's institutions were an ocean away from the country. Unlike Lord Durham nearly three decades before, they made no fact-finding trip to the other side of the Atlantic. Of course they talked to the Canadian delegates who had come to London, and they corresponded with British officials in the British North

American colonies. But to a large extent it was the "Canada" that they had been able to imagine for themselves, reflecting previous British attitudes towards the country, which determined their own attitudes to the political questions of Confederation. There was another element, too. The Canada of their imaginations also reflected how they wanted to see themselves as a free, more-or-less democratic society. Perhaps inevitably, the Canada that UK ministers helped call into being in the *British North America Act, 1867* was, in part, a reflection of how they imagined British politics at the time.[3]

By the late 1860s the great expanses of British territory in Australia and North America were starting to get filled in on the map. But what did having all that territory really mean to the British? As some of them were more than willing to point out, most of Australia was dry, and Canada was not all that it might seem. One of these sceptics about the value of Canada was Sir Charles Dilke. In 1866–7, the young Dilke, destined for a political career, went on a round-the-world tour of the British Empire and the United States. Out of this came his book, *Greater Britain*, published in 1868. With Canadian Confederation having come into effect the year before, Dilke's volume marked a new level of awareness in the United Kingdom about the size and potential of the British overseas empire. But Dilke had his doubts about the real importance of all that empty land. Indeed, he spent far more of the volume on the United States than he did on the British territory to the north. Why had he put his book together in this way? The usual map projection made some parts of the globe seem bigger than they really were, as he had told his father in a letter written off the coast of Ceylon:

> With regard to the value of the British North American possessions generally – Mercator's Projection – (the common chart map of the world) – has a great deal to answer for. Few atlases contain any separate map of these countries, + consequently the ideas of most of us as to their size are derived from this source. Now Mercator – in order to preserve certain proportions for the convenience of navigators – has made his chart correct at the equator – but grossly out at high latitudes; – hence – by way of example – the enormous size of Greenland on our maps, – + hence also much nonsense about the Canadas – wh. are made to look at least twice their real area. People look at their map + say – dear me! – British America is half as large

again as the U.S.; – + then straightaway make up their minds that in a country so vast, there must be something of value. Again they neglect the nine months' winter with wh. a great portion of this territory is blessed.[4]

So "the Canadas" – which for Dilke seemed to stand for all of British North America – were not so big as all of that, and they were too frozen over to be of much importance.

Better informed British and Canadian writers, many of whom had spent rather more time in British North America than Dilke, never minimized the severity or length of the Canadian winter. But they also explained to the British reader how the Canadians had managed to build a country despite the snow. Back in 1851, the catalogue of the Great Exhibition discussed this issue:

> The agriculture of the Canadas is greatly influenced by the climate, and is mercenarily of a peculiar character. During one half of the year the surface of the country is covered with snow and ice, and thus remains totally unproductive. The farmer is consequently constrained to select such plants or varieties of plants, for his cultivation, as will perfect their growth in the brief summer of the country.[5]

Fortunately the land sprung to life in a way England never did: "When the ice departs, at about the end of April, vegetation commences, and proceeds with a rapidity unknown in our climate. In Upper Canada the seasons are not so severe as in Lower Canada, or the provinces of Nova Scotia or New Brunswick, and the spring sets in about a month earlier."[6] Further, the wheat was of good quality and came in abundantly, although the produce was not as good as in "more favoured climates." But nonetheless the place had its own charm, as the Great Exhibition *Catalogue* tried to convey. We hear about sleigh rides, crisp air, and snow:

> Sleighing forms the chief and most highly relished amusement of the Canadians during winter. To follow it all business is suspended, and certainly a more invigorating exercise can scarcely be imagined. Seated in one of these light and elegant carriages, wrapped in the warmest furs, ornamented with the gayest colours, and tempted abroad by a sky that exceeds that of Italy in brilliance, the Canadian thoroughly enjoys himself, even if the thermometer be sometimes 30 degrees below the freezing point. It is no uncommon a thing to see a score or thirty at one time careening over the frozen snow in the "fashionable drives."[7]

What had the Canadian colonies sent to the Great Exhibition? How had they represented themselves? Newfoundland sent only cod liver oil. In 1865, *All the Year Round*, the weekly literary magazine Charles Dickens had founded in 1859, would note, with more sarcasm than accuracy, that "[s]o completely fishy is Newfoundland, that all the chief articles of export smell of fish in some form or other."[8] But the rest of the North American colonies sent a wider variety of things: minerals, timber, blankets, horse clothes, Indian crafts, and furs, of course – mainly raw commodities as this was "a comparatively new country," the catalogue explained; but there was also a finely crafted piano to show the British what could be done with the woods available.

The Canadians also sent a fire engine that could shoot water farther than any other and with a better design.[9] Quebec had suffered a number of terrible fires. In 1867 the *Times* ran a letter from a country clergyman complaining that now that the subscription to relieve the victims of a large fire in Quebec was drawing to a close, people ought to have remembered that a similar tragedy had occurred in that city about twenty years before. Perhaps this time the Canadians could rebuild in a material less inflammable than wood? Besides, Canada should not need this kind of financial assistance – as "it is a richer country than England, for if the riches of this country are great, they are not so great as its poverty."[10]

In Great Britain, Canada was understood to be a rich country, and rich not only in raw materials. It was a modern country, too. As was discussed in the pages of *All the Year Round* in 1867, in Canada there was a network of railroads, there were fine hotels (even if some of them were still under construction), and there were major navigation works completed or in progress. Lake St Peter had been dredged to make a deep channel. When the plan of Sir John Young to widen and deepen the Lachine and Welland canals was complete, "first-class steamers could ply between Liverpool and the great American lakes with as much regularity and comfort as they now ply between Liverpool and New York, and grain from the overflowing corn-fields of the bounteous West could reach the British manufacturing districts without the cost and delay of transhipment."[11] And "the Victoria-bridge at Montreal is, in its way, quite as great a wonder of the world as the Falls at Niagara," the same journal had reported a year before.[12]

By 1868, the cities of Canada were seen to be part of the modern world, and for *All Year Round* they held lessons for the imperial capital:

In one sentence, London must have tramways such are established in America, and which work so satisfactorily to the public in all the great cities of the United States and Canada ... The tramway will be laid down in London, as it has been laid down in Philadelphia, Baltimore, Boston, Washington, Chicago, San Francisco, Toronto, Montreal, Quebec, and in scores and hundreds of populous towns and cities.[13]

Meanwhile Canadian public works were well known as arenas for investment. References to Canadian railroads and railroad shares in the British press in the 1860s were legion. To promote and safeguard this investment, certain UK businessmen formed special interest groups to lobby Whitehall. The British North American Association, founded in 1862 in the wake of a financial crisis, was one of these groups, and it especially sought to promote Confederation, as historian Andrew Smith has shown. Another body, the Canada Club, had been founded in 1810, and it was still holding dinners four times a year for bankers and politicians in the 1860s and beyond.[14]

By the time Confederation came, an idea was widespread that the North American colonies were rich and modern and large enough to absorb British emigration – both in cities and in the wilderness. The image of Canada as a destination for British emigrants was hardly a new one. Canada had long been seen as a place of settlement for the poorer folk of the overcrowded United Kingdom. In the 1860s British reformers continued to send impoverished migrants across the North Atlantic. Promoters would announce their emigration projects and solicit donations in the *Times*.[15] The fact that there were still (supposedly) empty places for the British poor to go – places where they could take refuge and build a new life when, for example, they were cleared out of the Scottish Highlands – could lend Canada a certain romance. Both clearances – the clearance of the Scottish Highlands and the disappearance of many Indigenous peoples – were alluded to in a short story published by a *Times* journalist in *Cornhill Magazine* in 1867:

[T]he Machaddies of Glen and Strath have spread over Canada, New Zealand, Australia – the isles of the sea, and the broad lands of the Far West. They will not have our convicts, and they will not have the aborigines; and lost in democratic whorls of independent self-satisfying existence, they have no respect for titles. No doubt, they are better and happier far than they would have been had their ancestors never dared the sea. Let us hope so, at all events.[16]

And so in the run-up to Confederation, in some British minds Canada was – as ever – full of natural resources, snow, and room for emigrants to better their lives. There were also those long, rough, self-sufficient villages of the French *habitants* lining the rivers. They received some attention, too.[17]

In the opinion of some British observers, this countryside was all there was to Canada. The grand political questions of the country at the time of Confederation paled in comparison. Arthur Hamilton Gordon, the son and private secretary to Prime Minister George Hamilton Gordon, the Earl of Aberdeen, in the early 1850s, served as lieutenant governor of New Brunswick from 1861 to 1866. He was very keen on the Canadian outdoors, publishing a book about his camping and canoeing trips across the province.[18] Although he did what he was told in getting New Brunswick to accept the Confederation proposals, his heart was not really in the task. For when he wasn't camping, he seemed to feel that his political duties were uninteresting and his colony unappealing. An intimate friend of William Ewart Gladstone, he told the future prime minister that the Fenians were no real threat, Canadian politicians were corrupt, the Intercolonial Railroad was not something that Great Britain should guarantee or write into the *British North America Act, 1867*, and Confederation itself was unreal and an example of jobbing. Meanwhile he lobbied Gladstone for a better post and left the country, seemingly with no regrets.[19]

There were others who doubted the significance of the North American colonies. As the *Spectator* wrote in 1866, if Nova Scotia, which seemed to be framing objection after objection to Confederation, kept insisting on a union with America instead, then the British government ought to agree happily and negotiate the terms of its annexation to the United States at once. The *Spectator* later changed its mind, but not in a way that suggested a new enthusiasm for Great Britain's North American empire. The *Spectator* told its readers in 1868 that the need to defend Canada by sea and the importance of adhering to the spirit of the *British North America Act, 1867* meant that Nova Scotia could never be allowed to join the American republic.[20] It seems that *not* having a Confederation was now more trouble for the Mother Country than having one, as it would produce a situation in which the colonies were too expensive to defend.

The fact did not escape the attention of interested parties in the United Kingdom that one of the main reasons why Confederation was needed was to defend Great Britain's North American colonies from the United States. Yes, certain other factors were appreciated, such as the way the population growth in Upper Canada had thrown out of kilter the political balance with the more French-speaking parts further down the Saint Lawrence.[21] But the big question looming over everyone was what the Americans might do with their army after the defeat of the South. With this concern in mind, Colonial Secretary Edward Cardwell, a Liberal, and his Tory successor, Lord Carnarvon, facilitated the intercolonial talks leading towards Confederation. Carnarvon himself was quite enthusiastic about pressing forward. Throughout his administrative career he was very friendly to the idea of setting up federations, from Canada to South Africa to the West Indies. Carnarvon stopped short at promoting federation only in Australia because he knew it would be unpopular among the colonists there.[22]

Canadian Confederation, or so Carnarvon believed, would serve to hold together Great Britain's monarchical empire intact and keep the United States within its own borders. Confederation would tie the colonies together and advance their civilization. As he explained when he introduced the British North America Bill in the House of Lords in 1867:

> English institutions, as we all know, need to be of a certain size. Public opinion is the basis of Parliamentary life; and the first condition of public opinion is that it should move in no contracted circle. It would not be difficult to show that almost in proportion to its narrowness Colonial Governments have been subject to disturbing influences.[23]

Once Canada grew to the right size through the mechanism of the *British North America Act, 1867*, the country would fill up with people, trade, and towns, he said, and it would develop a mature rather than an overly narrow administrative tradition. Canada might one day "even overshadow this country."[24]

Carnarvon and Cardwell were not alone in dreaming of a great future for Great Britain's colonies of settlement at this time. In 1868 some of the more imperialistic thinkers in the United Kingdom founded the Colonial Society (now the Royal Commonwealth Society) to promote imperial interests.[25] But anti-imperialist pressures existed in Great Britain too, and often the concern about empire centred on the need to save money. By 1864 the British government wanted to withdraw all British troops from North America, never mind what some segments of the British public might have felt about the move. In the 1950s historian C.P. Stacey argued the government of the United Kingdom had supported Confederation chiefly as a way to conserve resources. The British needed the troops at home so the government could have full room of manoeuvre against Napoleon III and Bismarck, Stacey explained, and this tactic was admitted at the time. (By 1872, Great Britain did indeed withdraw all its troops save those at the naval base and garrison at Halifax, Nova Scotia, and the small, ungarrisoned naval base at Esquimalt, British Columbia.)[26]

The clear need in the short term to send *more* British troops to Canada to counter the Fenian threat prompted Benjamin Disraeli, who did support this late dispatch of troops, to reject sending any more after them in the future. Canada with its responsible government should defend itself, he wrote. He added, "What is the use of these Colonial Deadweights who *we do not govern*?" (And at least one other person agreed with these sentiments, for as the editors of Benjamin Disraeli's letters make clear, he borrowed the phrasing and indeed the whole tenor of his discussion of the topic from a man named Ralph Earle, who had written to him on the matter a few days before.)[27]

But it wasn't only the cost of defending the place that made the more anti-imperialistic elements in the British political class turn up their noses at Canada. There were other grounds for scepticism. Settlers and officials in the United States had horribly mistreated Indigenous peoples, and it was widely believed that given the chance, the Canadians would probably do the same. The founder of the 1868 pro-imperial Colonial Society, Lord Bury, had lived in Canada for a time as native affairs commissioner, where he married the daughter of Allan MacNab, the prime minister of the province of Canada (1854–6). He wrote at length about the rough way the Canadians treated the original population, squatting on their land and driving them to extinction if not for British protection. He did not tell his in-laws at the top of Canadian politics what he was thinking.[28]

Not everyone would have agreed with his views, however. On balance Canada might not be thought to be so bad a place as far as these frontier societies went. Even the sometimes patronizing Charles Dickens could publish a more positive (if entirely speculative) assessment in *All the Year Round* in 1866. He was not in his own voice (it is true) but in that of a representative citizen of Montreal whom he invented: "[I]f you are curious about redskins, we can show you plenty of Indians – fat, copper-coloured, prosperous, and happy, instead of the gaunt, dwarfed, half-starved wretches who are being 'improved' off the face of the earth by restless Yankees."[29] Canadian tolerance was visible in other ways too. A traveller in Lower Canada reported finding "the usual confusion of French and English nomenclature, and of Protestant and Romanist places of worship, and of people of Saxon and Celtic race along the road; but, as seems happily the case in Canada, the Gaul and the Saxon, the follower of Peter and the disciple of Martin, seemed to get along pretty well together."[30] Perhaps this tolerant picture reflected the way the British liked to see themselves, as a tolerant people.

Canadian Confederation, specifically because it came in 1867 and not some other year, touched on another vital aspect of Britain's self-image. At the very moment when the foundations of a modern nation were being laid in Canada in 1867, they were also being established in the United Kingdom itself by the *Representation of the People Act, 1867*, better known as the Second Reform Bill. Seeing Canadian developments through the lens of the struggles over the bill – key disagreements on the meaning of British democracy – also affected how Canada was perceived in 1867.

The Second Reform Bill, on which there was vastly more debate in parliament and across the country than there was on the *British North America Act, 1867*, expanded the franchise from the top one-seventh of the adult male population to the top one-third. Most everyone taking part in the great parliamentary and popular discussion surrounding reform understood that any such bill meant an irrevocable step on the road to democratization. Because the right to vote in Great Britain was determined by the property that one had, or the rates one paid under the bill as it was finally enacted, certain high-rate areas like Central London saw something like universal male suffrage. Accordingly, as Catherine Hall and others have argued, the Second Reform Bill meant the forging of a new sense of national identity. Freeborn Englishmen who had now earned the franchise or who might someday do so began to see themselves as part of a single voting public, rather than feeling that they were still part of a country divided class from class. They were now a single entity of white voters who defined themselves, to some degree, against non-whites abroad. If previously England had been divided within itself, now it would be united against both internal minorities and the other so-called races of the world.[31]

The debates over the Second Reform Bill, or over some version of a second reform bill, had raged in England almost from the moment that Prime Minister Lord Palmerston died in 1865, passing the torch to a new and less complaisant generation. Disraeli and Derby brought the Liberal government down over its reform proposals in 1866, and they led a Tory minority administration from 1866 to nearly the end of 1868. They then proceeded to "dish the Whigs" by passing a more extreme version of reform than what they had excoriated the Liberals for proposing. All of this tumult and discussion over what popular governance in the modern world should look like, and how much of the population was ready to participate in politics intelligently, resisting the blandishments of demagogues, dominated the upper levels of English life and politics in the very period that Cardwell and Carnarvon were engineering the Confederation talks, and also when Carnarvon and his officials were moving the British North America Bill through parliament. The debates on the nature of democracy at home had to affect those on the nature of Canadian democracy in some way.

One older current of opinion in Great Britain – and we saw something of this view reflected when Arthur Gordon dismissed the politicians of New Brunswick as corrupt and jobbing – was that Canada was too small and too undeveloped to be able to govern itself without falling prey to the inevitable demagoguery. So when Confederation was first discussed in the late 1850s, T.F. Elliot of the Colonial Office wrote that the proposed federal body could never referee interprovincial disputes, because federations are always too weak to do so; while if the new federation were

> restricted to objects of a really federal character, it may well be doubtful whether they will have business enough to occupy them, and in that case, there will arise the risk that men placed in so high a station, without sufficient legitimate employment, will turn their attention to objects which might prove mischievous or dangerous.[32]

And yet for all of that Elliot was *less* hostile to the proposed federation than Colonial Secretary Edward Bulwer-Lytton, who was his chief. Indeed, Bulwer-Lytton personally derailed Confederation in the late 1850s without ever quite explaining why. But something of an explanation can be teased out. Politically a Tory, in his role as a prolific novelist and cultural critic Bulwer-Lytton had pondered in a number of writings that key question of whether democracy must decline into demagoguery – and whether democracy must fail in this way in England itself. As colonial secretary he seems to decide that the Confederation proposal being put forward by a single party in Canada was an example of the demagoguery that one might well expect, and so it needed to be stopped, and stopped privately rather than with any publicity.[33] As Bulwer-Lytton explained the matter in a letter to Henry Drummond Wolff, "democracy" threatened the world and could not be prevented from taking over everywhere. English society was already marked by a democratic struggle for dominance and survival, and so was colonial society.[34]

As something like democracy in Great Britain approached in 1867, not everyone would see Canada in this way, as the harbinger of populism and political decline. Even the Tory leadership of the United Kingdom felt itself swept along towards widening the franchise, and there seemed to be few who disagreed that this was where the nation needed to go.[35] With this mood of democratic enthusiasm in the British political classes, Canada might provide an example of what might go right with democracy, not what must go wrong with it. It was against this background that in the spring of 1867 Henry Reeve noticed in the *Edinburgh Review* a very detailed new book on British parliamentary practice. It was written not by a Westminster expert but by none other than the clerk of the Legislative Assembly of Canada, Alpheus Todd. Reeve (Alexis de Tocqueville's first English translator) used this proof of Canadian parliamentary expertise to embrace, on his own part, the similarity of Mother Country and colony at this moment of democratic optimism:

> We trust that the publication of so sensible a book by a Canadian gentleman, at this time, may be propitious to the constitutional welfare of the Great Northern Confederation now about to be inaugurated with the cordial good wishes of the British people; and we hope that the future statesmen of that nation will never forget that if their independence is to be maintained, it will be by contrasting the principles of British Parliamentary Government in Canada with the purely republican and democratic institutions of the United States.[36]

The governing principle that united the United Kingdom and newly confederated Canada was that of responsible government, Reeve explained – the practice of a government being formed by whichever group had the controlling majority in the lower house and could pass budgets and acts of supply. This system of responsible government contrasted with the older British system of leaving real executive power in the hands of the Crown or the colonial governor, who would then have to look for allies in the legislature. Responsible government, not that many decades old in the United Kingdom itself, was a rare and delicate kind of political system requiring great statesmanship, or so Carnarvon explained at a dinner for the Canadian Confederation delegates, and it was a marvellous thing to see it operating in the United Kingdom and some of its colonies alike.[37]

Yet for all the delicacy and all the political artistry required to maintain this very new Anglo-Saxon hothouse plant of a political system, and for all the pride that Reeve and Carnarvon took in how responsible government had taken root across the British world, to other observers the precise pattern that responsible government must take would have to be different on either side of the Atlantic. Confederated Canada was likely to become more democratic than the Mother Country, some thought, for Canada lacked deep aristocratic traditions.[38]

There were other factors that might also lead towards divergence. Before Confederation, Canada was *already* more democratic than the United Kingdom in at least one respect: the Province of Canada itself had a broad (although not universal) male franchise. Anyone with property *or* an income could vote, and this included almost all men and some women. The situation in the Maritimes was similar.[39] As one British writer noted in 1868, while confederated Canada would retain a property qualification for voting, the social picture was different than in England. Most of the Confederation's new legislators would still have to work for a living in addition to attending to their parliamentary duties. So they would have to work harder than they would have in England to rise above their own daily concerns and think of the public good. Thus they would find it more difficult to master the art of nation-building than did the legislators of Westminster – whose nation was already built in any case.[40]

Still, according to the same analyst, the challenge of carrying on parliamentary government in this more egalitarian society was by no means an insurmountable one. He too had caught the spirit of optimism. For much had already been achieved:

> [Canada] now possesses over and above the parliaments of its several provinces, a federal parliament, by which all matters pertaining to the common interests of the whole, such as defence, fiscal regulations, and

finance, are considered and determined. Thus a "dominion" has been constituted, not unlike, in some respects, its great republican neighbour, and for all practical purposes as free and self-reliant.[41]

Other areas of divergence between the systems of responsible government on either shore of the Atlantic were noted too. The federal element of Confederation attracted some scepticism from British observers, perhaps because federalism did not match anything in British constitutional practice.[42] For many people, the American Civil War stood as only the latest example of how federations tend to be unstable. So there were some who predicted that the confederated provinces in North America would eventually break apart from each other. An alternative would be to allow the provincial governments themselves to decline into municipal-level institutions, with all real power being exercised by Ottawa.

The writers considering these issues also speculated that as democracy advanced in the New World as it would in the Old, Canada would one day separate from Great Britain. It would either become a republic or it would set up its own monarchy under a cadet branch of the royal family. Such were the predictions of Arthur Mills, an official in the Colonial Office.[43] Lord Bury, the founder of the 1868 Colonial Society and MacNab's son-in-law, agreed with most of this. In *The Exodus of the Western Nations*, which he published in 1865, he too looked forward to a unified, independent Canada that would defend itself without outside help. The title of his book bears noting. In two thick tomes, the work follows the locus of Western civilization down through the millennia from the Middle East to Greece, then Rome, then England, then Canada. And so the centre of Western civilization moves on the great circle route, skipping over Iceland on its way to the Great Lakes.[44]

Canada would become independent, but this status would not lessen Great Britain's achievement in helping to create this great country. The *Spectator* made a similar point in 1867:

> It is not by a formal federation, but by the conversion of colonies into allies, bound together by principles formally accepted on both sides, that this great Empire is to be held together. We have much to give – splendid careers, and absolute security; and they also have much to give – trustworthy aid in every quarter of the world, and endless additions to British careers; and it is upon that basis that we and they must at last consent to treat. A great power ringed in with subordinate but most cordial allies, – that, as it seems to us, is the future of Great Britain.[45]

In 1867, then, the questions of democratic nation-building in Canada and in the United Kingdom were running in parallel. The *British North America Act, 1867* and the *Representation of the People Act, 1867* both helped to constitute a democratic nation. On the British side, Confederation came from the way Canadian political and social life could now be imagined as interesting and complex, and worth cultivating still further. Lord Carnarvon helped to imagine the future community of Canada in this way. At the same time, the whole mass of the British political classes were trying to imagine what kind of community should be able to vote within England itself, how educated that community had to be, and how much informed discussion the electorate would be capable of. It was against this background that Carnarvon framed his argument that a confederated Canada, in becoming a larger society, would rise up to the level of informed political discussion which it deserved.

NOTES

1 Andrew Porter, *Absent-Minded Imperialists* (New York: Oxford University Press, 2004); Catherine Hall and Sonya O. Rose, eds., *At Home with the Empire: Metropolitan Life and the Imperial World* (Cambridge: Cambridge University Press, 2006). Patricia Rozema's film *Mansfield Park* (1999) introduces a slave ship where Jane Austen had no such thing.
2 For later perceptions of Canada, reflecting a period of greater imperial consciousness in Great Britain, see R.G. Moyles and Doug Owram, *Imperial Dreams and Colonial Realities: British Views of Canada, 1880–1914* (Toronto: University of Toronto Press, 1988).
3 Of course there was Canadian agency, too, not only in framing the proposals but in dreaming of unity. See L.F.S. Upton, "The Idea of Confederation, 1754–1858," in *The Shield of Achilles: Aspects of Canada in the Victorian Age / Le Bouclier d'Achille: Regards sur la Canada de l'ère victorienne*, ed. W.L. Morton (Toronto and Montreal: McClelland & Stewart, 1968), 184–207.
4 Dilke to his father, 16 March 1867, Dilke Papers, BL Add. MS 43901, fols. 36–8. The passage appears in *Greater Britain* itself in a somewhat cleaned-up version that discusses why, compared to the much larger United States, Canada will always fail to thrive. Charles Dilke, *Greater Britain: A Record of Travel in English-Speaking Countries in 1866 and 1867*, 2 vols. (London: Macmillan, 1868), 1:74–7, quotation, 75. Dilke also explains that America is friendlier to England than Canada is, the colonies cost the poor of England

a lot of money, and in no circumstances would Canada come to Britain's aid in a war over Serbia, 1:80, 2:148–51.

5 Great Exhibition of the Works of Industry of All Nations, *Official Descriptive and Illustrative Catalogue*, 3 vols. (London: Spicer Brothers; W. Clowes and Sons, 1851), 2:963.

6 Ibid.

7 Ibid., 2:968.

8 Great Exhibition, *Catalogue*, 2:971; "Our Colonies," *All the Year Round*, 9 September 1865, 150–3 at 152. See also E.A. Heaman, *The Inglorious Arts of Peace: Exhibitions in Canadian Society during the Nineteenth Century* (Toronto: University of Toronto Press, 1999), 143–50, 167–74. Heaman demonstrates that after making substantial preparations for the Great Exhibition of 1851, the colony of Canada made far less of an effort in the Great Exhibition held in London in 1862, while the Maritimes redeemed their poor performance in 1851 by sending more substantial exhibits to the later exhibition.

9 Great Exhibition, *Catalogue*, 2:957, 962. For more about the fire engine and another like it, both produced by the politically important Perry family, see Heamon, *Inglorious Arts of Peace*, 148–9, 161–2.

10 *The Times*, 26 January 1867, 7.

11 "With Jean Baptiste," *All the Year Round*, 31 August 1867, 232–7 at 233.

12 "Cuagnawagha," *All the Year Round*, 16 June 1866, 543–8 at 544.

13 "Locomotion in London," *All the Year Round*, 7 March 1868, 295–8 at 298.

14 Andrew Smith, *British Businessmen and Canadian Confederation* (Montreal and Kingston: McGill-Queen's University Press, 2008); J.G. Colmer, *The Canada Club (London): Some Notes on Its Origin, Constitution and Activities* (London: The Canada Club, 1934).

15 H.J.M. Johnston, *British Emigration Policy, 1815–1830: "Shovelling Out Paupers"* (Oxford: Clarendon Press, 1972); Elizabeth Jane Errington, *Emigrant Worlds and Transatlantic Communities: Migration to Upper Canada in the First Half of the Nineteenth Century* (Montreal and Kingston: McGill-Queen's University Press, 2007), chap. 1; John F. Kitto, "East-End Distress and Emigration," *The Times*, 20 September 1867, 4; Maria S. Rye, "Female Emigration," *The Times*, 10 April 1868, 10; "Emigration from the East End," *The Times*, 22 May 1868, 5.

16 [William Howard Russell], "Jacques in the Forest," *Cornhill Magazine* 13, no. 75 (March 1866): 307–15 at 314. In Francis Verney's novel *Stone Edge*, serialized in *Cornhill* in 1867, Canada played the same role as an indistinct forest for the oppressed to move to – this time the oppressed agricultural population of England fifty years before. See [Frances Verney], "Stone Hill," *Cornhill Magazine* 16, no. 93 (September 1867): 323–45 at 335, 337, and 344–5 (the end of the novel). For the period in which the novel is set,

see the first page, which ran in *Cornhill Magazine* 15, no. 89 (May 1867): 586–605 at 586.
17 "With Jean Baptiste," 234–5.
18 Arthur Gordon, *Wilderness Journeys in New Brunswick in 1862–3* (Saint John, NB: J. & A. M'Millan, 1864).
19 Gordon to Gladstone, 27 February 1865, 26 March 1866, given in Paul Knaplund, ed., "Gladstone-Gordon Correspondence, 1851–1896: Selections from the Private Correspondence of a British Prime Minister and a Colonial Governor," *Transactions of the American Philosophical Society*, new series 51, no. 4 (1961): 1–116 at 45–8; J.K. Chapman, *The Career of Arthur Hamilton Gordon, First Lord Stanmore: 1829–1912* (Toronto: University of Toronto Press, 1964), chap. 2; Ged Martin, *Britain and the Origins of Canadian Confederation, 1837–67* (Vancouver: UBC Press, 1995), 252–3.
20 "The Grievance of Nova Scotia," *Spectator*, 6 October 1866, 1103–5; "The Grand Remonstrance from Nova Scotia," *Spectator*, 4 March 1868, 310–11.
21 Leader, "The British North America Bill," *The Times*, 16 February 1867, 9.
22 Martin, *Britain and the Origins of Canadian Confederation*, chap. 7; W.P. Morrell, *British Colonial Policy in the Mid-Victorian Age* (Oxford: Clarendon Press, 1969), 110–11, 116–17, 446.
23 *House of Lords Debates*, 19 February 1867, vol. 185, cc575–7.
24 Ibid.
25 Edward Beasley, *Empire as the Triumph of Theory: Imperialism, Information, and the Colonial Society of 1868* (London: Routledge, 2005); Edward Beasley, *Mid-Victorian Imperialists: British Gentlemen and the Empire of the Mind* (London: Routledge, 2005).
26 C.P. Stacey, "Britain's Withdrawal from North America, 1864–1871," *Canadian Historical Review* 36 (September 1955): 185–98. For the idea that any money spent on defending Canada or keeping troops there was a waste, and that Canada could only be defended by a wider attack on the United States far away from the border, see Robert Lowe in the House of Commons in 1865: *House of Commons Debates*, 13 March 1865, vol. 177, cc1578–85.
27 Disraeli to Derby, 30 September 1866, given in Michel Pharand, Ellen H. Hawman, Mary S. Millar, Sandra den Otter, and M.G. Wiebe, eds., *Benjamin Disraeli Letters*, vol. 9, 1865–1867 (Toronto: University of Toronto Press, 2013), 9:158–61. For more of Disraeli's willingness to defend Canada in the near term, see *House of Commons Debates*, 13 March 1865, vol. 177, cc1576–7.
28 Bury to Edmund Head, 5 December 1855, given in Great Britain Parliament, *Copies or Extracts of Recent Correspondence Respecting Alterations in the Organization of the Indian Department in Canada*, no. 247 (1856), 16–37; Beasley, *Empire as the Triumph of Theory*, chap. 6.

29 "Cuagnawagha," 544.
30 Ibid., 545, 547.
31 Catherine Hall, "The Nation Within and Without," in *Defining the Victorian Nation: Class, Race, Gender, and the Reform Act of 1867*, ed. Catherine Hall, Keith McClelland, and Jane Rendall (Cambridge: Cambridge University Press, 2000), 179–233; Satnam Virdee, *Racism, Class, and the Racialized Outsider* (Basingstoke: Palgrave Macmillan, 2014), 58–9.
32 Given in Reginald G. Trotter, "The British Government and the Proposal of Federation in 1858," *Canadian Historical Review* 14, no. 3 (September 1933): 285–92 at 287–9.
33 I summarize and comment on the historical literature on this topic in my book *Mid-Victorian Imperialists*, chap. 7.
34 Bulwer-Lytton to Henry Drummond Wolff, 1 April 1859, given in Victor Bulwer-Lytton, *The Life of Edward Bulwer, First Lord Lytton*, 2 vols. (London: Macmillan and Co., 1913), 1:308.
35 [Henry Reeve], "Todd on Parliamentary Government," *Edinburgh Review* 19, no. 256 (April 1867): 578–96.
36 Ibid., 579.
37 "The Canada Club," *The Times*, 10 January 1867, 9.
38 [James Moncrieff], "Extension of the Franchise," *Edinburgh Review* 123, no. 251 (January 1866): 288.
39 John Garner, *The Franchise and Politics in British North America* (Ottawa: University of Toronto Press, 1969); Janet Ajzenstat, *Once and Future Canadian Democracy: An Essay in Political Thought* (Montreal and Kingston: McGill-Queen's University Press, 2003), 61, 168–9.
40 [John Robinson], "Colonial Parliaments," *Cornhill Magazine* 18, no. 106 (October 1868): 486.
41 [Robinson], "Colonial Parliaments," 484.
42 Duncan Bell, *The Idea of Greater Britain: Empire and the Future of World Order, 1860–1900* (Princeton and Oxford: Princeton University Press, 2007), 94–7. Bell goes on to show that Canadian Confederation helped to inspire schemes to create a federal structure for the whole empire.
43 [Mills], "Report of the Resolutions," 195–9. For more on Mills, see my *Mid-Victorian Imperialists*, chap. 2. For another evocation of Canadian self-reliance and independence, see J.B. Smith, *House of Commons Debates*, 6 April 1865, vol. 178, c828.
44 Lord Bury [William Coutts Keppel, later 7th Earl of Albemarle], *The Exodus of the Western Nations*, 2 vols. (London: Richard Bentley, 1865).
45 "The Reorganization of the British Empire," *Spectator*, 5 January 1867, 7–8.

10 The Impact of Canadian Confederation in Ireland

THOMAS MOHR

Canadian Influence before Confederation

The strongest link between Canada and Ireland has always been people. Countless sea voyages brought Irish emigrants across the Atlantic to Canada in the nineteenth and twentieth centuries where their more numerous descendants still thrive. Political models for self-government and autonomy also travelled across the Atlantic but in the other direction. In the nineteenth and twentieth centuries constitutional models developed in Canada were promoted as realistic solutions to the perennial Irish question. Why Canada? Canada provided the first laboratory within the British Empire for experiments in granting responsible government and in creating federal political systems. In the first half of the nineteenth century Canada presented Irish nationalists with a working model of autonomy that did not challenge the integrity of the Empire.

The emergence of responsible government in Canada in the 1840s had a powerful impact on contemporary Irish politics. The nationalist writer Thomas Davis imagined that Canada was calling to Ireland across the Atlantic, "Sister Ireland, my chains are breaking. Why sleepest thou, oh! my sister?"[1] In later decades Irish politicians would parody British politicians of the 1830s and 1840s who had made dire predictions when opposing the prospect of responsible government in Canada. These included predictions of civil war and the emergence of "a French Republic in Lower Canada."[2] This mockery was intended to discredit similar predictions of doom concerning the creation of an autonomous Irish parliament in the late nineteenth and early twentieth centuries.

The Irish liberal politician William Sharman Crawford was an early voice in promoting the adoption of the Canadian model for Ireland in the 1840s. In 1844 Crawford created a draft bill to establish a local legislature for Ireland that was modelled on the Canadian *Act of Union* of 1840. The provisions of the bill linked the legislative powers of a future Irish parliament to the position of Canada in key areas such as religion, custom duties, and the exchequer.³ Crawford's plans never came close to capturing the support of the constitutional nationalist movement in Ireland in the mid-nineteenth century, but they did represent the future. Proposals for constitutional reform that followed Canadian models offered a more realistic and, on close inspection, a more desirable solution than the more popular alternative of restoring the status quo that had existed in Ireland before it had been incorporated into the United Kingdom in 1801.

Irish nationalists always had mixed feelings concerning the Canadian *Act of Union* of 1840 that would set the stage for the development of responsible government on the far side of the Atlantic. Irish nationalists acknowledged its perceived association with the Durham Report, which had advocated the granting of responsible government in Canada.⁴ On the other hand, they insisted that the union of the provinces of Upper and Lower Canada had been based on the precedent of the Irish *Acts of Union* of 1800. Durham himself had actually described the Irish and Scottish *Acts of Union* as successful expedients for "compelling the obedience of a refractory population."⁵ This led Daniel O'Connell, leader of the constitutional nationalist movement in Ireland until his death in 1847, to protest that an unequal union was being forced on the French Canadians just as one had been forced on the Irish in 1801.⁶ O'Connell insisted that "[t]here was example enough of the effect of such an unequal union in the case of Ireland."⁷

Confederation

Irish reactions to Canadian Confederation in 1867 comprise three important aspects. The first was that attention to Confederation was often overshadowed by reactions to the Fenian raids on the British North American colonies.⁸ The second concerns the Irish "Father of Confederation," Thomas D'Arcy McGee. Although Irish newspapers did pay close attention to McGee's political career, he was seldom mentioned in connection with the achievement of Canadian Confederation in 1867. This omission may have been a consequence of McGee's exclusion from the substantive negotiations at the London Conference of 1866 and 1867 that hammered out the final form of the *British North America Act, 1867*.⁹

In 1867 and 1868 the attention of Irish newspapers was focused on McGee's electoral fortunes, his reactions to the Fenian raids, and finally on his assassination in Ottawa and subsequent funeral in Montreal.[10]

The third aspect of Irish reactions to Canadian Confederation in 1867 reflects the long-established unionist/nationalist division. Irish unionists in parliament and in the press overwhelmingly welcomed the advent of Confederation. Chichester Fortescue, a Whig member of parliament (MP) for County Louth, welcomed "the birth of a large British community in North America" and was confident that a bright future awaited the new Dominion.[11] Unionists often contrasted the loyalty of the people of the embryonic Dominion of Canada, as shown by their determined resistance to the Fenian raids, with the unhappy position of Ireland in 1867. Earl Beauchamp noted: "We should all be heartily glad if the same love of peace and desire for union which prevails in our North American Colonies existed in every other portion of the British Empire."[12] It should be remembered that the Fenians were active in Ireland itself as well as in North America. Beauchamp and others contrasted Canadian rejection of Fenianism with the "widely-spread conspiracy" that had taken root in Ireland in 1867.[13]

The *Irish Times*, a liberal unionist newspaper in the 1860s, was strongly supportive of the process of Canadian Confederation. It maintained a correspondent in Canada who provided extensive details on the military and economic prospects of the proposed Dominion.[14] Opponents of Canadian Confederation at Westminster were dismissed as "crotchety men … who don't believe in the retention of these colonies at all."[15] The arguments made by these opponents of Confederation were dismissed as being "weak and unpatriotic."[16] The *Irish Times* had no objection to the proposal that the new Confederation be called a "kingdom," but did have difficulties with the official use of the name "Canada" on the grounds that it excluded the identity of the Maritime provinces. The newspaper preferred the "United Provinces of British North America" or the "United Provinces of Canada and Acadia." However, the *Irish Times* conceded that the new Confederation could be called "Canada" for short in an unofficial capacity, just as the name "England" was often used in this period to refer to the United Kingdom of Great Britain and Ireland. Alternatively, it suggested that the new entity could be called the "United Provinces" in similar fashion to the designation of its southern neighbour as the "United States."[17]

The reaction to Canadian Confederation in 1867 among nationalist newspapers varied between indifference and outright hostility.

The second response was most apparent in the nationalist newspaper *The Nation*. It insisted that the *British North America Act, 1867* had been passed in unseemly haste and that the entire scheme of Canadian Confederation had been motivated by underlying fears of annexation by the United States of America and by the immediate impact of the Fenian raids. In this context *The Nation* mocked Confederation by asking, "Does the mighty Briton retire from the field before American menace and Irish impetuosity?"[18]

Some British parliamentarians drew analogies between Canadian Confederation and the 1801 union between Great Britain and Ireland during the Westminster debates that preceded the enactment of the *British North America Act, 1867*. The events in Ireland of 1800 and 1801 were used as a precedent to show that a political union might legitimately take place without directly consulting the electorate, as was being proposed for British North America in 1867.[19] These comparisons were not lost on Irish nationalists, who began drawing similar analogies but from a very different perspective. As noted earlier, Irish nationalists had once compared the Canadian *Act of Union* of 1840 with the Irish *Acts of Union* of 1800 to support the argument that French Canadians were being forced into a union against their will. In the late 1860s a similar comparison with the Irish *Acts of Union* was used in relation to Nova Scotia to support the argument that a forced union had taken place.[20] The pro-Confederation *Irish Times* admitted difficulties with Nova Scotia but liked to stress, as a counterweight, the strong desire expressed by British Columbia, parts of the Northwest Territories, and Rupert's Land to join the new Dominion.[21]

A good example of Irish nationalists making use of Nova Scotia to attack Confederation is reflected in an article that appeared in *The Nation* on the public ceremonies in British North America that took place in July 1867. According to *The Nation*, the celebrations "fell dead on the public mind generally, and there were unmistakable evidences, especially at Halifax, of a wide-spread discontent at the involuntary Confederation forced upon the people of the provinces by the British government and its agents." This newspaper added, "Such was the feeling in Halifax, that flags were hung at half-mast, and half the stores closed, as if for death, and two of the daily papers appeared with their columns in mourning."[22] *The Nation* often emphasized the unhappy position of Nova Scotia in the Dominion of Canada in the late 1860s, while the *Freeman's Journal* concluded that this province would have been more prosperous if it had instead joined the United States of America.[23]

The unhappy position of Nova Scotia provided a useful basis for comparisons with Ireland's place in the United Kingdom. *The Nation* asked its readers, "We would now ask is there one single evil feature in connexion with this Canadian 'Union' which does not apply with tenfold force to the Union – the untouched Union – of this island with Great Britain."[24] The position of Nova Scotia also proved useful in accusing the British press of hypocrisy. *The Nation* argued, "The organs of public opinion in England are with the Nova Scotians in their demands. But let Ireland ask for the same, on a thousand-fold stronger grounds, and we are immediately told by the same journals that our demands are absurd and can never be granted."[25]

Yet there was also evidence of a very different attitude among some Irish nationalists in 1867, in particular among the diaspora in Canada. *The Nation* reported a speech made in April 1867 by Bernard Devlin, president of the St Patrick's Society of Montreal and a notorious enemy of Thomas D'Arcy McGee,[26] in which he concluded that Ireland should have "the same liberty and freedom as Canada – a legislature of its own, and a government of its own people." Devlin was confident that if all this were granted, "Fenianism would soon die out."[27] In late 1868 *The Nation* reprinted an article from the *Irish Canadian* newspaper that concluded with the hope that "Ireland may lawfully claim, and will yet obtain, what has made Canada what it is, a free nation and a great people, bearing but a nominal friendship to England, while she retains the fostering protection of the British Empire."[28] In early 1868 a letter from an anonymous correspondent was published in the *Irish Times* advocating that Ireland be granted autonomy within a federal United Kingdom in a settlement modelled in many particulars on the new Dominion of Canada.[29] These attitudes towards the new Dominion and the nature of Canadian Confederation soon became dominant among constitutional nationalists in Ireland and overwhelmed the initial hostility voiced in 1867.

The 1870s saw the emergence of a campaign for a new form of parliamentary autonomy in Ireland while remaining within the embrace of the United Kingdom, an objective that was popularly known as "home rule." Its emphasis on the Canadian model was evident from the outset and grew with the passage of time. Isaac Butt, founder of the Irish Parliamentary Party, popularly known as the "Home Rule Party," had seen the potential offered by Canadian Confederation earlier than most Irish nationalists. Butt praised the model offered by Canadian Confederation for an autonomous Ireland within a federal United Kingdom in his 1870 publication *Irish Federalism*.[30] He concluded, "Why should not the self-government which has made Canada contented and loyal be equally successful in Ireland in attaining the same results?"[31] This argument, based on glorification of the Durham Report and the *British North America Act, 1867*, would become deeply entrenched in the canon of Irish constitutional nationalism.[32]

The Nature of the Canadian Model

Canada was presented by constitutional nationalists as offering a model for Ireland in three distinct areas: federalism, tolerance, and autonomy. The first of these concerned turning the United Kingdom into a federation along similar lines to the Dominion of Canada with Ireland, Scotland, Wales, and England forming separate provinces. This solution had advocates in Canada itself, for example the future prime minister William Lyon Mackenzie King.[33] The Canadian analogy ensured that these federal schemes could be presented as being entirely consistent with the laws and traditions of the British Empire. Proposals to federate the United Kingdom, popularly known as "home rule all round," could also be built into even more ambitious schemes to federate the British Empire as a whole, an ideal known as "Imperial federation." One difficulty with these federal schemes concerned the position of England. Should it be retained as a single "province," or, as a consequence of its considerable population, should it be subdivided into several autonomous areas? Another difficulty concerned the position of Scotland and Wales, which in the nineteenth and early twentieth centuries did not possess campaigns for autonomy that could in any way be compared with that in Ireland. Irish nationalists argued that they could not wait while Scotland and Wales caught up.[34] This lag meant that Ireland would have to strike out alone and set the foundations for a future federal United Kingdom. Irish unionists responded that if the United Kingdom must be federalized, Ulster should have its own autonomous "Canadian province," separate from the rest of Ireland.[35] Most Irish nationalists rejected these calls and so were placed in the awkward situation of promoting the merits of autonomy in one context while denying it in another.

Canada was also promoted as a model for Ireland in terms of tolerance. In 1885 Charles Gavan Duffy, an Irish nationalist and former premier of the Australian state of Victoria, recalled meeting the Canadian delegates sent to London to negotiate the final stages of Confederation in 1866 and 1867. He concluded that the Canadian delegates were "an encouraging spectacle for an Irish nationalist to see," as they were a mixture of Catholics and Protestants and persons of British, Irish, and French descent. Duffy noted, "The old antagonists have become friends and colleagues. I could not fail to reflect that on the same conditions we, too, could make our country prosperous and glorious."[36] He would later write an article analysing the provisions of the *British North America Act, 1867* with the conclusion, "What we may learn from Canada is how races long hostile have come to live peacefully, and to work harmoniously, together. The lesson is a very simple one – it is by respecting their separate rights, and carefully sheltering them from the possibility of invasion."[37] Thomas D'Arcy McGee had made similar arguments in the 1860s, including shortly before his assassination.[38]

The province of Quebec attracted particular attention in the context of promoting values of tolerance. It was touted by Irish nationalists as proof that a Protestant minority could prosper free from discrimination under a Catholic majority.[39] Unionists responded by arguing that the position of the Protestant minority in Quebec was not nearly as enviable as nationalists liked to argue. One unionist concluded, "Those who know Ireland are well aware that a Dublin Parliament, like the Quebec Legislature, would be at the mercy of the priests."[40]

The third aspect regarding the use of Canada as a model for Ireland concerned nationalist hopes of autonomy from London. This model had a competitor drawn from the Irish past in the form of the parliament in Dublin that had existed before the Irish *Acts of Union*. This Irish parliament had enjoyed an exceptional degree of autonomy between 1782 and 1801. This period was later associated with Henry Grattan, one of the leading figures in the Irish parliament, and became popularly known as "Grattan's parliament." However, memories of Grattan's parliament became heavily romanticized in the years that followed its abolition, and its many failings were largely forgotten. In any case, a literal restoration of the antiquated and, with the benefit of unsentimental scrutiny, undesirable model provided by an eighteenth century all-Protestant parliament was no longer a realistic objective by the late nineteenth century.[41] By contrast, the model provided by Canada offered a practical and successful example of autonomy within the British Empire. In any case, Irish politicians found ingenious ways of uniting the Canadian model with the popular and heavily idealized image of Grattan's parliament. John Redmond, leader of the Irish

Parliamentary Party from 1900 to 1918, insisted that Irish nationalists were asking "for a parliament as free at least from English control as was the parliament of Grattan, and for a constitution as free at least as that under which the Australian colonies and Canada had become not only prosperous but contented."[42]

One of the great advantages of drawing analogies with Canada was in persuading sceptical British audiences that the objective of Irish home rule was perfectly consistent with the history and traditions of the British Empire. The most important British convert to the cause of Irish home rule was the Liberal leader William Ewart Gladstone, who had served as colonial secretary during the 1840s when responsible government was developing in Canada. When he returned to power as prime minister in 1886, the prospect of Irish home rule inched closer to reality.

Gladstone began his research into how a scheme for Irish home rule might operate in 1885. One of his first actions was to order copies of the Canadian *Act of Union* of 1840 and the *British North America Act, 1867*. This was a logical course of action as Canada had provided Westminster with its first and most prominent example of granting responsible government and enhanced autonomy to a constituent part of the British Empire. Gladstone made extensive use of the 1867 Act during the drafting of the first Irish Home Rule Bill that was presented to parliament in 1886.[43] By the end of the drafting process, Gladstone's copy of the *British North America Act, 1867* was heavily defaced, with key phrases underlined and many annotations in the margins.[44] The heavy reliance on the 1867 Act was also evident in the structure and contents of the first home rule bill itself.

The 1886 bill, which served as the model for all subsequent home rule legislation, began with the familiar reference to creating a legislature in Ireland to make laws for "peace, order and good government."[45] Executive authority would be vested in the King or Queen, as in Canada, and would be exercised by a representative of the Crown who was intended to perform a similar role to his equivalent under the *British North America Act, 1867*.[46] John Kendle has observed that Gladstone "often lifted whole phrases, even clauses, in the preparation of his first draft" from the *British North America Act, 1867*.[47] A good example was Section 91 of the 1867 Act dealing with the legislative powers of the Canadian parliament, which was substantially reproduced in the Irish bill.[48] The power of the Crown to withhold royal assent to Canadian legislation was also reproduced in the Irish bill.[49] Gladstone reassured Irish nationalists, "It shall be understood that the Royal Veto shall be exercised upon the same principles as in the Dominion of Canada and other great legislative dependencies of the Crown."[50] The final arbiter of the limits of Irish autonomy would be a court that sat in London known as the "Judicial Committee of the Privy Council."[51] This mirrored the position in Canada in which the Judicial Committee of the Privy Council served as the final arbiter of the provisions of the *British North America Act, 1867*. No Irish MPs were to sit at Westminster under the 1886 bill, although this would be reversed in future measures for Irish home rule.[52] The parliament at Westminster retained the amending power in relation to the *British North America Act, 1867* and in relation to all the measures intended to grant Irish home rule.

Prime Minister Gladstone made numerous references to Canada and the *British North America Act, 1867* when promoting his Irish Home Rule Bill during parliamentary debates at Westminster.[53] The use of parallels with the 1867 Act proved useful in refuting allegations that Gladstone was breaking with precedent and attempting to create new constitutional principles. In addition, Gladstone attempted to convince parliament that granting responsible government would strengthen and not weaken the imperial link in Ireland, just as it had in Canada. Gladstone quoted Charles Gavan Duffy when introducing the first home rule bill to the House of Commons: "When it was determined to confer Home Rule on Canada, Canada was in the precise temper attributed to Ireland. She did not get Home Rule because she is loyal and friendly, but she is loyal and friendly because she got Home Rule."[54] Gladstone was aware that there were dangers in pushing the analogy with Canada too far and insisted that his home rule bill was "not parallel" but "strictly and substantially analogous" to the *British North America Act, 1867*.[55] The bill appeared to give Ireland more autonomy than a Canadian province but less than the Dominion of Canada as a whole. For example, the legislative competence of the Canadian provinces was limited to a number of named areas under the *British North America Act, 1867*, while the proposed Irish parliament would have full legislative powers with the exception of a number of named areas.[56] On the other hand, the anticipated Irish parliament would not have equivalent autonomy to the Dominion of Canada in the important spheres of defence, taxation, currency, and trade.[57] There were also far more stringent religious safeguards in the Irish bill than existed in the *British North America Act, 1867*.[58] Nevertheless the link with Canada was now firmly planted in the public consciousness, and *The Times* summarized Gladstone's policy as being one of "Ireland as Canada."[59]

The Irish Home Rule Bill of 1886 was defeated in the British House of Commons but survived as the model for the subsequent home rule measures of 1893, 1914, and 1920. Consequently, Canadian influence remained intact in the structure and content of the various proposals for Irish home rule. In addition, the parallels between Ireland and Canada and the other self-governing colonies promoted by Gladstone became further entrenched in public discourse concerning Irish home rule. These parallels provided a major incentive for the Irish Parliamentary Party to recruit Canadian politicians of Irish descent into its ranks. Examples include Charles Ramsay Devlin, a former MP in the Canadian parliament who became an MP at Westminster in 1903 for the Irish Parliamentary Party. Even more important was Edward Blake, former leader of the Canadian Liberal Party and an expert on the Canadian constitution, who joined the ranks of the Irish Parliamentary Party as an MP at Westminster in 1892.

By the early twentieth century analogies with Canada and the other self-governing dominions had become so common among supporters of Irish home rule that L.S. Amery, a future colonial secretary, could conclude:

> There is no argument in favour of Home Rule for Ireland which is more frequently used to-day than that which is based on the analogy of our Colonial experience ... The ablest, as well as the most courageous, piece of Home Rule advocacy which has so far appeared, Mr Erskine Childers's "Framework of Home Rule" is based from first to last on this analogy and on little else.[60]

Childers' book, published in 1911, contained a lengthy account of Canadian constitutional history, including the achievement of Confederation, and drew numerous parallels to contemporary Ireland. Childers even recommended that the process of establishing responsible government in Canada "ought to be studied carefully by every voter, however lowly, who has a voice in deciding the fate of Irish Home Rule."[61]

Unionists also made use of Canadian analogies to attack the objective of Irish home rule. Some unionists were satisfied to simply deny that any accurate comparisons could be made between the situations of Ireland and Canada on the grounds of geography and history. Others argued that nationalists needed to clarify their intentions when they used Canada as a model for their ambitions. Was Ireland being compared to a Canadian province such as Ontario or Quebec, or to the

Dominion of Canada as a whole? In other words, were the proposed relations between Ireland and Westminster under a home rule settlement to be analogous to the relationship between Ontario and the federal institutions in Ottawa, or would they be analogous to the relationship between Ottawa and London? Many unionists found the first analogy troubling, while the second analogy provoked outright horror.[62] They were convinced that granting Ireland the status of Canada as a whole would undermine any effective oversight from London. Unionists pointed out that many of the constitutional limits on Canadian autonomy under the *British North America Act, 1867* had proved to be ineffective in practice.[63] Would constitutional limits on Irish autonomy prove equally ineffective under a future home rule settlement? Unionists insisted that even if these limits were effective, the autonomous Irish authorities would exploit every opportunity to dismantle them.[64] They were convinced that granting Canadian autonomy to Ireland would give almost full sovereignty to a people who could not be compared to Canadians in terms of their past, present, and future attitudes towards the United Kingdom and the British Empire.[65] In addition, unionists and many dominion statesmen insisted that responsible government had only been granted to the dominions because great distances had precluded their representation at Westminster.[66] These realities imposed by vast geographical distance simply did not apply to Ireland. Unionists had little doubt that the granting of full Canadian autonomy would place Ireland on a path to complete independence.[67]

The absence of clarity in drawing parallels between Ireland and Canada was a constant feature of Irish politics in the late nineteenth and early twentieth centuries. On some occasions members of the Irish Parliamentary Party claimed that Ireland was seeking the autonomy of a Canadian province, while on other occasions they drew analogies between Ireland and the Dominion of Canada as a whole.[68] Thomas Sexton, a prominent member of the Irish Parliamentary Party, attempted to smooth over the lack of clarity on this vital issue by arguing, "The analogy between Canada and Ireland rests not on details but on principles."[69] It was necessary for the Irish Parliamentary Party to maintain a certain amount of ambiguity, as many Irish nationalists were not prepared to accept a final settlement that placed Ireland in the same position as a Canadian province. This was made clear to John Redmond in 1910 when a severe backlash forced him to repudiate a newspaper interview in which he had suggested that Ireland was only seeking the level of autonomy enjoyed by the Canadian provinces.[70]

Unionists attacked all the proposed legislative measures for Irish home rule on the basis that they offered far more legislative powers than those enjoyed by the Canadian provinces.[71] They were seldom convinced by arguments that Irish home rule would be the first step in creating a federal United Kingdom in which Ireland "is to be set up as an experimental Quebec, and the other provinces will follow suit shortly."[72] Some nationalists openly admitted that the whole idea of Irish autonomy being slotted into a wider federal settlement was a chimera.[73] Unionists remained convinced that Irish home rule would not create a federation. "What it will set up will be a national or Dominion government in Ireland, separate and exclusive, but subject to certain restrictions and interferences which it will be the first business of the Irish representatives, in Dublin or Westminster, to get rid of."[74] They asked whether a Dominion such as Canada, having achieved union, would now tolerate the secession of one its component parts.[75] Unionists also liked to point out that John A. Macdonald had made it clear that he would have preferred union to Confederation in Canada under ideal circumstances.[76]

Conclusion

The absence of clarity as to whether Irish constitutional nationalists were advocating autonomy for Ireland along the lines of a Canadian province or whether they were aiming for the autonomy enjoyed by the Dominion of Canada as a whole was a major stumbling block in the late nineteenth century campaigns for Irish home rule. This ambiguity was finally resolved in the changed circumstances of the twentieth century and in the aftermath of the Easter 1916 rising. In 1922 a new "Irish Free State" that comprised most of the island of Ireland was recognized by Westminster as having the same constitutional status within the British Empire as the Dominion of Canada.[77] Yet all this lay in an unknowable future during the home rule debates of the Victorian and Edwardian periods. In these years the persistent refusal of leading members of the Irish Parliamentary Party to clarify their ambitions added fuel to unionist distrust. Did the leaders of the Irish Parliamentary Party really want a final settlement based on autonomy within the United Kingdom, or were they searching for a pathway towards a fully sovereign state such as that being gradually forged by Canada after 1867? In this way the impact of Canadian Confederation on nineteenth century Ireland can be seen as a double-edged sword. It provided a model that could be used in campaigns for greater Irish autonomy, but also stirred up powerful incentives to resist this movement whatever the cost.

NOTES

1 Richard Davis, *The Young Ireland Movement* (Dublin: Gill and Macmillan, 1987), 212–3.
2 See *Hansard*, House of Commons, 21 May 1886, vol. 305, col. 1750–2; 25 May 1886, vol. 306, col. 127.
3 B.A. Kennedy, "Sharman Crawford's Federal Scheme for Ireland," in *Essays in British and Irish History*, ed. H.A. Cronne et al. (London: Muller, 1949), 235–54.
4 For example, see Erskine Childers, *The Framework of Home Rule* (London: Arnold, 1911), 94–9. A more skeptical perspective on the significance of the Durham Report is found in Ged Martin, "The Influence of the Durham Report," in *Reappraisals in British Imperial History*, ed. Ronald Hyam and Ged Martin (Toronto: Macmillan, 1975), 75–87.
5 Report on the Affairs of British North America, General Review and Recommendation, accessed 1 November 2016, https://en.wikisource.org/wiki/Report_on_the_Affairs_of_British_North_America/General_Review_and_Recommendation.
6 *Hansard*, House of Commons, 3 June 1839, vol. 47, col. 1286–7. The Irish *Acts of Union* of 1800 came into force on 1 January 1801.
7 *Hansard*, House of Commons, 3 June 1839, vol. 47, col. 1287.
8 See chapter three by William Jenkins in this volume.
9 David A. Wilson, *Thomas D'Arcy McGee*, vol. 2, *The Extreme Moderate, 1857–1868* (McGill-Queen's University Press, 2011), 288–90, 295–6.
10 For example, see "Canada," *Irish Times*, 1 October 1867, 3; "A Protest from Canada," *The Nation*, 9 June 1866, 9–10; "Ireland and Canada," *Anglo-Celt*, 2 May 1868, 2; "Assassination of D'Arcy McGee," *Irish Times*, 24 April 1868, 3; "Funeral of the Late Hon. D'Arcy M'Gee," *Irish Times*, 1 May 1868, 4.
11 *Hansard*, House of Commons, 28 February 1867, vol. 185, col. 1195.
12 *Hansard*, House of Lords, 5 February 1867, vol. 185, col. 10.
13 *Hansard*, House of Lords, 5 February 1867, vol. 185, col. 10–11.
14 "Canada," *Irish Times*, 23 January 1867, 4; "Canada," *Irish Times*, 22 March 1867, 3.
15 "Canada," *Irish Times*, 22 March 1867, 3.
16 Ibid.
17 Ibid.

18 "British American Confederation," *The Nation*, 9 March 1867, 9–10.
19 For example, see *Hansard*, House of Lords, 19 February 1867, vol. 185, col. 580–1; 26 February 1867, vol. 185, col. 1012.
20 "A Political Parallel," *The Nation*, 4 April 1868, 10.
21 "Canadian Difficulties," *Irish Times*, 21 October 1867, 4.
22 "Canada," *The Nation*, 20 July 1867, 3.
23 "A Political Parallel," *The Nation*, 4 April 1868, 10; "Editorial," *Freeman's Journal*, 26 December 1868, 2.
24 "A Political Parallel," *The Nation*, 4 April 1868, 10.
25 Ibid.
26 Wilson, *Thomas D'Arcy McGee*, vol. 2, 308–11.
27 "A Voice from Canada for an Irish Parliament," *The Nation*, 27 April 1867, 6.
28 "Give Ireland What Canada Has," *The Nation*, 9 September 1868, 12.
29 "Correspondence – The Irish Question, letter from G.T.M.," *Irish Times*, 6 January 1868, 4.
30 Isaac Butt, *Home Government for Ireland: Irish Federalism! Its Meaning, Its Objects and Its Hopes*, 1st ed. (Dublin: John Falconer, 1870).
31 Isaac Butt, *Home Government for Ireland: Irish Federalism! Its Meaning, Its Objects and Its Hopes*, 3rd ed. (Dublin: Falconer, 1871), 87.
32 For example, see a review in the *Freeman's Journal* of a pamphlet written by T.P. Gill, an MP with the Irish Parliamentary Party, on "The Home Rule Constitutions of the British Crown," in which he was seen as drawing "a striking parallel" between Canada and Ireland. "The Home Rule Constitutions of the British Crown," *Freeman's Journal*, 25 January 1887, 5.
33 John Kendle, *Ireland and the Federal Solution: The Debate over the United Kingdom Constitution, 1870–1921* (Kingston and Montreal: McGill-Queen's University Press, 1989), 117.
34 Childers, *The Framework of Home Rule*, 199–201.
35 Kendle, *Ireland and the Federal Solution*, 158, 163.
36 "Colonial Constitutions," *Freeman's Journal*, 28 August 1885, 6.
37 "Constitution of Canada," *Freeman's Journal*, 15 October 1885, 5.
38 "Ireland and Canada," *Anglo-Celt*, 2 May 1868, 2.
39 For example, see *Hansard*, House of Commons, 12 April 1893, vol. 11, col. 159–60.
40 Peter Kerr-Smiley, *The Peril of Home Rule* (London: Cassell, 1911), 74–8.
41 This was admitted by Isaac Butt in the early days of the home rule movement. See Butt, *Home Government for Ireland*, 3rd ed., 1871, 55.
42 "The National League – The Prospects in the North," *Freeman's Journal*, 9 September 1885, 2.
43 Kendle, *Ireland and the Federal Solution*, 35, 41, 44–51.

44 Ibid., 45.
45 Government of Ireland Bill, 1886, Section 2, in *What Home Rule Means Now, with An Appendix Containing the Home Rule Bill of 1886 and Sections 25 to 28 of the Land Purchase Bill of 1886* (Dublin: The Liberal Union of Ireland, 1893), Appendix A. This printed source is also available online at https://archive.org/details/whathomerulemean00dubliala.
46 Government of Ireland Bill, 1886, Sections 7 and 26.
47 Kendle, *Ireland and the Federal Solution*, 45.
48 Government of Ireland Bill, 1886, Section 3.
49 Government of Ireland Bill, 1886, Section 7(2).
50 Alan J. Ward, *The Irish Constitutional Tradition: Representative Government in Modern Ireland, 1782–1992* (Washington, DC: Catholic University of America Press, 1994), 64.
51 Government of Ireland Bill, 1886, Section 25.
52 For example, see Government of Ireland Bill, 1893, Section 9, in *An Examination of the Home Rule Bill of 1893, with an Appendix Containing the Full Text of the Measure Itself* (Dublin: Liberal Union of Ireland, 1893), Appendix. This printed source is also available online at https://archive.org/details/examinationofhom00libe.
53 For example, see *Hansard*, House of Commons, 10 May 1886, vol. 305, col. 585–8; 7 June 1886, vol. 306, col. 1221–30.
54 *Hansard*, House of Commons, 10 May 1886, vol. 305, col. 587.
55 *Hansard*, House of Commons, 10 May 1886, vol. 305, col. 585.
56 *British North America Act 1867*, Sections 92, 93, and 95.
57 Government of Ireland Bill, 1886, Sections 3 and 4.
58 Government of Ireland Bill, 1886, Section 4.
59 "Editorial," *The Times*, 16 April 1886, 9.
60 L.S. Amery, "Home Rule and the Colonial Analogy," in *Against Home Rule: The Case for the Union*, ed. S. Rosenbaum (London: Warne, 1912), 128.
61 See Childers, *The Framework of Home Rule*, 95.
62 For example, see Kendle, *Ireland and the Federal Solution*, 112.
63 For example, see Amery, "Home Rule and the Colonial Analogy," 130; and Ward, *The Irish Constitutional Tradition*, 83–4.
64 See Amery, "Home Rule and the Colonial Analogy," 142.
65 For example, see *Hansard*, House of Commons, 9 April 1886, vol. 304, col. 1194 and 1254.
66 See Amery, "Home Rule and the Colonial Analogy," 131–3.
67 Ibid., 142.
68 Ibid., 129–30; Michael Wheatley, "John Redmond and Federalism in 1910," *Irish Historical Studies* 32 (2001): 343–64.

69 *Hansard*, House of Commons, 1 June 1886, vol. 306, col. 701.
70 See Wheatley, "John Redmond and Federalism in 1910."
71 For example, see *Hansard*, House of Commons, 1 June 1886, vol. 306, col. 694–8.
72 See Amery, "Home Rule and the Colonial Analogy," 141.
73 See Childers, *The Framework of Home Rule*, 198–203, 205–6.
74 See Amery, "Home Rule and the Colonial Analogy," 142.
75 Ibid., 140.
76 Ibid., 147–8.
77 See Article 2 of the "Articles of Agreement for a Treaty between Great Britain and Ireland," in Second Schedule, Constitution of the Irish Free State (Saorstát Éireann) Act, 1922 (Irl).

11 Distant Relations: Australian Perspectives on Canadian Federation

ANN CURTHOYS

When the new nation of Australia was inaugurated on 1 January 1901, Canadian residents of Sydney, headed by the Canadian trade commissioner, participated in the city's celebrations. On their horse-drawn float, surmounted by a blue silk canopy, stood two women holding hands, symbolizing sister nations. One, clothed in white, represented Canada, and the other, clothed in blue, Australia; at the front of the float were the words "Canada welcomes her sister Australia."[1] There had been no equivalent Australian participation, however, at Canada's inauguration celebration thirty-four years earlier, on 1 July 1867. Australia as a nation did not yet exist, and the Australian colonies had little overseas identity. Nevertheless, references to Canadian Confederation in Australia, especially in colonial newspapers – one of the cornerstones of the public sphere in this period – indicated an interest in Confederation framed by Australian colonists' particular ideas and anxieties. While interest at the time was relatively modest, it was to increase two decades later, when the Australian colonies themselves came to face the question of their own federation.

For much of the twentieth century, historians of both Canada and Australia understood their national history as part of a broader British imperial and Commonwealth history. They sought to understand how the political institutions of these societies were forged and the processes whereby they changed from settler colonies under direct British control to largely self-governing settler colonies, to dominions, and ultimately to independent nations.[2] This assumption of a common and connected history declined after the middle of the twentieth century as historians in each country set about developing their own national and sometimes nationalist histories. In the last two decades of the twentieth century, however, political, institutional, and legal developments, as well as a revived historiographical interest in comparative and transnational histories, led to a revival of mutual interest, this time with different historical questions, arising from labour, feminist, immigration, and multicultural histories, in mind.[3] Especially important has been scholarship comparing and connecting the history of Indigenous-settler relations in the two countries, as Indigenous people's claims, especially to land, prompted interest in each other's history, particularly in relation to colonialism and the law.[4] This chapter draws on both the older tradition of imperial political history and more recent concerns with questions of race, gender, and identity.

Australia and Canada: The Broader Framework

Canadian political events of the late 1830s and 1840s had important consequences for the Australian colonies. The rebellions in Upper and Lower Canada in 1837–8, the ensuing Durham Report advocating responsible government, and the subsequent political struggles between Britain and the Canadian colonies all had implications for Britain's settler colonies on the other side of the world. Indeed, Canadian and Australian colonial history came briefly together when over 150 participants in the rebellions of 1837–8 were transported in 1839, the French-speaking rebels to Sydney and the English-speaking to Hobart.[5] The Australian story diverged from the Canadian one, however, in certain crucial ways. Since there was only ever one empire, the British Empire, proclaiming possession of the continent, there was no history of the imperial competition that so marked Canadian history, and consequently, no equivalent of the French-speaking population of the Canadian colonies. Furthermore, the creation of most of the Australian colonies as penal settlements meant the establishment of an authoritarian political system with none of the trappings of legislative assemblies and councils that had been common in North America for two centuries. Yet New South Wales and Van Diemen's Land (Tasmania) were never purely convict colonies, and the growth of free populations and of their colonial economies necessitated the development of several key institutions essential for a freer public sphere: the public meeting, the petition, and a free press. When convict transportation was suspended to New South Wales in 1840 (though continued to Van Diemen's Land), a lively political culture developed, with competing liberal, conservative, and radical ideas jostling for attention. Importantly, suspension of convict transportation in New South Wales allowed the development of a limited form of representative government from 1843.

As a result, when Nova Scotia, New Brunswick, and the United Canadas gained responsible government in the late 1840s, political reformers in New South Wales were in a position to demand something similar for themselves. A mass movement in the late 1840s against British plans to revive convict transportation to New South Wales and to continue it to Van Diemen's Land stimulated stronger demands for self-government. Colonial reformers wanted what they called "the Canadian system" and insisted that what was good enough for the Canadian colonies was good enough for them.[6] Rising political figure Archibald Michie moved at a meeting in Sydney on 18 June 1849 a resolution that the government of the colony "should no longer be administered by the remote, ill-informed, and irresponsible Colonial Office, but by Ministers chosen from and responsible to the colonists themselves, in accordance with the principles of the British constitution."[7] They were following, he said, the views of Lord Durham and Herman Merivale, and the proven example of Canada. Robert Lowe, then a member of the New South Wales Legislative Council and later to become a leading figure in the Gladstone government in Britain, attributed British determination to continue transportation despite overwhelming colonial opposition to their lack of responsible government. Of the forty-five dependencies of the British Crown, he pointed out, only Canada, New Brunswick, and Nova Scotia had responsible government, and it was clear that the British government would never contemplate sending convicts to *them*.[8]

Partly as a means of shifting costs from Britain to the colonies, and partly in order to preserve the loyalty of these increasingly restive British settlers, British authorities by this time were already moving towards granting to the Australian colonies some form of self-government (if not quite the "Canadian system" of responsible government). In doing so, they had to consider the demands from colonists in the southern districts of New South Wales for separation to form a new colony. While sympathetic to these demands, since distance made government from Sydney extremely difficult, Earl Grey, as secretary of state for the colonies, saw a need for some kind of federal mechanism to draw what would now be five colonies closer together; he proposed in 1847 a General Assembly to deal with matters such as import and export duties, railways, and mail services. By this time, colonists of various political persuasions, though wary that it might enhance the power of their local opponents, welcomed self-government, but strongly opposed Grey's plans for a federation. There was, as yet, little sense of a common Australian identity, and proposals coming from the pro-transportationist Grey were in any case automatically suspect. So vociferous was colonial opposition to the proposal for a General Assembly that in 1849 the British government deleted the relevant clauses from the forthcoming bill on Australian colonial government.[9] This ready acquiescence to the Australian colonial refusal to federate provides a telling contrast with British policy in southern Africa a little later, where, as Tim Stapleton shows, federation was imposed with disastrous consequences.[10]

After several years of deliberation, the British parliament passed the *Act for the Better Government of Her Majesty's Australian Colonies, 1850*, which established a framework for the development of greater self-government. The contrast with India clearly indicates a racial dimension to British policy; colonies regarded as being populated by predominantly British settlers were seen as far more ready for self-government than those that were not. Two years later, in 1852, with gold rushes in southeastern Australia transforming the character and size of both the population and the economy, the British government went further, specifically allowing the four eastern Australian colonies to devise constitutions similar to that of the United Canadas.[11] By 1856, Britain had granted responsible government to the colonies of Victoria, New South Wales, South Australia, and Tasmania; when Britain in 1859 formed Queensland from the New South Wales Northern Districts, it gave the new colony responsible government immediately. Only Western Australia, with its small settler population and its new role as a receiver of British convicts, was without responsible, or indeed even representative, government. The colonies would remain separate, with no linking mechanism.

The idea of federation, however, never quite went away. In the early 1850s, there was occasional reference to it, notably by Presbyterian reverend and radical politician John Dunmore Lang, who combined it with republicanism in his notable 1852 text *Freedom and Independence for the Golden Lands of Australia*. While Lang's vision of a federated Australian republic was too radical for most, it was not long before some journalists and politicians began to discuss the idea of a federal assembly more favourably than before. In February 1857, leading conservative politician W.C. Wentworth, at this point living in London, presented to the Colonial Office a memorial, along with a draft bill, proposing such a body. Secretary of State Labouchere, unsure of the status of the proposal, asked the colonial governors to seek local opinion. Legislatures in New South Wales, Victoria, and South Australia appointed select committees to consider the question; all three subsequently agreed that it would be worth holding an intercolonial conference to discuss the matter.[12] The lack of any sense of urgency or external threat, however, led them all to quietly drop the idea, and they held no such conference.[13] As William Westgarth, a leading politician and writer in Victoria, commented in 1861, the enthusiasm of the colonists for their new governments was proving an obstacle to federation: "They will not readily abandon, to the comparatively irresponsible and independent deliberation of a federal body, the great questions of their public policy." For several decades after gaining self-government, newspapers and politicians frequently supported the idea in vague and general terms, only to let it go when the particular problem that had prompted the suggestion was in some way resolved or set aside.[14]

In these newly self-governing colonies, the colonists' conception of their political rights was closely tied to the idea that they had built free societies with the taint of the convict era behind them. Furthermore, they had proved themselves as colonizers. In their view, they had transformed the colonies, once a wilderness inhabited only by Indigenous people whom they thought savage and uncivilized, into prosperous, civilized, progressive societies. They also saw themselves as exceptionally democratic, having introduced universal male suffrage and the secret ballot within two years of gaining responsible government.[15] This was a masculine democracy, resting on the notion of manhood rather than universal suffrage. As John Stuart Mill wrote to the initiator of the secret ballot, Henry Chapman, in 1858, he could praise the colony for enfranchising men, but could only deplore its failure to include women.[16] It would also become a *Herrenvolk* democracy, imbued with the idea that true democracy rested on a racially and culturally homogenous population. In the 1850s and again in the 1870s and 1880s, restriction of Chinese immigration was justified on the basis that the colonies had to protect their social and political system, and thus the British character of the community. Colonists regarded Indigenous people not as political subjects but as people to be managed and controlled.

The people of these newly self-governing colonies were, then, overwhelmingly people of the Empire. They regarded themselves, largely, as British or as having joined a British community, and were intensely interested in Britain and British peoples elsewhere. Many of them had direct connections with this worldwide British diaspora. Pastoral projects and expansion in the Australian colonies were intimately connected with economic developments in the British world generally, some of it funded by the massive compensation to former slave owners following the end of slavery in British settlements after 1833.[17] Trade, investment, and migration all meant many had moved between colonies themselves, and retained connections and relations across the British Empire.[18] They followed imperial news through local newspapers, which informed their readers of events largely through reprints from British and sometimes American newspapers, a very common practice in the nineteenth century. In the colonies, they could read articles from the London *Times*, the *Irish Times*, the *Spectator*, the *New York Tribune*, the *Pall Mall Gazette*, and especially from the *Saturday Review*, a Peelite liberal conservative paper founded in 1855. Colonists read avidly about events such as the Indian Rebellion of 1857, wars in Cape Colony and elsewhere in southern Africa, the Crimean War, and the New Zealand Wars of the 1860s. They also followed the American Civil War with great interest and at times concern, some fearing that if Russia allied with the Union and Britain recognized the Confederacy, it could result in a major war involving both Britain and Russia, endangering other British possessions like themselves.[19]

Despite this common sense of belonging to the British Empire, extreme distance impeded the development of close relations between the Australian and Canadian colonies. In the 1860s, there was neither cable communication nor a direct shipping route linking the two sets of colonies. Exchange between them – of people, goods, newspapers, and ideas – tended to be indirect, mediated through Britain or the United States. Nevertheless, the Australian and Canadian colonies had a great deal in common, notably their shared loyalty to the British monarch; Australian colonists were particularly interested in and envious of the Royal tour of Canada in the summer and autumn of 1860. The *South Australian Advertiser*, for example, saw the official announcement of the forthcoming visit by the Prince of Wales to the Canadas as "striking proof of the growing importance of our colonies," the notion of "our colonies" here referring in familial terms to British colonies in Canada and Australia alike.[20] Australian colonial newspapers saw the Canadian Royal tour as an affirmation of the importance of settler colonies like themselves, and hoped that they, too, would receive a Royal tour before long. (They did, in 1867–8, when, to their immense embarrassment, an Irishman falsely claiming Fenian connections shot Prince Alfred in Sydney). Newspapers reprinted British accounts of the Canadian tour throughout, and in the following years, many papers included other items of interest about Canada from British papers, including land and immigration policies, and especially the building of economic infrastructure, in particular railways and bridges.[21]

Australian Interest in Canada in the 1860s

When debates in the Canadian colonies concerning Confederation intensified in 1864, especially in the context of the Charlottetown Conference held in early September, Australian newspapers covered the debates mainly through reprinted material from British newspapers, and occasionally from American papers such as the *New York Tribune* and Canadian ones such as the Ottawa *Times* and the *Toronto Herald*. These reprints ranged from brief notices to quite long descriptive and analytical pieces, and mostly they appeared without local comment.[22] Sometimes, however, there *was* direct comment, offering interpretations of events or drawing out the implications for the Australian colonies. There were two peaks of commentary, coming after heightened moments in the Confederation process (a result of delays in news reaching Australia), that is, from the middle of 1864 to mid-1865, and then again in the middle months of 1867. The focus of interest in each case was very different.

Through 1864 and into 1865, Australian colonial observers saw Confederation as a response to the possibility of military threat from the United States, and interpreted it within the larger problem, which concerned them too, of whether Britain or the settler colonies themselves were responsible for colonial defence. Since 1846, Britain had been trying to shift responsibility for defence to her colonies wherever possible; by the 1860s there were strong views within Britain that she should not assist her colonies at all.[23] In March 1862, the House of Commons resolved that self-governing colonies ought to defend themselves; and by July 1864 British ministers were supporting the confederation of Britain's North American provinces on the basis that it would fend off their annexation by the United States without committing Britain militarily.[24] In August and September 1864, Australian newspapers reprinted items from British newspapers reporting the British view on colonial defence, notably a London *Times* editorial arguing that Britain had no responsibility to come to the defence of her colonial dependencies, and a *Saturday Review* article also making it clear that Britain wanted the colonies to defend themselves. Dismayed by the *Times* editorial, a small rural Victorian paper, the *Mount Alexander Mail*, asked on 25 August 1864,

"Is England Bound to Protect Her Colonies?" Of course she was, the *Mail* predictably responded. Not only were the colonies of enormous economic benefit to Britain but also, given Britain's role in establishing the colonies in the first place, taking territory and encouraging emigration, she now had a profound obligation to protect them.[25]

It is not surprising, then, that when Australian colonial newspapers, both urban and rural, from September 1864 began explaining and discussing the proposals for federation emanating from Canada, they did so with these shared questions of colonial defence in mind.[26] In New South Wales, the leading newspaper, the *Sydney Morning Herald*, on 15 September 1864 thought Britain would support Confederation, since she would prefer a united Canada to the colonies joining with the United States and would see it as a way of sparing Britain the cost of defending the North American colonies in the case of war.[27] Canadians, the paper suggested, would soon come to have a strong sense of themselves as a nation, and Britain would find a federation easier to deal with than a set of separate colonies: "Her politicians will probably be larger-minded men, her finances certainly broader, and her necessity for securing the alliance of Great Britain certainly much greater." Nine days later, the *Herald* added that, in relation to the United States, "Canada lies defenceless across the frontier, and could be quickly gobbled up." While the *Herald* did recognize other issues were at stake in Confederation, notably the difficult relationship between the former Lower and Upper Canada (the "forcible union," it observed, "of Lower and Upper Canada has always been a source of trouble"), it continued to regard the strengthening of defence capability as primary.[28] In Victoria, the Melbourne-based conservative *Argus* was also concerned on 20 April 1865 that there might be war between Britain and the United States, with Russia as a possible ally of the United States, but this time added the fear that Canadian Confederation itself might prompt such a war. So convinced was the paper of the imminence of war, that it urged the Victorian government to seek help from the home government, and if that was not forthcoming, then from private sources, to enable the colony to acquire without delay what it needed: "guns of greatest calibre, ammunition, iron-plates, and iron-clads if need be."[29] By May the paper had learned that war was not so likely after all, but it still pressed hard for British protection, just in case.[30] The question of colonial defence was also raised at this time in the Victorian Legislative Assembly.[31] If Canada needed support, some speakers said in debate, so too might Victoria, though others pointed out in debate that the danger of military attack was small indeed compared to that facing Canada.[32]

From around the middle of 1865, when it became clear that the fears of war were not to be realized, the concerns with colonial defence – for both Canada and Australia – that had so far dominated commentary faded into the background. The sense of danger to Canada declined, and interest now turned to the *political* implications for Australia. Commentators felt they were witnessing a political transformation within the British Empire that could ultimately affect Australia too. The *South Australian Register* was typical when it commented on 26 May 1865, "Canada is making an experiment which Australia can afford to watch with patience" since "[f]ederation would be a good thing for us in some respects."[33] There was little discussion of Confederation through 1866, though a great deal of the Fenian raids at Niagara and their failure. The idea that one day the Australian colonies might follow the Canadian example persisted through 1867 as newspapers of various political persuasions sympathetically covered the passage of the British North America Bill through parliament.[34] The *Australasian*, a relatively new weekly paper published by the conservative *Argus*, on 6 April 1867 welcomed the news, commenting that British North America was "walking ahead of us in our own prospective path."[35] The Australian colonies, it thought, would follow eventually; compared to the huge differences between the Canadian colonies, "our provincial difficulties ought to vanish like snow in sunshine." (This seems to have been as close as any newspaper came to commenting on the Canadian colonies' cultural and linguistic diversity.) The generally conservative Hobart *Mercury* two weeks later was similarly enthusiastic. It was impossible, it said, to overestimate the importance of the measure, and it was evident that Canadian Confederation would pave the way for a similar Australian Act.[36] They had difficulties just as we do, and they had overcome them.[37] The *Maitland Mercury*, a liberal newspaper based in a town northwest of Sydney, was impressed: "It is not easy," it wrote on 2 May 1867, "to persuade an individual to exchange the full control of his private affairs for a simple voice amongst others in disposing of them."[38] For the *Sydney Morning Herald* four days later, Confederation, now imminent in Canada, was "some day, doubtless, to be a fact in Australasia."[39] An article appearing in several colonial newspapers two weeks later noted the enthusiasm for the bill in both Britain and Canada.[40] "We Australians," it said, "ought to throw a hearty note of encouragement into this confederation chorus" since it "concerns us prospectively almost as much as it does the British Americans." The writer noted, however, that those proposing confederation had not taken it to the ballot box and insisted that the hard practical work was yet to come. "The Federation scheme, so blatantly eulogized in London, is, in short, the mere starting-point of Federation." A little later, there were also occasional letters to the editor in various papers wondering whether the time had arrived for Australian federation.[41]

There was little urgency, however, behind these musings, and the question of federation did not become a central one in colonial politics for some time. Not only were the colonies themselves only tepidly interested, but also a succession of British governments did not press the issue. Earl Carnarvon, secretary of state from July 1866 to March 1867 and mover of the British North America Bill in the British House of Lords, thought the Australian colonies were not yet ready for federation.[42] His successor, the Duke of Buckingham, in 1867 rejected a proposal from New South Wales for a Federal Council, primarily to manage intercolonial postage.[43] Britain's focus on the Australian colonies in these years was less on encouraging federation than on persuading them to look after their own defence. The last British forces left the Australian colonies in September 1870. The Sydney-based liberal newspaper, the *Empire*, noted on 31 December 1870 that governors in Canada, the Australian colonies, and New Zealand were all making speeches insisting that the colonies would have to cease to rely on British troops and maintain their own defence forces, except in the case of an attack from a great power at war with Great Britain.[44] Responsible government, the *Empire* agreed, had brought with it an expectation of self-defence – as the *Times* had recently said, for Britain to continue to support the colonies militarily "would retard the growth of [that] manly spirit and self-reliance, without which colonial self-government is a mockery." The *Empire* supported the general rule "that when colonies claim to be exempt from the exercise of home authority, they ought to be prepared to maintain the defence of their own borders."[45]

It was only when fears grew in the 1880s that the colonies were militarily insecure in the face of French and German activity in the Pacific that proposals for an Australian federation finally gained real traction.[46] Political theorist William Riker's suggestion that all federations are based on some sense of military threat seems to be well borne out by both Canada and Australia.[47] Concerns about Australian military security led the British government to ask Major General Bevan Edwards, commander of British troops in China, to report on the state of colonial defences. His report was scathing. Colonial defences were weak and disorganized, and the only way to place them on a proper footing was to federate the colonies.[48] In a landmark speech on 24 October 1889, now generally credited with launching the federation proposals in earnest, veteran liberal politician in New South Wales, Henry Parkes, stressed their great need for a federal system of defence, and especially the creation of a single "great Federal army."[49] In a federal parliament, moreover, he argued, "All great questions will be dealt with in a broad manner just as the Congress deals with the national affairs of the United States and as the Parliament of the Dominion of Canada deals with similar questions."[50] Parkes, and those who took up his call, were now applying to their own situation their observation made in relation to Canada in 1864, that federation might be the best way to enhance their military capability and national security.

The Canadian Model and the Federation Movement in the 1890s

The growing support for federation was by no means based only on the question of military security. Desires to facilitate intercolonial commerce, strengthen immigration controls, and protect white racial identity were all very much involved.[51] Despite many opposing voices, including those of the smaller colonies wary of political domination by the larger, and of the growing labour movement wary that federation might favour its conservative opponents, the push towards federation gathered momentum from the late 1880s. Leading political figures representing all the Australian colonies held a conference in Melbourne in February 1890 to consider a new federal constitution; and here the Canadian constitution came under serious consideration. The *British North America Act, 1867* was of particular interest, since Canada was the only example they had of a federation under the British Crown. They considered other federations, too, notably the American and the Swiss; many of those present had legal backgrounds and were well read in the literature on constitutional law and history. In the early stages of the convention, many speakers spoke favourably of the Canadian constitution, and it seemed it might provide the model for Australia. There was, however, an influential intervention by Tasmanian liberal lawyer and politician Andrew Inglis Clark. An expert on both the Canadian and US constitutions, Clark argued strongly against the Canadian model on the grounds that it gave too much power to the federal government and too little to its constituent elements, the provinces. Given that the colonies had now been self-governing for several decades and thus were likely to protect their independence on many matters, Inglis Clark's arguments carried the day. As Helen Irving and other historians point out, the delegates agreed that the Canadian model, in which residual powers lay with the federal rather than the state governments, was too centralized for Australian purposes.[52] From then on, delegates looked instead to the US constitution as a better model for protecting individual states' rights. Through the ensuing debate that lasted to the end of the decade, Canada became the symbol of a centralized system overriding state rights.

Yet, as Irving suggests, in other respects Australian politicians *did* consider Canadian precedents as worth following, and at a second convention the following year, in 1891, adopted many of Canada's provisions, such as those concerning the role of the governor general and the nature of the upper and lower houses of the new federal parliament.[53] They also drew on the Canadian model for defining some of the federal powers, notably marriage and divorce law, which was in the Canadian but not the US constitution.[54] Australian legislators, aware of the huge variety in divorce law between the colonies, with New South Wales and Victoria granting women much greater rights to initiate divorce than did the other colonies, saw the American situation of state-based marriage and divorce laws as having caused much "pain and grief."[55] Marriage and divorce, they concluded, perhaps surprisingly, was a national rather than a state matter.

One of the key differences between Australian and Canadian federations concerned their effect on existing systems of governing and controlling Indigenous people. In Australia, the granting of responsible government in the 1850s (1890 in Western Australia) was accompanied by the complete and immediate withdrawal of the British government from Indigenous policy. Federation in 1901 made little difference, as Indigenous policy, long controlled by each colonial government, now became a state matter only, until a change in the Australian constitution in 1967. In Canada, by contrast, Britain retained a role in Indigenous policy for some years after the granting of responsible government, and it was Confederation, not responsible government per se, that marked the final transfer of governing authority on Indigenous matters to the new Canadian state. Since Indigenous groups had signed treaties with Britain, however, the Crown would remain a factor in settler-Indigenous relations, and Indigenous people continued to see the treaties, and the Crown, as transcending the national government.

Conclusion

The sense of a family connection, of being sister nations in the British Empire, shown by the Canadians in Sydney who helped celebrate Australian federation on 1 January 1901 had a lot going for it. Both countries had achieved nationhood by drawing together a group of geographically connected but separately governed British settler colonies, and both would retain strong British connections and institutions long after political independence had become a reality. Most important, however, from a modern perspective, is the fact that both had been through a history of settler colonialism, of significantly displacing and disrupting Indigenous populations to build new European societies. In both cases – though in different ways – continuing Indigenous activism against dispossession, assimilation, and incorporation meant that the nations that emerged from this particular imperial and colonial history finally had to confront Indigenous claims a century later. The sense of family had become, in some eyes at least, not a matter of pride in belonging to a powerful Empire but rather recognition of a family disgrace, requiring new ways of thinking about national identity, sovereignty, and governance. Paradoxically, perhaps, tackling these questions brought Indigenous and non-Indigenous populations in the two countries closer together than they had ever been before.

NOTES

1 *Sydney Morning Herald (SMH)*, 2 January 1901, 9; Helen Irving, ed., *The Centenary Companion to Federation* (Cambridge: Cambridge University Press, 1999), 342.
2 See essays by William Roger Louis, D.R. Owram, and Stuart Macintyre, in *The Oxford History of the British Empire*, vol. V, *Historiography*, ed. Robin Winks (Oxford: Oxford University Press, 1999).
3 *Labour/Le Travail*, vol. 38, 1996, vii–294 is devoted to comparative Australian/Canadian labour history.
4 A.J. Ray, "Aboriginal Title and Treaty Rights Research: A Comparative Look at Australia, Canada, New Zealand, and the United States," *New Zealand Journal of History* 34, no. 1 (April 2003): 5–21; Kent McNeil, *Emerging Justice? Essays on Indigenous Rights in Canada and Australia* (Saskatoon: Native Law Centre, University of Saskatchewan, 2001); Peter Russell, *Recognizing Aboriginal Title: The Mabo Case and Indigenous Resistance to English-Settler*

Colonialism (Toronto: University of Toronto Press, 2005); Henry Reynolds, *Law of the Land* (Melbourne: Penguin, 1987), esp. 49–50, 167–9; Penelope Edmonds, *Urbanizing Frontiers: Indigenous Peoples and Settlers in 19th-Century Pacific Rim Cities* (Vancouver: UBC Press, 2010), 12; Amanda Nettelbeck, Russell Smandych, Louis A. Knafla, and Robert Foster, *Fragile Settlements: Aboriginal Peoples, Law and Resistance in South West Australia and Prairie Canada* (Vancouver: UBC Press, 2016); John Weaver, *The Great Land Rush and the Making of the Modern World, 1650–1900* (Montreal and Kingston: McGill-Queen's University Press, 2003).

5 Brian Petrie, *French Canadian Rebels as Australian Convicts* (Melbourne: Australian Scholarly Publishing, 2013).
6 Zoe Laidlaw, "The Victorian State in Its Imperial Context," in *The Victorian World*, ed. Martin Hewitt (London: Routledge, 2012), 333.
7 *SMH*, 19 June 1849, 2.
8 *SMH*, 19 June 1849, 2; see John M. Ward, *Colonial Self-Government: The British Experience, 1759–1856* (Toronto: University of Toronto Press, 1976), 300.
9 Ward, *Colonial Self-Government*, 292–4.
10 See chapter thirteen by Timothy Stapleton in this volume.
11 Ward, *Colonial Self-Government*, 296.
12 Robert Garran, *The Federation Movement and the Founding of the Commonwealth* (1933; repr., Sydney: University of Sydney, 2001), 9. See also W.G. McMinn, *Nationalism and Federalism in Australia* (Melbourne: Oxford University Press, 1994), 73–80.
13 William Westgarth, *Australia: Its Rise, Progress, and Present Condition* (Edinburgh: Adam and Charles Black, 1861), 82. See also John Williams, "The Emergence of the Commonwealth Constitution," in *Australian Constitutional Landmarks*, ed. H.P. Lee and George Winterton (Melbourne: Cambridge University Press, 2003), 7–8.
14 McMinn, *Nationalism and Federalism in Australia*, 71.
15 Marian Sawer, "Inventing the Nation through the Ballot Box," in *From Subject to Citizens: A Hundred Years of Citizenship in Australia and Canada*, ed. Pierre Boyer, Linda Cardinal, and David Headon (Ottawa: University of Ottawa Press, 2004), 61–80; Mark McKenna, *Building a 'Closet of Prayer' in the New World: The Story of the Australian Ballot*, London Papers in Australian Studies, no. 6 (London: University of London Institute of Commonwealth Studies, 2002).
16 Mill to Chapman, 8 July 1858, reproduced in R.S. Neale, "John Stuart Mill on Australia: A Note," *Historical Studies in Australia and New Zealand* 13, no. 50 (1968): 240–1.

17 Catherine Hall, Nicholas Draper, Keith McClelland, Katie Donington, and Rachel Lang, *Legacies of British Slave Ownership: Colonial Slavery and the Formation of Victorian Britain* (Cambridge: Cambridge University Press, 2014).
18 Angela Woollacott, *Settler Society in the Australian Colonies: Self-Government and Imperial Culture* (Oxford: Oxford University Press, 2015).
19 *SMH*, 13 July 1861, 4. The *South Australian Register* warned on 23 August 1864 of "a great war possibly impending," 23 August 1864, 2.
20 *South Australian Advertiser*, 7 May 1860, 2.
21 *SMH*, 16 May 1861, 3; 23 October 1862, 4.
22 Examples include reprints from the *Saturday Review* in the *Empire*, 28 September 1864, 2 and 13 May 1867, 2; reprint from the *New York Tribune* in the *Empire* on 5 November 1864, 2; reprint from the London *Times* in the *SMH*, 28 Jan 1865, 8.
23 Peter Burroughs, "Defence and Imperial Disunity," in *The Oxford History of the British Empire*, vol. III, *The Nineteenth Century*, ed. Andrew Porter (Oxford: Oxford University Press, 2001), 327.
24 Burroughs, "Defence and Imperial Disunity," 327–31.
25 *Mount Alexander Mail*, 25 August 1864, 2.
26 See, for example, the *Empire*, 13 October 1864, 3.
27 *SMH*, 15 September 1864, 2.
28 *SMH*, 24 September 1864, 4; 4 April 1865, 4.
29 *Argus*, 20 April 1865, 4.
30 *Argus*, 16 May 1865, 4.
31 Victoria, Legislative Assembly, Parliamentary Debates, 22 June 1865, reported in the *Argus*, 23 June 1865, 6–7. Victoria, Legislative Council, Parliamentary Debates (VLCPD), 4 July 1865, reported in *Argus*, 5 July 1865, 6.
32 VLCPD, 11 July 1865, reported in the *Argus*, 12 July 1865, 6.
33 *South Australian Register*, 26 May 1865, 2.
34 *SMH*, 6 May 1867, 4.
35 *The Australasian*, 6 April 1867, 16.
36 *Hobart Mercury*, 22 April 1867, 2.
37 See also the Melbourne *Argus*, 23 April 1867, 4.
38 *Maitland Mercury*, 2 May 1867, 2.
39 *SMH*, 6 May 1867, 4.
40 *South Australian Register*, 18 May 1867, 2.
41 David Randall, in *South Australian Register*, 16 August 1867, 2; "Australian," *Adelaide Observer*, 29 June 1867, 1.
42 B.A. Knox, "Carnarvon, Fourth Earl of," *Australian Dictionary of Biography*, http://adb.anu.edu.au/biography/carnarvon-fourth-earl-of-3166.
43 Garran, *The Federation Movement*, 10.

44 The *Empire*, 31 December 1870, 6.
45 Jeffrey Grey, *A Military History of Australia*, 3rd ed. (Melbourne: Cambridge University Press, 2008), 22–4.
46 Burroughs, "Defence and Imperial Disunity," 336–7.
47 William Riker, *Federalism: Origin, Operation, Significance* (New York: Little Brown, 1964), 12.
48 A.J. Hill, "Sir James Bevan," *Australian Dictionary of Biography*, http://adb.anu.edu.au/biography/edwards-sir-james-bevan-3470.
49 Garran, *The Federation Movement*, 13.
50 *SMH*, 25 October 1889, 8.
51 Marilyn Lake and Henry Reynolds, *Drawing the Global Colour Line: White Men's Countries and the Question of Racial Equality* (Melbourne: Melbourne University Press, 2008).
52 Helen Irving, *To Constitute a Nation: A Cultural History of Australia's Constitution* (Cambridge: Cambridge University Press, 1997), 64; John Williams, "'With Eyes Open': Andrew Inglis Clark and Our Republican Tradition," *Federal Law Review* 23, no. 2 (1995): 149–79, at 165; Helen Irving, "Sister Colonies with Separate Constitutions: Why Australians Chose Not to Follow Canada," in *Shaping Nations: Constitutionalism and Society in Australia and Canada*, ed. Linda Cardinal (Ottawa, University of Ottawa Press, 2002), 27–37.
53 Helen Irving, "The Over-Rated Mr Clark? Putting Andrew Inglis Clark's Contribution to the Constitution into Perspective," *Papers on Parliament*, No. 61, Canberra, May 2014, http://www.aph.gov.au/~/~/link.aspx?_id=35A426B090A1488F962A8E4A9724E8C9&_z=z.
54 Irving, *To Constitute a Nation*, 69.
55 Irving, *To Constitute a Nation*, 92.

12 The Delinquent Colony: The New Zealand Press and Canadian Confederation

KENTON STOREY

Canadian Confederation was a news subject of interest in New Zealand throughout the period between the Charlottetown Conference in 1864 and the creation of the Dominion of Canada in 1867. Opinions varied, though. Some newspaper editors typeset benign platitudes – that Canadian Confederation was symbolic of an advancing British civilization and the evolution of imperial governance since the days of George III and the American Revolution.[1] But more often than not, when editors discussed Canadian Confederation at length, they focused on the unsettling aspects of these events and their implications for New Zealand's future. This thematic response resonates with a key insight in Arjun Appadurai's monograph *Modernity at Large: Cultural Dimensions of Globalization*: that information spread by global networks becomes indigenized according to the "imagined worlds" of constituent audiences.[2] In this way, Confederation became local news.

This chapter is a study of how newspaper editors in New Zealand encountered and then responded to news about Canadian Confederation between 1864 and 1867.[3] It builds on previous work on the subjects of news transmission and press culture, where I have tracked New Zealand's location within imperial communications networks.[4] In that study, I revealed how settlers were sensitive to accusations of mistreatment against New Zealand's Indigenous Maori population. To defend against the epithet of a "nigger despising temper,"[5] colonial editors crafted their editorial manifestos to resonate "at home" in Great Britain, infusing their rhetoric with humanitarian language to characterize their relations with the Maori positively. A key insight of this study is that settlers in New Zealand experienced anxiety related to metropolitan surveillance of colonial affairs and that the local press attempted to mitigate this danger by appealing to readers abroad. This research suggests that editors conceptualized multiple audiences for their editorial manifestos: local subscribers in a given newspaper's host community and then readers across New Zealand, the Australian colonies, and Great Britain. The chapter builds on this work with a two-part analysis: The first section elaborates the significance of the New Zealand press and discusses how the mechanics of news transmission influenced editors' encounter with news about Canadian Confederation. The second section considers how both the New Zealand Wars and local political conflict mediated responses to news from British North America.

The New Zealand Press and News Transmission in the 1860s

The press occupied an iconic status across the British Empire in the mid-nineteenth century. It certainly captured cross-class support in both the Canadian colonies and New Zealand, where communities of newspapers in both metropolitan and provincial centres functioned as vital forums for the exchange of ideas and information.[6] It was not uncommon in this period for a relatively small colonial town to have several newspapers, meaning that cumulatively across New Zealand in the mid-1860s there were many newspapers in existence.[7] The prescribed role of the press, or the "Fourth Estate," in this period was to reflect public opinion, thereby mediating relations between social classes.[8] But the press did not simply reiterate an aggregate of individual opinions; rather, it played an active role in disseminating strongly voiced arguments and points of view.[9] A community of newspapers in a given city was expected to present the breadth of local political discourse, empowering an interested citizenry and facilitating the democratic process. In this way, the press was believed to be a quintessentially English institution, the enemy of tyranny, and an agent of the moral, social, and political transformation of the world.[10] Of course this idealism about the representational qualities of the press collided with reality; newspapers everywhere across the British Empire were first and foremost commercial enterprises, often operated to advance the political careers of their owners. Mid-nineteenth century newspapers were often hybrid institutions too, consumed with party politics but also operated for profit and oriented to capture a popular audience. In this way, newspapers of the mid-nineteenth century resembled neither the purely political journals of decades earlier nor the fully commercialized press of the late nineteenth century.[11]

The popularity of the press in New Zealand can be illustrated in several ways. One quantitative measure is to examine newspaper subscription rates. For example, while subscription rates are sparsely available from the mid-nineteenth century, my previous research has suggested that in 1858 the press within New Zealand's capital Auckland may have published sufficient newspapers for 88 per cent of adult colonists within the city, or 35 per cent in the wider Auckland province.[12] This limited data set suggests that local papers saturated the available market rather than only appealing to local elites. Perhaps more significantly, though, it is clear that newspapers in this period oriented their editorial manifestos towards a broad audience and were encountered by colonists within a variety of public settings such as public houses and popular reading rooms.[13]

Editors in New Zealand had reason to believe that their editorial manifestos were also read "at home" for two reasons. First, they knew that large numbers of their papers were sent abroad to metropolitan readers. For example, in 1864 colonists dispatched 849,094 newspapers away from New Zealand, with 71 per cent of this total posted to the United Kingdom and most of the remainder to the Australian colonies.[14] Second, the mechanics of "cut and paste" journalism resulted in the wholesale replication of local news articles within foreign papers. It was a common practice across the anglophone world in this era for newspaper editors to reproduce verbatim news articles from foreign papers. Thus an anglophone newspaper reader in 1864 would expect to encounter an eclectic collection of news in any given edition: up-to-date local news and editorials compiled for a host paper itself but also older articles of note from other provincial centres, British colonies, and Great Britain. In this way, extended editorials from New Zealand were republished within both Australian and metropolitan newspapers, thereby amplifying the potential audience of a local editorial manifesto by the given circulation of the host paper. For example, when an article from a New Zealand paper was republished within *The Times* of London, its circulation would increase from several hundred subscribers in, say, Auckland to 70,000, not to mention the paper's additional readers across the Empire. Cut and paste journalism amplified the voices of colonial editors far beyond their local subscriber lists. This republication of dated news continued to occur because New Zealand did not garner telegraphic news via Melbourne until 1871, and even then the prohibitive cost of telegraphic communication ensured that only news that was concise, time sensitive, and economically valuable was sent near instantaneously.[15]

Thus our first insight is this: colonists in New Zealand encountered a great deal of dated news about Canadian Confederation between 1864 and 1867. This news came from two principle sources. First, news about Confederation appeared within the hundreds of thousands of metropolitan papers transmitted to New Zealand from Great Britain. Second, readers in New Zealand encountered news about Confederation within both Australian and New Zealand papers, most commonly in the form of reproduced foreign articles but also within interpretive editorials penned by local New Zealand writers. Perhaps most interestingly, though, the cut and paste journalism synonymous with this era entailed that sample articles from Canadian newspapers were accessible in New Zealand. In this way, New Zealand did not have to have strong or direct communications links with Canada to garner a sample of local press perspectives about Confederation. So while colonists in New Zealand received stale news several months distanced from its original date of publication and transmitted to them primarily by rail and sail transportation technologies rather than the telegraph, they were still relatively well informed about events occurring so far away. Indeed, local editors were aware of many facets of the Confederation process. They knew that colonial debts, the proposed construction of railway infrastructure, and easier access to credit were all motivating factors;[16] that Confederation had its origins in a political impasse in Upper and Lower Canada and that enthusiasm varied among the Maritime colonies;[17] that both the threat of American aggression and the Fenian raids contributed to support for Confederation; and, finally, that controversy erupted in Nova Scotia in the aftermath of 1867.[18]

However, a lack of direct press connections with the British North American colonies meant that it was difficult for editors in New Zealand to assess the biases of the news they received. Here I am making a distinction between the large quantity of news about Confederation that New Zealand received versus the very limited ability of editors to assess the reliability of this news and the motivations of its authors. Again, the mechanics of news production in this period are key here. Most New Zealand papers in this era were operated by a small staff of editors, journalists, and printers, and had limited capacity for investigative journalism. Because foreign news was not generated in-house, interpreting the reliability of news from afar depended upon two factors: the capacity to receive contrasting editorial perspectives from a given press community, and institutional knowledge about the specific economic and political motivations of a given foreign paper. We can imagine that an editor's ability to assess and interpret news diminished in proportion to the distance from and personal knowledge of a news source. Not surprisingly, it was easier in New Zealand to assess news from the nearby Australian colonies or the content of prominent London papers such as *The Times* or the *Saturday Review* with their well-known political biases. New Zealand editors, then, had far more difficulty gauging the accuracy of news articles from the Canadian colonies, especially if they did not receive contrasting Canadian editorial perspectives for a given news story.

Related to this theme, the *Otago Daily Times* in 1867 commented on the discrepancies within the emergent reports:

> The accounts from Canada, which filter through English papers, represent everything as most satisfactory. If we are to believe these statements, the people are not only perfectly content with the change of Government, but sanguine of a brighter future than they had previously dared to expect ... The accounts which reach us through America represent an entirely opposite state of affairs. The new form of Government, the American journals declare, is not popular; it is accepted only because of the rich bribe which accompanies it – the guaranteed loan of some millions for railway purposes.[19]

The *Otago Daily Times* writer concluded, "Something, probably, of both these accounts is based on truth."[20] Here we see mid-nineteenth century custom at work: how editors read emergent news narratives about Canadian Confederation against the grain and took for granted that ideological motivations coloured each news source's characterization of the event. At the same time, this *Otago Daily Times* article suggests that metropolitan papers tended to reiterate positive rather than negative perspectives of Confederation, which was certainly not an accurate representation of the breadth of political viewpoints in the press communities of British North America. These challenges to the interpretation of Canadian news help explain why there was not a great deal of commentary within the New Zealand press on their counterparts within the Canadian colonies and the press's role as agents both for and against Confederation. More commonly, editors in New Zealand characterized Confederation as a product of imperial policy and in relation to local politics.

The New Zealand Wars and Canadian Confederation

Confederation occurred during a troubling time for New Zealand. War had first broken out between the Crown and several Maori *iwi* (tribes) in 1860 over a controversial land sale in the province of Taranaki. Despite the efforts of several thousand British imperial troops during a year-long campaign, the Taranaki War sputtered to an inconclusive end with a ceasefire in 1861. Then a larger-scale conflict broke out in the Waikato region of the central North Island in July 1863 and continued to the end of 1864. The war in Waikato pitted the Crown against the Kingitanga, a Maori political movement that had elected its own king in 1858 as a symbol of its commitment to end land sales with the Crown and to implement an alternative code of laws. While the British military was more successful during the Waikato campaign, new Maori insurgent groups continued to emerge in the late 1860s and sporadic outbursts of armed conflict did not end until the early 1870s. Thus New Zealand was either at war or on a war footing throughout the period during which Canadian Confederation was occurring.

The New Zealand Wars were fought between the Maori and the Crown over control of the land, the implementation of British sovereignty, and a defence of Maori *mana* (that is, prestige, authority, and/or spiritual authority).[21] These were large-scale conflicts too. At its height, over 20,000 British imperial troops were mobilized during the war in Waikato. The wars were also controversial. During the Taranaki War especially, New Zealand's settler society was deeply divided over the war's legitimacy because Governor Thomas Gore Browne had used military force to enforce a controversial land purchase, wherein one party of Maori had sought to sell a parcel of land to the Crown but were opposed by their kinsmen who claimed a communal interest in the land and the right to block the sale. Indeed, during this conflict the Te Ati Awa Maori insurgents had many defenders among New Zealand's well-established community of missionary humanitarians. The fierce debates over the war's legitimacy resulted in a parallel pamphlet war, as published pro and con arguments were forwarded to Great Britain to win over policy makers in London. These lengthy and complicated discourses attempted to explain how the colony's founding document, the Treaty of Waitangi, had defined the nature of Maori land title, but they simply confused metropolitan commentators. What British observers could agree on, though, is that the New Zealand Wars were enormously expensive and surprisingly difficult to win.[22]

Indeed, during the New Zealand Wars the British military unexpectedly suffered a number of controversial battlefield defeats.[23] With the conflicts dragging on and on, the imperial government eventually concluded that wars with the Maori might continue forever. As historian James Belich has noted, by 1865 the imperial government had had enough and decided to withdraw the majority of troops and disengage the remaining garrison from active operations.[24] Of course, this withdrawal was enormously controversial and resented, especially when many settlers believed the wars had actually been instigated by the rash and short-sighted actions of the imperial government's own governor, Thomas Gore Browne.

It should not surprise, then, that New Zealand editors viewed both Canadian Confederation and the withdrawal of imperial troops from New Zealand as common products of imperial colonial policy. But whereas New Zealand settlers had been censured by metropolitan papers and lost tangible imperial support, the Canadian colonies were fêted by London papers and garnered additional resources as a reward for Confederation. For example, the editor of the *New Zealand Advertiser* in 1865 reflected bitterly on how Canadian ministers were able to secure a loan of £200,000 per annum from the imperial government to defray the costs of purchasing additional local armaments.[25] As the editor noted, "How different is this treatment to that which New Zealand has received ... though New Zealand has given far stronger proofs of its willingness to provide for its future defence, as well as to suppress a rebellion which originated in Imperial mismanagement." Here we see how the receipt of news stories that celebrated the benefits of Confederation for the defence of the Canadian colonies against military threats elicited jealousy in New Zealand.

On a similar vein, a strong theme within the New Zealand press was to interpret Canadian Confederation primarily as a product of British colonial policy. This perspective elided the colonial political personalities at the centre of events and instead focused on how Confederation depended upon metropolitan assent and was authorized by an act of parliament. As *The Oamaru Times, and Waitaki Reporter* remarked in April 1865, Confederation had "the cordial approval of the mother country and its rulers" and would result in the establishment of "a third great Anglo-Saxon community, which, although still connected with the home country, will virtually occupy the position, and have all the rights and privileges, of a free and independent nation."[26] As the writer also noted, Confederation was supported in Great Britain because of a desire among its political classes to rid themselves of their colonies:

> There is, in the home country, a class of politicians who regard the colonial empire of Great Britain as a useless and expensive encumbrance, which should be got rid of as quickly as possible; and it is to be feared that the protracted and expensive New Zealand wars have constituted a too convincing argument with the English people generally, many of whom think that were the Colony made more independent of the home country, the war would soon be brought to an end.[27]

As the writer noted, there were many "anxious to quit of us" but "no one can maintain, with any show of reason, that the time has arrived for entirely abandoning this Colony to its own insufficient resources."[28] If Confederation was an act of imperial abandonment, then perhaps New Zealand's future would not be of its own choosing.

Later in 1867, the *Otago Daily Times* reiterated this theme by characterizing Canadian Confederation as an expedient that was only staving "off the settlement of the Colonial question."[29] According to this interpretation, Great Britain had not solved its problems yet:

> She has to decide between one of two things: Either she must make up her mind to part with her Colonies, at the first convenient opportunity, or else she must aid them to become powerful allies in case of the Empire being threatened. They are sources of weakness to her at present, because they not only are unable to do anything to aid her in the way of aggressive war, but they cannot defend themselves in case of attack ... Money only is required to make the Colonies useful allies, and if Great Britain would supply the means, she might multiply her power the world over.[30]

In this article, we see the writer is making an appeal to the British government to invest the necessary resources in its colonies to provide them with real strength. But this was not the popular viewpoint in Great Britain, where a prominent paper like the *Saturday Review* lauded the Confederation of the British North American colonies as a means to reduce imperial liabilities: "Our true course is to narrow our responsibilities, and to concentrate our means of action."[31]

Another common response in the New Zealand press was to view Canadian Confederation as a harbinger of the future. New Zealand's position within the Empire would change because of it. *The Press* made this point in December 1864, stating: "Every colony must, sooner or later, become free from the control of the country that planted it."[32] What was not clear, though, was what shape that change would take.

Indeed, one does not get the impression that very many New Zealand editors considered a union with the Australian colonies to be realistic in the mid-nineteenth century, though writers did assert that colonies in Australia and at the Cape would follow the Canadian example.[33] Perhaps editors were not enthusiastic about a confederation scheme with other Australasian colonies because New Zealand's own political classes were riven over the merits of their own federal system of governance during this period.

New Zealand's "Provincial System" and Canadian Confederation

A fact noticed by several members of the New Zealand press was that Canadian Confederation was inaugurating a model of federal governance that was remarkably similar to New Zealand's own political structure.[34] As the *Wellington Independent* remarked, the Canadian model was "exactly the system of Government which at present exists in New Zealand. The Federal Legislature of Canada with its two Houses, one elective and the other nominated, corresponds with the House of Representatives and the Legislative Council in New Zealand."[35] However, what made Canadian Confederation a cause for comment, though, was that in this period New Zealand's own "provincial system" was being challenged by two divergent campaigns. On the one hand, advocates for "separation" promoted the dissolution of New Zealand's provinces into separate British colonies; on the other hand, advocates of "centralism" promoted the dissolution of the colony's constituent provinces in favour of a stronger central government. In this context, news about Canadian Confederation offered supporters and opponents of these rival schemes the opportunity to appraise the merits of federalism.

As Bruce A. Knox has argued, the origins of New Zealand's *Constitution Act* lay in the efforts of the third Earl Grey, who had attempted "to promote federations in Australasia, South Africa, and British North America" between 1846 and 1851, but "failed (except, in a sense, in New Zealand) partly because his schemes were more visionary than practically suited to existing colonial conditions."[36] Worth recognizing, then, is that New Zealand's governing structure was a precursor to the Canadian federal model, but the product of imperial policy in 1846 rather than a local grass-roots campaign for responsible government. Partly because of its initial impracticality for a colony numerically dominated by its Maori population in the 1840s, Governor George Grey postponed its implementation for five years until 1852.

When the *Constitution Act* was implemented, New Zealand was divided into six provinces, each with its own legislature and executive, and an elective central assembly.[37] While the General Assembly featured lawmaking powers and the prerogative to supersede provincial legislation, Provincial Councils had control over revenues from land sales, immigration, and public works.[38] The business of shaping colonization on the ground largely occurred in the Provincial Councils. But while the Act provided a measure of responsible government, the governor still retained substantial power.[39] For example, Grey's successor, Thomas Gore Browne, controversially reserved control over Maori affairs for himself, arguing that these were "imperial matters."[40] Browne's decision reflected both the advice he had received from prominent missionary humanitarians and his own view that many colonial legislators "know as little of the New Zealanders as they do of the Japanese ... talk rubbish on the subject and what is more, refuse or grudge the smallest support."[41] For both Browne and his successor, the returning Governor George Grey, the maintenance of gubernatorial control over Maori affairs proved to be enormously controversial, especially because both the purchase of Maori land and war policy were of utmost importance to settler society. Of course the situation in the Canadian colonies was very different, where by 1860 the Indian Department responsible for Indigenous peoples was fully supported by local monies and operated by the government of the Province of Canada rather than by imperial authorities.[42]

Thus by the time news of Confederation reached New Zealand, the colony's provincial system had proven to be both controversial and unwieldy. Yet one strategy in the New Zealand press was to comment on Canadian Confederation as a rationale for chastising proponents of the separatist movement. For example, in 1865 the editor of *The Oamaru Times, and Waitaki Reporter* argued:

> Just at the time, for instance that the news of the Toronto [sic] Conference reached this country, New Zealand was extremely busy getting up Separation Leagues – one in Auckland and another in Dunedin ... No; the spirit to be cultivated is that displayed lately in North America, where the most anxious consideration was shown for the interests of every member of the federation, the weakest as well as the most powerful.[43]

Here we see how the writer praised the display of unity by supporters of Confederation as exemplars of the correct colonial spirit.

On a similar theme, the *Wellington Independent* in 1866 warned its readers that "should separation meet with the support of a majority in the New Zealand Parliament ... they will be looked upon at home as wanting in foresight."[44] The writer's point was that Great Britain was at that time encouraging its colonies in Canada to federate. Thus the separation movement was out of step with both imperial policy and antithetical to the perceived evolution of colonies.

Not surprisingly, given the divisions within New Zealand society, rival papers took an opposing tack. For example, the *New Zealand Herald*'s writer stated, "The plan of the proposed Confederation of certain of the North American States cannot but be of interest to us in New Zealand at a time when public attention is drawn to our system of government and when we are on the eve of a great political struggle between Provincialism and Centralism."[45] The *Herald* writer then noted how the opponents of separation identified parallels between New Zealand's provincial system and the federal system to be inaugurated in North America "as a convincing argument against the policy of Separation." Against this argument, though, the *Herald* writer asserted that unlike the colonies of North America, there was no compelling economic rationale to retain connections between New Zealand's North and South Islands, as they were trading competitors rather than ready markets for each other's trade goods. For this writer, Canadian Confederation functioned as an object lesson, but one revealing the flaws of the local system of governance because New Zealand's provinces were not comparable to the Canadian colonies.

Adding to this theme in another editorial, the *New Zealand Herald* writer commented on the Dominion of Canada's new constitution in a bid to criticize local supporters of a stronger central government. Here the structure of federalism in Canada offered an object lesson:

> Now it is most noteworthy that the Constitution of Canada is almost a reproduction of that of New Zealand. Except in so much that in following out our system of Provincial Institutions greater power is accorded to the several Provincial Governments of the dominion of Canada than the New Zealand provinces possess. So far from having deemed it wise to curtail the power of the Provinces and place a larger balance of power in the hands of the General Government, the framers of the new constitution for Canada have taken a contrary course. Here, then, given in an indirect manner, is a direct verdict delivered by the British Parliament and the Canadas against the centralising policy of Mr. Stafford and his Government.[46]

Clearly the *New Zealand Herald* writer was an advocate for the greater separation of New Zealand's provinces, and supported this position with the assertion that "the Canadian Provinces are not content to be ruled from Ottawa, as the advocates of centralism would have us ruled North and South, from Wellington."

Interestingly enough, both the opponents and proponents of the separatist movement drew on news about Confederation to support their political discourses. While each editor highlighted a divergent aspect, say the unity of Confederation's supporters or the retention of significant power within Canadian provincial legislatures, they generally accepted that Confederation itself was a positive step for British North America.

Conclusions

A question this chapter has not answered is whether Canadian Confederation was more or less noteworthy in comparison to other foreign news. It is impossible to know whether readers responded enthusiastically to this news. Our only suggestive guide is whether editors published large quantities of this news to answer popular interest. Anecdotally speaking, coverage of Canadian Confederation does not compare with that of the 1857 Indian Rebellion, which garnered pervasive interest within New Zealand papers. In contrast, New Zealand papers paid periodic attention to Confederation as fresh news became occasionally available. Likewise, news about the Fenian raids in the Canadian colonies also garnered comparable interest within the New Zealand press. Thus we can say that war news emergent from British North America was just as interesting as news about Canadian Confederation. All this is to say that given the large quantity of news about Confederation forwarded to New Zealand within metropolitan papers and then republished within the New Zealand press, local readers would likely have been well aware of events in British North America between 1864 and 1867 but not overwhelmed or inundated by related local editorial commentary.

Another interesting aspect of the New Zealand press's response to Confederation is that editors did not attempt to influence the Confederation process by appealing to metropolitan policy makers, either for or against events occurring in British North America. I draw attention to this point because my earlier work on the New Zealand press has made the argument that members of the New Zealand press often crafted their editorial perspectives for an audience "at home" in a bid to protect the interests of local settlers. This type of advocacy does not appear to have included lobbying to influence metropolitan policy makers to intervene in the Canadian colonies for the benefit of New Zealand colonists.

However, it could be argued that the editorials previously mentioned in this chapter which criticized imperial policy, particularly the mistreatment of New Zealand versus the Canadian colonies, can and should be interpreted as messages of discontent intended for an audience in Great Britain. By drawing attention to the unfair treatment of New Zealand versus the Canadian colonies, editors sought to garner metropolitan support for the colony. Likely editors in New Zealand also limited their criticism to decision makers in the United Kingdom because they understood that with the six-month time lag between their receipt of news and then the receipt in London of their own response to that news, New Zealand perspectives on events across the Empire were useless contributions to any sort of debate. While it might have been practical to attempt to influence interpretations of local events in the United Kingdom, the New Zealand press could not easily participate in events in British North America itself. In this way, editors in New Zealand were interested observers of Confederation, cognizant of the event's significance but unable to influence or direct Canadian affairs.

In Ged Martin's study *Britain and the Origins of Canadian Confederation*, he characterizes New Zealand as a delinquent colony; this comment is in the context of the enormous debts accrued by New Zealand during the New Zealand Wars, which were reluctantly guaranteed by the imperial government.[47] But perhaps symbolically, the descriptor "delinquent" fits with the themes encountered within this chapter's analysis of press coverage of Canadian Confederation. The general sense is that editors in New Zealand perceived themselves on the outs; both the New Zealand Wars and local political conflict reflected poorly on local settler society. In contrast, the Canadian colonies were the recipients of imperial favour and on the cutting edge of imperial development. All in all, the period between 1864 and 1867 was not an encouraging time for New Zealand as compared with Canada.

NOTES

1 *Otago Witness*, 3 December 1864; *Wellington Independent*, 22 December 1864; *The Press*, 24 December 1864; *The Oamaru Times, and Waitaki Reporter*, 30 August 1867.

2 Arjun Appadurai, *Modernity at Large: Cultural Dimensions of Globalization* (Minneapolis: University of Minnesota Press, 1996), 32–3.
3 I utilized the website Papers Past to conduct research. Key word searches for content related to Confederation generated tens of thousands of hits; extensive notes were taken from editorials in the *Otago Witness; Lyttelton Times; Wellington Independent; The Press; Otago Daily Times; Oamaru Times, and Waitaki Reporter; New Zealand Herald; Lake Wakatip Mail; Wairarapa Standard; Nelson Evening Mail; Daily Southern Cross; Nelson Examiner;* and *New Zealand Chronicle.*
4 Kenton Storey, *Settler Anxiety at the Outposts of Empire: Colonial Relations, Humanitarian Discourses, and the Imperial Press* (Vancouver: UBC Press, 2016).
5 *Saturday Review,* 3 November 1860.
6 P.B. Waite, *The Life and Times of Confederation, 1864–1867: Politics, Newspapers, and the Union of British North America* (Toronto: University of Toronto Press, 1961); Jeffrey L. McNairn, *The Capacity to Judge: Public Opinion and Deliberative Democracy in Upper Canada, 1791–1854* (Toronto: University of Toronto Press, 2000); Michael Eamon, *Imprinting Britain: Newspapers, Sociability, and the Shaping of British North America* (Montreal and Kingston: McGill-Queen's University Press, 2015); Storey, *Settler Anxiety at the Outposts of Empire.*
7 For example, the website Papers Past features forty-two digitized newspapers from the era between 1860 and 1870. This list of titles, though, is by no means a complete representation of all the newspapers published in this period.
8 F. Knight Hunt, *The Fourth Estate: Contributions Towards a History of Newspapers and the Liberty of the Press,* vol. 1 (London: David Bogue, 1850), 7–8.
9 McNairn, *The Capacity to Judge,* 7.
10 James Grant, *The Newspaper Press: Its Origin – Its Progress – and Present Position,* vol. 2 (London: Tinsley Brothers, 1871), 459–60.
11 See Gerald J. Baldasty, *The Commercialization of News in the Nineteenth Century* (Madison: University of Wisconsin Press, 1992).
12 Storey, *Settler Anxiety at the Outposts of Empire,* 133–5.
13 For an analysis of the culture of reading in Auckland, see Jeremiah Rankin, "Science and Civic Culture in Colonial Auckland" (MA thesis, University of Auckland, 2006).
14 Registrar General, *Statistics of New Zealand for 1864* (Auckland: W.C. Wilson, 1865), no. 46.
15 See Eric Pawson and Neil Quigley, "The Circulation of Information and Frontier Development: Canterbury 1850–1890," *New Zealand Geographer* 38, no. 2 (October 1982): 65–76.

16 *Lyttelton Times*, 13 May 1867.
17 *New Zealand Herald*, 24 April 1867.
18 *The Press*, 24 December 1864; *Lyttelton Times*, 27 July 1866; *Otago Daily Times*, 19 December 1867; *Nelson Evening Mail*, 14 October 1868.
19 *Otago Daily Times*, 19 December 1867.
20 Ibid.
21 Danny Keenan, *Wars without End: The Land Wars in Nineteenth-Century New Zealand* (Auckland: Penguin, 2009).
22 Ged Martin, *Britain and the Origins of Canadian Confederation, 1837–67* (Vancouver: UBC Press, 1994), 256.
23 See James Belich, *The New Zealand Wars and the Victorian Interpretation of Racial Conflict: The Maori, the British, and the New Zealand Wars* (Montreal and Kingston: McGill-Queen's University Press, 1986).
24 Belich, *The New Zealand Wars*, 211.
25 "Imperial Treatment of Canada & New Zealand Contrasted," *Lake Wakatip Mail*, 28 October 1864. Article originally published in the *New Zealand Advertiser*, no date.
26 *The Oamaru Times, and Waitaki Reporter*, 27 April 1865.
27 Ibid.
28 Ibid.
29 *Otago Daily Times*, 27 May 1867.
30 Ibid.
31 *Saturday Review*, 17 June 1867.
32 *The Press*, 24 December 1864.
33 *Wellington Independent*, 2 April 1867; *The Oamaru Times, and Waitaki Reporter*, 27 April 1865;
34 See Waite, *The Life and Times of Confederation*, 96, 285, 287. Waite details how New Zealand's *Constitution Act* functioned as a benchmark for John A. Macdonald.
35 *Wellington Independent*, 2 July 1867.
36 Bruce A. Knox, "The Rise of Colonial Federation as an Object of British Policy, 1850–1870," *Journal of British Studies* 11, no. 1 (November 1971): 92.
37 R.D. McGarvey, "Local Politics in the Auckland Province, 1853–62," (MA thesis, University of New Zealand, 1954), 1.
38 "The Provincial Period, 1853–76," An Encyclopedia of New Zealand 1966, accessed 20 November 2013, http://www.teara.govt.nz/en/1966/history-constitutional/page-5.
39 W. David McIntyre, "Self-Government and Independence – Crown Colony," Te Ara – the Encyclopedia of New Zealand, accessed 24 July 2016, http://www.teara.govt.nz/en/self-government-and-independence/page-1.

40 McIntyre, "Self-Government and Independence."
41 Gore Browne to Gordon Gairdner, 18 October 1856, "Sir Thomas Gore Browne Letterbook," QMS-0284, Alexander Turnbull Library.
42 James Douglas Leighton, "The Development of Federal Indian Policy in Canada, 1840–1890" (PhD thesis, University of Western Ontario, 1975), 178.
43 *The Oamaru Times, and Waitaki Reporter*, 27 April 1865.
44 *Wellington Independent*, 23 August 1866.
45 *New Zealand Herald*, 4 June 1867.
46 *New Zealand Herald*, 10 July 1867.
47 Martin, *Britain and the Origins of Canadian Confederation*, 256.

13 "The Word Is Steeped in Blood and Violence": Canadian-Style Federation in Southern Africa

TIMOTHY STAPLETON

During the late nineteenth and early twentieth century, most people in Southern Africa likely did not know much about the 1867 Confederation of Canada. Nevertheless, tens of thousands of them would suffer and die in wars related to failed attempts to impose this model on the region's settler states, which also involved the subjugation of the area's last independent African communities. While late nineteenth century British imperialists and some local settler elites came to think that Southern Africa's settler societies were prime candidates for a Canadian-style federation, the situation in the region was very different from circumstances in North America or Australia. The main difference was that white settlers in Southern Africa represented a small but dominant minority among a vast African population. Another major issue, and one that impacted directly on federal experiments in the region, was that the two main communities of white settlers, Britons and Boers (the latter eventually called Afrikaners), each had their own set of autonomous settler states with different agendas, systems of government, and legal status. To complicate matters further, not all Boers lived in the Boer republics, with many inhabiting the British Cape Colony, which had been their original point of settlement; and from the 1890s many British subjects came to live in the Boer republic of the Transvaal. Although the main motivation for federation in Southern Africa in the late nineteenth century was the discovery of diamonds and gold, and the consequent rise of a capitalist mining economy, the dream was continued into the twentieth century by white British settlers in mostly agricultural Southern Rhodesia (now Zimbabwe), where it also led to armed conflict. This paper will demonstrate that attempts to implement Canadian-style federation programs in Southern Africa, none of which succeeded, led to a series of deadly wars from the late nineteenth to the late twentieth century. At the same time, these failed attempts represented some of the most significant processes in the region's history and did much to shape its current political situation.

Background

By the end of the 1850s the area of what is now South Africa was dominated by a number of settler colonial territories and independent African states. Established by the Dutch in the seventeenth century, the Cape Colony had been taken over by the British at the start of the nineteenth century and granted responsible government with a non-racial but qualified franchise in 1853. Adjacent to the eastern border of the Cape Colony was the separate and smaller territory of British Kaffraria, which was home to the recently conquered Xhosa people under direct rule by the Cape governor. While the Cape was home to an expanding settler society, which was developing its own interests, the main purpose of Dutch and then British occupation was to secure the strategic position of Cape Town on the oceanic route between Europe and Asia. From the imperial perspective, a large territorial empire in the impoverished and agrarian region had never been desirable. The colony of Natal, established by expansionist Boer (Dutch-speaking) settlers from the Cape in the late 1830s, had been occupied by the British in 1843 for similar strategic reasons: to protect the southeastern coast from potential maritime rivals who could possibly ally with the Boers. The high grassland of the interior (the Highveld) was home to two independent Boer republics, which had been founded in the late 1830s during what later Afrikaner nationalists called the "Great Trek." In the early 1850s the British, seeing little value in trying to control the interior of South Africa, had recognized the suzerainty of the Boer-ruled Orange Free State and the South African Republic (or Transvaal). Although many African communities had been subjugated by these British and Boer colonial entities or had lost land to them, a few powerful and independent African states occupied the periphery, including the Gcaleka Xhosa on the Cape's eastern frontier; Lesotho, which was in conflict with the Orange Free State; and the Zulu Kingdom, which was adjacent to Natal and the Transvaal.

Although it is now an almost forgotten element of South African history, the prospect of federating colonial territories in the region was first raised by Cape Governor Sir George Grey in 1859. The federation plan had little to do with Canada. Grey's proposal was influenced by his previous experience as governor of New Zealand where, in the early 1850s, he had overseen the creation of a number of provinces under a central government. In the late 1850s Grey proposed to the British government that the Cape Colony, Natal, and the Orange Free State should form a federation of self-governing territories under a federal government and that other settler territories (particularly the Transvaal) and even African states could join later as similarly self-governing entities. He also proposed that the Cape absorb British Kaffraria, where the colonial administration had taken advantage of chaos caused by a millenarian movement to further dispossess the Xhosa. However, the Colonial Office instructed Grey to take no action on the matter without approval from the British parliament. At the time, London feared that the proposed federation in South Africa might result in great expense and cause the more unified white settlers to embark on warfare against the blacks. Nevertheless, without authorization from the Colonial Office, Grey obtained a resolution from the Orange Free State *volksraad* (legislature) supporting the proposed union with the Cape, and he presented this to the Cape parliament, stating that it would ensure the colony's security and success. The Orange Free State's willingness to join the Cape had been informed by recent conflict with the Transvaal to the north and Lesotho to the east. Once Grey reported his actions to London, a disapproving British government recalled him in June 1859. However, a change in government in Britain prompted Grey's sudden reappointment as governor of the Cape, though he was forbidden to further pursue the federation scheme, and this ambition fizzled when he was sent back to New Zealand in 1861. The only part of Grey's plan to come to reality was the 1865 annexation of British Kaffraria by the Cape. Some early historians of South Africa would see Grey's imagined federation as a tragic missed opportunity that could have steered the region away from a long period of warfare from the late 1870s to the early 1900s.[1]

South Africa: The Failure of Imposed Federation (1874–81)

British imperial policy towards Southern Africa changed dramatically with the discovery of diamonds in the Northern Cape in the late 1860s and the subsequent development of the diamond fields around what became the mining town of Kimberley. This occurred at a time when British imperial policy had moved towards the creation of self-supporting and self-governing settler colonial federations, the first of which was Canada. According to historian Ronald Hyam, "After the successful establishment of the Canadian Confederation in 1867, the 'federal panacea' almost became an imperial obsession."² The British disinterest in the South African interior that had characterized much of the previous two decades gave way to a sudden desire to control the potential location of valuable resources. In 1868 Cape Governor Philip Wodehouse told the Cape parliament that he supported federation with the Boer republics, and the Natal legislature voted in favour of such a policy. Nonetheless, the way the British used legal trickery in the early 1870s to ensure that the Cape Colony annexed the diamond fields, which were located in an area with uncertain borders and overlapping claims, alienated the Boers of the Orange Free State and Transvaal.

In 1874 Lord Carnarvon, who had ironically been involved in Grey's dismissal over proposed federation at the end of the 1850s, returned for his second term as Britain's colonial secretary. In that role, he quickly became determined to apply his 1867 experience with Canadian Confederation to South Africa, but in a more top-down fashion. While Canadian Confederation had been a British North American initiative, Carnarvon's reputation within imperial circles had benefited from the perception that he had been its successful architect. The recent unifications of Germany and Italy were also inspirational in London's desire to bring together the South African territories. The older British strategic considerations in Southern Africa were not lost, as Carnarvon believed a South African federation would serve as a more stable host to the important naval facility at Simon's Town in the Cape. There was some general support for the concept of a broad South African federation in the Cape Colony, which had gained responsible government in 1872, including from among diverse parliamentarians such as Afrikaner Bond leader Jan Hendrik Hofmeyr and Eastern Cape separatist John Paterson and from Chief Justice John de Villiers. Frustrated by the conflicts and intrigues of the existing separate British and Boer colonial states and their African neighbours, these men developed a vision of a grand union of self-governing territories that would bring together Boers and Britons under a British governor general and extend from the Cape as far north as the Zambezi River.³

In 1875, however, the Cape parliament turned down Carnarvon's plan for federation given concern that most of the cost of the scheme would fall on the Cape Colony, which had the region's largest economy (especially since it had gained the diamond fields), and that it would endanger the Cape's non-racial franchise as Natal and the Boer republics had exclusively white political systems with no plans for black representation. Furthermore, the Cape government was not completely opposed to the principle of a Canadian-style federation but believed that the process should originate in South Africa and not Britain, and that the tumultuous region was not yet ready. The proposed federation was also undermined by a failed conference held in London in 1876 and Transvaal plans to establish a rail link with Portuguese Mozambique on the East African coast, which would certainly reduce economic dependence on the more distant ports of the British colonies.

The frustrated Carnarvon then opted for direct imperial intervention. Given the military defeat of Transvaal forces by the Pedi Kingdom in 1876, Carnarvon dispatched Theophilus Shepstone, Natal's secretary for native affairs, with some British troops to the Transvaal, which was summarily annexed by Britain in May 1877. The penniless Boer government did not resist. Around the same time the Colonial Office drafted legislation, modelled on the *British North America Act, 1867* that had created Canada, to facilitate the South Africa federation. This legislation was sent to the British parliament where, in August 1877, it became the *South African Act*. In addressing parliament on the bill, Carnarvon was frank, stating that unlike the federation process in Canada, which had been a home-grown initiative, Britain would be forcing this system on South Africa where there were still many problems to be resolved. In early 1877 Sir Bartle Frere was appointed as governor of the Cape Colony and high commissioner of Southern Africa with a mandate to create the federation of regional territories and an understanding that he would become its first governor general. With the departure of the previous governor, Henry Barkly, and Frere's dismissal of John C. Molteno's Cape government, sceptics of federation in Cape Town were sidelined. The Cape was central to the federation scheme as it controlled the economically important diamond fields, and its population of 237,000 white settlers was double that of the combined white population of Natal and both Boer republics.[4]

For Carnarvon and Frere, the key to white South African support for federation was the elimination of independent African states, which were seen as a potential threat as well as a source of additional land and labour. As such, the British army and hosts of African auxiliaries fought a series of wars of conquest in South Africa during the late 1870s. In 1877–8 Xhosa groups along the Cape's eastern frontier were further subdued; in 1879 the Zulu Kingdom was invaded and its monarchy overthrown, which threw the state into a disastrous civil war; and later the same year the Pedi Kingdom was conquered, becoming part of the Transvaal. While the Zulu Kingdom had been an ally of the British colony of Natal against the Transvaal Boers for some time, Frere reversed this policy, portrayed the Kingdom as a threat to regional peace, and issued it an impossible ultimatum. The surprising massacre of British troops by the Zulu at the Battle of Isandlwana in January 1879, though it simply delayed the inevitable given the superiority of British firepower, might have inspired the Transvaal Boers to resist annexation.[5]

Three rebellions at the start of the 1880s destroyed Carnarvon's ambition for a federal South Africa. In the eastern part of the Cape Colony, the Mpondomise and some Thembu, who had recently accepted colonial rule through treaty, rebelled against colonial officials who were undermining traditional leaders. In Basutoland (present day Lesotho), where local rulers had volunteered to come under British protection in the late 1860s to forestall conquest by the Boers of the Orange Free State, there was a rebellion against the Cape administration which had tried to disarm Africans. This "Gun War" of 1880–1 led to a negotiated settlement in which the British imperial government reassumed direct authority over Basutoland, which would remain separate and therefore protected from the regional settler states. Most importantly, the Boers of the Transvaal, now liberated from the Pedi and Zulu threats, rebelled against British taxation and the arrival of British businessmen, clergy, and soldiers. The Boers besieged British garrisons within the Transvaal and blocked the mountain passes through which British relief forces landed at Natal would have to travel. In late February 1881 the Boers, though they lacked formal military training, inflicted a stunning defeat on the British army at the Battle of Majuba Hill where Britain's new high commissioner, George Pomeroy Colley, was killed. Given that the war was unpopular in Britain and that there were troubles in Ireland, Gladstone's new liberal government concluded a settlement with the Transvaal. As stipulated in the Pretoria Convention of August 1881, British soldiers withdrew from the Transvaal, which regained autonomy under nominal British supervision. Later, in the 1884 London Convention, Britain surrendered its sovereignty over the Transvaal. Since the Transvaal was a poor agricultural area with no known valuable resources, Britain lacked the political will to sacrifice the "blood and treasure" needed to overwhelm it, which meant that the federation scheme was effectively abandoned.[6] In 1881 Francis Statham, an anti-imperialist newspaper editor in the Cape and Natal, compared the attempted imposition of Canadian-style confederation on South Africa to a person who was expected to wear a coat that did not fit. Of confederation, he wrote: "The word is steeped in blood and violence, and all the perfumes of Arabia will not sweeten it. This is the result of Lord Carnarvon's day-dreaming over Canadian Acts of Parliament."[7]

South Africa: War and Union (1890–1910)

The discovery of gold in the newly independent Transvaal in the late 1880s once again impelled a change in British policy towards the interior of South Africa and resurrected the possibility of a federation of settler-ruled territories in the region. With a fortune made on the diamond fields, British imperialist Cecil Rhodes was elected premier of the Cape Colony in 1890. Rhodes was committed to forming a federation of South African territories, similar to the autonomous Canadian model, which he dreamed would become part of a global British imperial federation of self-governing settler states. Rhodes and other mining capitalists also saw the Transvaal republican government as an inefficient and even backward partner in the development of the local gold mining industry. Partly to give the Boers confidence in the federation scheme, Rhodes's Cape administration increased voting qualifications, which disenfranchised many black voters, and implemented the *Glen Grey Act*, which deprived Africans of agricultural land and pushed them into low-paid wage migrant labour. Furthermore, Rhodes privately orchestrated the British colonization of what became Southern Rhodesia (now Zimbabwe), located north of the Transvaal, and he believed that the white settlers moving there from the Cape would one day join a wider South African federation. Believing that Southern Rhodesia would be the location of a second major gold discovery, Rhodes facilitated the conquest of the Ndebele Kingdom in 1893 and the suppression of Ndebele and Shona rebellions in 1896–7. Initially, Rhodes approached the regional federation issue with patience, working towards gradual economic integration through building railways from the Cape to Johannesburg and Pretoria in the Transvaal, and proposing a customs union for the region. However, with the Transvaal republic's continued opposition to federation and the lack of anticipated gold sources in Southern Rhodesia, Rhodes organized a sudden armed incursion into the Boer republic with the aim of overthrowing the government of President Paul Kruger. But this raid failed as a planned uprising by foreign white mine workers (called "uitlanders" by the Boers) did not happen. The scandal brought about by the disastrous 1895 Jameson Raid ended Rhodes's government at the Cape and, given that London appeared to have been implicated in the plot, made war between Britain and the Boer republics almost inevitable. As such, it also terminated the ambition of a locally initiated British federation of British and Boer territories.[8]

During the late 1890s mounting tensions between the British imperial government and the Transvaal centred on the potential enfranchisement of the large number of uitlanders who were mostly British subjects. While Britain demanded that the uitlanders be granted voting rights so as to elect a pro-British regime in the Transvaal that would then join a regional union under Britain, the Kruger administration resisted this pressure in order to maintain the Boer republic's independence. To make matters worse, the Boer republic conscripted the disenfranchised uitlanders for military campaigns to extend the authority of the Transvaal over the last remaining independent African communities in the area. Enflaming regional tensions, Rhodes's imperialist South African League was formed in 1896 with branches in the Cape, Natal (which had been granted responsible government in 1893), and Transvaal; the League campaigned for the federation of South African territories under Britain and called for direct British intervention. After the Jameson Raid, British officials also feared that the growing wealth of the Transvaal would enable it to form its own republican regional grouping that would pull in the Cape, Natal, and the Orange Free State, and potentially form alliances with imperial rivals such as Germany, which had established the neighbouring colony of German South West Africa (now Namibia). The purchase of German weapons by the newly enriched Boer republics seemed to confirm these anxieties. These British strategic concerns were in some way similar to worries about the possible expansion of the post–Civil War United States that had informed Canadian Confederation. As Lord Selborne, under-secretary to British Colonial Secretary Joseph Chamberlain, wrote in a memorandum from the Colonial Office: "If we can succeed in uniting all South Africa into a Confederacy on the model of the Dominion of Canada and under the British flag, the probability is that that confederacy will not become a United States of South Africa."[9]

In October 1899, with negotiations over the uitlander issue going nowhere, the Boer republics launched a pre-emptive military strike on the British territories. The Boers, thinking about their victory in 1881, hoped to seize the railway centres of the Northern Cape and occupy all of Natal, which would make it difficult for the British to bring in large military forces and therefore compel London to offer a favourable settlement. This did not happen: the Boers failed to secure their initial military objectives, and the British eventually shipped massive numbers of soldiers, including thousands from the Dominions of Canada, Australia, and New Zealand, to overwhelm the republics. The desire to conquer the gold fields of the Transvaal generated the political will that had been lacking during Britain's previous conflict with the Boers. After a series of battlefield disasters in the conventional phase of the war, the British occupied the Boer republican capitals of Bloemfontein and Pretoria, and the mining centre of Johannesburg, and declared British rule over the Boer territories. When desperate Boers vowed to fight to the bitter end and embarked on a guerrilla campaign against British occupation, the British responded with a brutal and thorough counter-insurgency program. Some 25,000 Boer non-combatants and 20,000 of their black servants died in British concentration camps. In total, the Second Anglo-Boer War or South African War of 1899–1902 cost around 75,000 lives, including 22,000 British imperial troops and 7,000 Boer combatants. The prospect of the extermination of their society and the rise of African resistance to them prompted the remaining Boer fighters to rethink what the bitter end actually meant.

In the May 1902 Treaty of Vereeniging, Boer leaders conceded independence, while the British declared a general amnesty, allocated funds for reconstruction, ensured the protection of the Dutch language, promised self-government for the former republics, and guaranteed that black political rights would not extend beyond the Cape. The British, in giving so many concessions, were eager to encourage Boer cooperation in the future administration of a united South Africa. In 1907, as promised, the Boers of both the Transvaal and Orange River Colony were granted responsible government. In 1910 the Cape Colony and Natal and the two former republics, now all British territories, were combined into the Union of South Africa, which was a self-governing British dominion with the same legal status as Canada, Australia, and New Zealand. Unlike Canada and Australia, however, the Union of South Africa was not a federation but a unitary state. For some, the unitary model would be more effective at promoting unity among Britons and Boers in South Africa than Canada's federal system, which seemed to keep anglophone and francophone people apart. Although westernized African elites had sent a delegation to Britain in 1909 to protest the racially exclusive nature of the South African central government that would be created by the *Act of Union*, only whites could vote in union elections. Inspiring the saying that "the Boers lost the war but won the peace," former Boer republican military leaders Louis Botha and Jan Smuts became the first and second prime ministers, respectively, of South Africa. On the other hand, the memory of the South African War became a powerful grievance for many Boers and an important factor in the rise of Afrikaner nationalism during the early twentieth century, which eventually led to the imposition of apartheid in 1948.[10]

Initially encouraged by the British government, Botha and Smuts believed that the union would gradually expand to include much of the Southern Africa region, perhaps adding Portuguese territory, just as Canada and Australia had also added new territories. This ambition informed the South African invasion of German South West Africa during the First World War and the subsequent granting of a League of Nations mandate to Pretoria to administer the former German colony. However, the emergence of Afrikaner nationalism and related tensions with Britain meant that the British High Commission territories of Bechuanaland (Botswana), Basutoland (Lesotho), and Swaziland, where African traditional leaders had worked against incorporation into a white-supremacist state since the 1890s, were never handed over to South Africa, and in 1922 (as discussed in the next section) the mostly white voters of Southern Rhodesia rejected inclusion in the union.[11]

Southern Rhodesia and the Central African Federation (1953–63)

Although their territory had been created by Rhodes's chartered British South Africa Company (BSAC) in the 1890s, Southern Rhodesia's small white settler minority quickly became interested in acquiring self-government within the British Empire. As noted earlier, Rhodes had encouraged this. White Rhodesian society very rapidly came to see itself as particularly British, despite some diverse origins, though also distinct because of its African frontier experience. As early as 1894 white Rhodesians began comparing themselves to the "Canadian ideal" of a self-governing British settler state. Many white Rhodesians saw participation in the First World War as an opportunity to ingratiate themselves to Britain, which would then, it was believed, logically grant political devolution as a reward.[12] In 1922, with the pending withdrawal of the financially troubled BSAC administration, the mostly white voters rejected union with South Africa, seen as too Boer (or Afrikaner) dominated, and decided to go it alone under responsible government, which was granted the following year. Many white

Rhodesians had been disgusted by the Boer uprising in South Africa during the First World War and the white mine worker rebellion on the Rand in early 1922. While white Rhodesians had long been interested in joining a larger British-themed settler-dominated regional federation that would become a military and economic power in its own right, the politics of the Union of South Africa prompted them to look north.

During the 1930s the now self-governing whites of Southern Rhodesia who were busy passing laws to undermine local black economic competition and the even tinier settler minority of Northern Rhodesia (now Zambia), which was a protectorate under Britain, began discussing the potential amalgamation of the two territories. In 1945, with the conclusion of the Second World War, the British Labour Party government rejected the consolidation of the two Rhodesias as it was concerned that the vast African majority of the north would become subjugated and exploited by the white minority of the south. In turn, local settler politicians proposed creating a federation in which African rights in Northern Rhodesia would be protected by a semi-autonomous territorial government. The 1948 South African electoral victory of the Afrikaner Nationalist Party with its policy of apartheid and hostility to Britain prompted London to support the federation of its south-central African territories, which now, at Britain's insistence, would also include the small colony of Nyasaland (now Malawi). The Central African Federation, created in 1953, would constitute a new regional ally for Britain and serve as a foil to apartheid South Africa, which was on the road to becoming a republic. For many Southern Rhodesian whites, participation in the federation was expected to lead to long-sought-after dominion status. The new federation sought to combine the administrative expertise and secondary industries of white-ruled Southern Rhodesia with the copper mining wealth of Northern Rhodesia and the African labour reservoir of densely populated Nyasaland. Britain assisted the federation by contributing modern military aircraft, which it could use to project power as far away as the Middle East, and encouraging a major hydroelectric project on the Zambezi River to facilitate economic growth. Although the Central African Federation was not a sovereign state in the same way as Canada or Australia and its constitution was not modelled on these existing dominions, the federal government in Salisbury (now Harare) had authority over defence, finance, and trade. However, the federation contained many contradictions, such as the different legal status of Southern Rhodesia, which enjoyed internal self-government, and Northern Rhodesia and

Nyasaland, which, in theory, remained British protectorates. Politically, the white minority–dominated federal government mobilized the rhetoric of "multiracialism," which paternalistically promised civil rights to the African majority when they were deemed ready, a stage that many whites believed would be a very long time in the future.[13]

British policy towards Africa changed a great deal during the decade-long life of the Central African Federation. In the early 1950s Britain was set to stay in much of Africa for the foreseeable future. But by the late part of the decade, conflicts in Kenya and Egypt as well as the changing international context of the Cold War and anti-colonialism prompted London to withdraw from Africa as quickly as possible. A white-dominated British federation in the heart of south-central Africa became an embarrassment. African nationalist movements in all three federal territories, inspired by decolonization in other parts of the continent, opposed the white-controlled federation and launched protest campaigns against it that were met with increasingly deadly force by the state. At the end of the 1950s and during the early 1960s, emergencies were declared in all three territories. In 1960 Britain's Monckton Commission, which included Canadian historian Donald Creighton, concluded that the Central African Federation could only be maintained through coercion and recommended dramatic political reform that would effectively bring about its demise.[14] In 1963 the British government disbanded the embattled federation and the following year granted independence under majority rule constitutions to Northern Rhodesia, which became Zambia, and Nyasaland, which became Malawi. Protectorate status allowed London to step in and oversee a quick transition in the former federation's northern territories.

A crisis developed over Southern Rhodesia's future given its long-standing system of internal self-government (responsible government), which had a qualified non-racial franchise inherited from the Cape but in which there were pitifully few black voters. Within Southern Rhodesia, disappointment over the end of the federation and fear that chaos in newly independent Congo would spread south had inspired the mostly white voters to elect the Rhodesian Front (RF), which pursued a conservative agenda. While Britain offered Southern Rhodesia dominion status if it guaranteed eventual majority rule, the RF government of Ian Smith demanded immediate and unconditional dominion status based on the territory's enthusiastic defence of Britain during both world wars and the claim that it was one of the last bastions of Western civilization in Africa. For Smith and his supporters, Britain's hesitance in supporting white minority rule in Southern Rhodesia represented a "great betrayal." This impasse was broken on the symbolic date of 11 November 1965 when Smith's administration unilaterally declared independence from Britain and gained support from neighbouring apartheid South Africa and sympathetic politicians in the United States. Since London did nothing about this illegal action, the much harassed and exiled African nationalist leaders of Rhodesia embarked on what would become a long armed struggle to liberate their country. They were backed by newly independent African states like Zambia and Tanzania, and within the Cold War context they were armed by the Soviet Union and Communist China. Smith's Rhodesia became an international pariah subject to economic sanctions and reviled even within Britain's settler dominions such as Canada, which had once served as its model. After a protracted guerrilla war that intensified during the second half of the 1970s, the British-sponsored Lancaster House negotiations of 1979 led to majority rule and independence for Zimbabwe in April 1980. The African nationalist leader Robert Mugabe then came to power and led an increasingly authoritarian and oppressive state.[15]

Conclusion

In Southern Africa, attempts to federate settler colonial states led to many wars that caused massive loss of life and destruction. Directly inspired by the Canadian model, which was imposed by London on unwilling regional participants, Carnarvon's failed scheme of the 1870s caused six major conflicts in what is now South Africa. Rhodes's aggressive revival of the Canadian-style federation program during the 1890s had more support among the region's white English-speaking settlers but prompted imperial intervention, triggered the South African War (1899–1902), and resulted in the imposition of a unitary South African state that eventually expanded racial segregation through apartheid. As such, instead of attracting its smaller neighbours such as Bechuanaland (Botswana), Basutoland (Lesotho), Swaziland, and Southern Rhodesia (Zimbabwe) to join the union, the nature of the South African state would encourage them to remain separate. While the Central African Federation of the 1950s was not directly or technically inspired by Canada, it was a product of unrealistic white Rhodesian ambitions to become a white settler British dominion like Canada and Australia, though situated in the heart of Africa and among a very large majority of subject African peoples. These thwarted federal and dominion dreams contributed to the Rhodesian crisis of the 1960s and a long guerrilla war during the 1970s that eventually brought Mugabe to power in Zimbabwe. The basic concept of uniting the small economies of Southern Rhodesia (Zimbabwe), Northern Rhodesia (Zambia), and Nyasaland (Malawi) was probably a sensible goal but the way it was applied, through a white-supremacist state, meant that these three colonial entities would become distinct independent states. In short, a series of failed Canadian-style federal schemes represent the context in which South Africa, Botswana, Lesotho, Swaziland, Zimbabwe, Zambia, and Malawi became the separate independent states of today.

NOTES

1 "The Recall of His Excellency Sir George Grey, Governor of the Cape of Good Hope," British Parliamentary Papers, April 1860; William Lee Rees and L. Rees, *The Life and Times of Sir George Grey*, vol. 1 (London: Hutchinson, 1892), 282–3; George Cockburn Henderson, *Sir George Grey: Pioneer of Empire in Southern Lands* (London: J.M. Dent, 1907), 262; A.P. Newton and E.A. Benians, eds., *The Cambridge History of the British Empire*, vol. 8, *South Africa, Rhodesia and the Protectorates* (Cambridge: Cambridge University Press, 1936), 407–8; Bernard M. Magubane, *The Making of a Racist State: British Imperialism and the Union of South Africa, 1875–1910* (Trenton, NJ: Africa World Press, 1996), 176.
2 Ronald Hyam, *Understanding the British Empire* (Cambridge: Cambridge University Press, 2010), 77.
3 *Cambridge History of the British Empire*, vol. 8, 426, 457.
4 Peter Gordon, ed., *The Political Diaries of the Fourth Earl of Carnarvon, 1857–1890* (Cambridge: Royal Historical Society, 2009), 22–3; "South African Act, 13 August 1877," in *Select Documents Relating to the Unification of South Africa*, ed. A.P. Newton (1924; repr., London: Routledge, 2006), 51–68; John Laband, *Zulu Warriors: The Battle for the South African Frontier* (New Haven: Yale University Press, 2014), 69–72; for a classic study see C.W. die Kiewiet, *The Imperial Factor in South Africa: A Study in Politics and Economics* (Cambridge: Cambridge University Press, 1937).
5 Peter Delius, *The Land Belongs to Us: The Pedi Polity, the Boers and the British in the Nineteenth Century Transvaal* (Los Angeles: University of California Press, 1984); John Milton, *The Edges of War: A History of Frontier Wars (1702–1878)* (Cape Town: Juta, 1983); John Laband, *Rope of Sand: The Rise and Fall of the Zulu Kingdom in the Nineteenth Century* (Johannesburg: Jonathan Ball Publishers, 1995); Laband, *Zulu Warriors*.

6 Clifton Crais, *The Politics of Evil: Magic, State Power and Imagination in South Africa* (Cambridge: Cambridge University Press, 2002); Oliver Ransford, *The Battle of Majuba Hill: The First Boer War* (London: Thomas Y. Crowell, 1967); John Laband, *The Transvaal Rebellion: The First Boer War, 1880–1881* (Harlow, UK: Pearson/Longman, 2005).

7 Francis R. Statham, *Blacks, Boers and British: A Three-Cornered Problem* (London: MacMillan, 1881), 246.

8 John Flint, *Cecil Rhodes* (Boston: Little, Brown, 1974); Robert Rotberg, *The Founder: Cecil Rhodes and the Pursuit of Power* (Oxford: Oxford University Press, 1988).

9 Martin Meredith, *Diamonds, Gold and War: The British, the Boers and the Making of South Africa* (New York: Public Affairs, 2007), 367.

10 Thomas Pakenham, *The Boer War* (London: Weidenfeld and Nicholson, 1979); Bill Nasson, *The South African War 1899–1902* (London: Hodder Arnold, 1999); Carmen Miller, *Painting the Map Red: Canada and the South African War, 1899–1902* (Kingston and Montreal: McGill-Queen's University Press, 1998); for the South African unitary system compared to Canada, see Brian D. Tennyson, *Canadian Relations with South Africa: A Diplomatic History* (Washington, DC: University Press of America, 1982), 35.

11 Ronald Hyam, *The Failure of South African Expansion, 1908–48* (London: MacMillan, 1972).

12 Julie Bonello, "The Development of Early Settler Identity in Southern Africa, 1890–1914," *International Journal of African Historical Studies* 43, no. 2 (2010): 341–67; Tim Stapleton, "Views of the First World War in Southern Rhodesia (Zimbabwe), 1914–18," *War and Society* 20, no. 2 (May 2002): 23–45.

13 Henry Franklin, *Unholy Wedlock: The Failure of the Central African Federation* (London: George Allen and Unwin, 1963); J.R.T. Wood, *The Welensky Papers: A History of the Federation of Rhodesia and Nyasaland* (Durban: Graham Publishers, 1983); Zoe Groves, "Transnational Networks and Regional Solidarity: The Case of the Central African Federation, 1953–63," *African Studies* 72, no. 2 (August 2013): 155–75; Julia Tischler, *Light and Power for a Multi-Racial Nation: The Kariba Dam Scheme in the Central African Federation* (London: Palgrave-MacMillan, 2013).

14 Donald Wright, *Donald Creighton: A Life in History* (Toronto: University of Toronto Press, 2015).

15 D. Martin and P. Johnson, *The Struggle for Zimbabwe* (New York: Monthly Review, 1981); P. Moorcroft and P. McLaughlin, *The Rhodesian War: A*

Military History (London: Pen and Sword, 2008); Ian Smith, *The Great Betrayal: The Memoirs of Ian Douglas Smith* (London: Blake Publishing, 1997); Carl Peter Watts, *Rhodesia's Unilateral Declaration of Independence: An International History* (New York: Palgrave-MacMillan, 2012); Luise White, *Unpopular Sovereignty: Rhodesian Independence and African Decolonization* (Chicago: University of Chicago Press, 2015).

14 The Federation Idea in the British West Indies and Canadian Confederation

FRANKLIN W. KNIGHT

The history of the establishment of Canadian Confederation in 1867 was not just a simple narrative of Canadian domestic aspirations and British political calculations. Rather Canadian Confederation reflected an extremely complex story in global imperialism that weaved together changing times, changing political circumstances, and specific geographical locations. The long nineteenth century presented the confluence of diverse circumstances that challenged the core conventional notions of empire. It was the turning point when the corrosive ideas of the long period of the Enlightenment began to be seen in the overpowering revolutionary concepts of industrialization, modernization, free trade, and industrial capitalism.[1] So it should not be surprising that this period also coincided with what has been called the "age of revolutions," the chaotic, century-long global political changes that occurred between the end of the Seven Years War (1756–63) and the great Indian Mutiny of 1857 that proved the death knell for the over-extended British East India Company.[2] Beside the transcendental political revolutions like the American Revolution (1776–83), the French Revolution (1789–1830), the Haitian Revolution (1789–1804), the Spanish American Wars of Independence (1810–30), and the Greek War of Independence (1821–32) were other significant accompanying social, cultural, and economic revolutions across the Atlantic world and Africa as well as much of India.[3] The political revolutions of the late eighteenth and nineteenth centuries suggested, perhaps, that all empires bear within themselves the seeds of their eventual dissolution. Over time the inherent conflicts between the metropolitan centres and their peripheries become increasingly more difficult to negotiate and resolve successfully. After a few generations Europeans in the Americas might still have identified spontaneously with their original homelands but they began to manifest differences of self and self-interests that inevitably generated conflicts with the imperial centres.⁴ By the nineteenth century the Atlantic world had changed profoundly. Marketing and commerce intensified, so it should not be surprising that new rationales were being articulated for new concepts of sovereignty, domination, and exploitation.⁵ As William Woodruff noted in *The Impact of Western Man*:

> European dynamism was a strange mixture of God, greed, and glory; of gunpowder and the Gospel. However badly the white man behaved in Africa, the hope that legitimate commerce would one day replace slavery and barbarism never died. Trade in goods should replace the traffic (especially in Africa) in human beings ... In this respect, what distinguishes European civilization from preceding civilizations is that it hoped not only to exploit the world but also to build a better world.⁶

Political changes in the nineteenth century were propelled not only by rapidly expanding acquisitive capitalist influences but also by modernizing concepts of administrative efficiency.⁷ Both were related in a seemingly irresolvable and troublesome way that often generated perpetual conflict, not only between colonial administrators and imperial entrepreneurs at the centre but also between metropolitan centres and their overseas peripheries. Such complexities applied equally to Canada and the British West Indies. Administrators at the centre wanted a simple and cost-efficient system of regulations with the widest application across the Empire. Sometimes that could not be achieved by local administrators, who took an interest in the special needs of their particular territories.⁸ Colonial civil servants preferred specific instructions designed for their peculiar situation. Those differences made conflict unavoidable. Moreover, within influential groups in Great Britain were found opponents to further expansion of the Empire. In the meantime entrepreneurs preferred loose regulations, free trade, and porous imperial boundaries. Resentment in the periphery gradually increased as the amount of the economic surplus appropriated by the imperial centre became larger, a sentiment encapsulated earlier in the British North American colonial resentment to taxation without representation. The granting of dominion status to Canada and elsewhere illustrated the complexities of administering a diverse global empire. The new political rearrangements also reflected the increased problems of race and colour within empires and across the nineteenth century world.

From the perspective of Great Britain, the Canadian colonies and the British West Indies were worlds apart. And indeed they were.

The Genesis of the Federal Idea in the Caribbean

The federal idea in the Caribbean long predated the Canadian example of 1867. It had its origins in the days of Charles II and the conversion of the Eastern Caribbean possessions from proprietary settlements to monarchical administered colonies.[9] After the Restoration in the later seventeenth century, some British bureaucrats started to think of a British West Indian confederation that sometimes included all the Eastern Caribbean possessions and at other times specifically considered only the British Leeward Islands. The idea from the point of view of the metropolitan bureaucrats was that a confederation would facilitate administration as well as maritime defence, especially of the Leeward Islands.

In 1674 Sir William Stapleton (d. 1686), an Anglo-Irish property holder who had followed Charles II (1630–85) into exile and after the Restoration accompanied Sir Tobias Bridge to Barbados in 1667, set up the first federation in the British West Indies.[10] The federation worked between 1674 and 1685 while Stapleton was actively acquiring estates and expanding his personal sugar businesses. The idea failed to find traction among the local island legislatures, especially in Barbados, as various islands retained their limited local representative assemblies while sharing a single governor and attorney general. It was a model that would remain fixed in the British bureaucratic mind.

The nineteenth century brought new attempts to impose a federal structure on selected groups of Eastern Caribbean islands. This project was driven by the anachronistic and incongruous nature of the Caribbean territories by the nineteenth century – some retained microcosmic aspects of British colonization while others were administered as Crown colonies. By the nineteenth century the original nature of the British Caribbean colonies had fundamentally changed from essentially European (British) settler colonies to demographically diverse exploitation slave colonies in which the original British settler component represented a small minority of the inhabitants.[11]

As settler colonies, the original European inhabitants who had arrived in the early decades of the seventeenth century sought to reproduce in the tropical Caribbean islands microcosms of their familiar British political, social, and economic norms. Directed by their proprietors, yeoman farming constituted the basic economic organization. Initially tobacco represented the most important cash crop. But the experiment did not last long. Within the first generation the system began to fall apart as larger tobacco exporters on the mainland overwhelmed the market. By the second generation the region was already undergoing a major transformation in the social and economic structures as a result of the all-encompassing sugar revolutions.[12] Yet the original colonies retained their unrepresentative elected legislatures with political power exercised by a decreasing minority of white men. The colonial incongruity was further accentuated by the practice whereby members of the local assemblies also served as members of the imperial parliament in London.

By the later eighteenth century the sugar revolutions had become a widespread Caribbean phenomenon. From Barbados in the middle of the seventeenth century to Cuba, Puerto Rico, Trinidad, and the Guianas in the nineteenth century, the experience was roughly similar. The expansion of a sugar industry fundamentally impacted demography, agriculture, culture, and society. The ideals of the original settlement society became transformed by the imperatives of the exploitation slave plantation society. Instead of recreating the norms of the metropolitan society, the local elites became intoxicated with the pursuit of efficient production and maximum profit. Exploitation slave societies were also potentially explosive.[13]

By retaining the original legislatures in the early settlement colonies, problems were inevitable when the new element of non-European and their mixed progeny begun to demand political enfranchisement and to enter the assemblies. This process obviously accelerated with the general abolition of slavery, although acceptance of this new element was stubbornly opposed in all the territories. In short, no meaningful expansion of the franchise accompanied the emancipation of the slaves who almost everywhere comprised the majority of the population. Instead, the local planter elites sought to continue the exploitation of the free non-white population by transferring to them the economic costs of adjusting to free labour. That resistance created divisions, not only between the colonies and the metropolis but also within aspiring segments of the colonial population.

The Colonial Office, especially during the middle of the nineteenth century, regarded the local assemblies as impediments to efficient local administration.[14] For that reason assembly government was never introduced to the newer colonies acquired after the Seven Years War. All the new territorial acquisitions were placed under governors appointed by the British government and directly accountable to it. At the same time strenuous efforts were made to convert the assemblies and subordinate them to Crown colony government too. But most imperial administrators, especially those at the centre, were not really interested in the general welfare of the lower sectors of society that comprised the greater majority of the population. The overriding concern was to reduce the cost of local sugar production and maintain production so that export duties could offset the administrative and military costs incurred in the region.[15] That proved inordinately difficult.

In 1816 the administration of the Leeward Islands was divided between two appointed governors. One governor administered St Kitts, Nevis, and Anguilla; the other administered Antigua, Barbuda, and Montserrat. The experiment lasted until 1833, when the Leeward Islands as well as Dominica (ceded along with Grenada, St Vincent, and Tobago to Britain by France at the Treaty of Paris that ended the Seven Years War) were placed under a single governor.[16] This expedient action combined islands with independent representative assemblies and islands that did not have that tradition. It simply did not work. Yet throughout the period, the confederation idea was alive and well.

At about the time that the Canadian colonists were contemplating their Confederation, the British government appointed one of their peripatetic colonial administrators, Sir Benjamin Chilley Campbell Pine (1809–91), as governor of the Leeward Islands, with the specific instruction to bring together under a single administrative entity the islands of Anguilla, Antigua, Barbuda, the British Virgin Islands, Dominica, Montserrat, Nevis, and St Kitts.[17] Pine was unsuccessful in getting the local legislatures, especially St Kitts and Nevis, to agree locally to any sort of confederation. Instead, in 1871 the British parliament passed the *Leeward Islands Act* that concentrated administrative authority under one governor and a single legislature, and imposed that solution on the territories.

Throughout the nineteenth century, if the bilious Oxford historian James Anthony Froude (1818–94) is to be believed, the British government sought assiduously to dispose of its non-revenue–producing colonies. In his curious travel account published in 1888 entitled *The English in the West Indies,* Froude wrote:

> In the recent discussion on the possibility of an organized colonial federation, various schemes came under my notice, in every one of which the union of the West Indian Islands under a free parliamentary constitution

was regarded as a necessary preliminary. I was reminded of a conversation which I had held seventeen years ago with a high colonial official specially connected with the West Indian Department, in which the federation of the islands under such a constitution was spoken of as a measure already determined on, though with a view to an end exactly the opposite to that which was now desired. The colonies universally were then regarded in such quarters as a burden on our resources, of which we were to relieve ourselves at the earliest moment. They were no longer of value to us; the whole world had become our market; and whether they were nominally attached to the Empire, or were independent, or joined themselves to some other power, was of no commercial moment to us ... The sooner, therefore, the connection was ended, the better for them and for us.[18]

One of Froude's big mistakes – and he made many – about the Caribbean was to think that the residents at the end of the nineteenth century were all culturally English, or British in the way that the Scots, Welsh, and Irish could be described.[19] The deeper implication was that without the small core of white residents the territories would quickly relapse into a sort of "African barbarity," which such contemporary thinkers mistakenly and pejoratively thought characterized the state of Haiti. It was a common mistake on the part of the people at the centres of empire.[20] British Caribbean societies were different from English society but they were not identical to Haiti.[21] Unlike independent Haiti, the British West Indies were an interesting combination of heterogeneous peoples coercively brought together under the imperatives of efficient cane sugar production and striving determinedly to create a new form of society. Most of their institutions and much of their culture reflected superficial English patterns of social organization. The new Canada was not a model during the nineteenth century. Indeed, Canada received very little newspaper notice at the time.

Any review of British Caribbean local newspapers during the nineteenth century indicates that they were quite provincial. Their names reflected a personal product with a highly commercial purpose. The leading newspaper in Jamaica started in 1834 (and remains in publication today) with the title *The Gleaner and DeCordova's Advertising Sheet*. It recycled about a column and a half of regional and international news gleaned from mainly British newspapers, and information on arrival and departures of trade vessels, with an additional three to four pages of local advertisements. Much the same applied to the leading newspaper published in the northwestern part of the island, in the major port of Falmouth. That newspaper, called the *Falmouth Post and Jamaica General Advertizer*, was printed and published for a number of years by John Castello. The subscription cost £2 per year. The newspaper consisted of four pages. The first page and a half provided local, regional, and international news, sometimes with an editorial or letters to the editor. The rest contained advertisements.

Local politics did not seem to be a major issue during the later nineteenth century, but that would change significantly during the twentieth century. A reform of general elementary education would broaden the readership base of newspapers, and the expansion of the middle classes would make political reform an increasingly urgent issue.

The Idea of Federation in the Twentieth Century

When the issue of political federation begun to attract renewed bureaucratic attention around the middle of the twentieth century, an author with the initials, H.P. contributed an interesting article to the Royal Institute of International Affairs journal, *The World Today*, which began:

> Most of the arguments for federation have been valid for generations. Many of the smaller communities, most of them poor for the last century or so, have been bearing the financial burden of administrations which would have been hard to justify at any time, and which were only economically practicable in the days when sugar brought exceptional prosperity to the colonies. The British West Indies have a common tradition and a common language and their social and economic life conforms, with minor variations, to one familiar pattern. In innumerable ways their common interests have long made some sort of association, whether federal or of some looser kind, seemingly imperative. How is it, then, that they are still separate?[22]

H.P. repeated the often-declared but highly unpersuasive assertions of geographical dispersal and historical accident. While the tyranny of distance has played a genuinely important role in the economic development of such far-away places as Argentina, Chile, Australia, and New Zealand, the same cannot be said for the Caribbean. Already by the middle of the nineteenth century steam-based technology was revolutionizing maritime and overland transportation, and air transport would accelerate the process further during the twentieth century. Distances became telescoped. Most of the Caribbean islands are located within a few hours sailing time from one another; and the distance between Kingston, Jamaica, and Georgetown, Guyana, is only about 2,375 kilometers (1,475 miles). The perceived problem of geographical isolation was, and remains, merely a figment of a weak imagination. Relatively speaking the Caribbean is not a vast region.

Nor does the case for historical accident seem any stronger as an impediment to regional cooperation. At the root of many of the arguments based on historical accident lies an assumption concerning the handicaps to progress and prosperity of a plural or diverse society. In other words, the "historical accident" argument is a coded form of racism – although in the case of James Froude it was not coded at all. While Caribbean populations may be more diversified than most, they are not unique. In addition, plural societies are commonplace across the Americas and around the world. Imperialism made that possible.

The pessimistic reservations about the plural society permeated even the arguments of H.P. in 1950. Nowhere was this clearer than when he (and I cannot properly explain why I believe the author to be male) wrote:

> With the development and dominance of the sugar industry, a vital change took place not only in the economic but also in the racial and social structure of West Indian life. A numerous population of white farmers and servants gave way to a small population of white planters, estate managers, and merchants, and a vast population of slaves of West African origin. The history of the West Indies is very largely a story of the painful adaptation of a structure of society, created by and for one group, to the needs of another more numerous group with fundamentally different ideas and traditions. The process of adaptation and fusion was necessarily long. No true community could, in fact exist in any of the West Indian Colonies before Emancipation, which took place in Antigua in 1834 and elsewhere in 1838.[23]

The author continued, surprisingly, by stating: "A homogenous society is essential to successful self-government, and the degree of homogeneity achieved in each of the colonies is closely related to the stage of constitutional development which it has reached."[24] Nevertheless, there was some merit in his argument that "British West Indian education has not automatically created a desire for federation, an idea less obviously implicit in our [*presumably he means British*] political traditions than in those of the Dominions and the United States, with whose institutions West Indians are for the most part less familiar."[25]

H.P was patently incorrect about the degree of Caribbean familiarity with political institutions in Canada and the United States – a familiarity that goes back to Alexander Hamilton (1757–1804) in the 1770s and grew stronger during the nineteenth and twentieth centuries. The idea of political reform along with ideas of political independence for the British Caribbean colonies had strong vocal supporters throughout the twentieth century. Three of these important early political agitators were Robert Love (1839–1914), William Galwey Donovan (c.1865–1929), and Theophilus Albert Marryshow (1887–1958).

Robert Love was born in the Bahamas and spent considerable time in the United States and Haiti before settling down in Jamaica in 1889.[26] He was an accomplished Episcopalian clergyman, missionary, medical doctor, publisher, journalist, and indefatigable propagandist for political reforms for Jamaica and the British West Indies. Love published the *Jamaican Advocate* between 1894 and 1905, and supported the Pan-African ideas of the Trinidadian Henry Sylvester Williams (1869–1911). His paper influenced the Jamaican nationalist Marcus Mosiah Garvey (1887–1940). The *Jamaican Advocate*, like its much older newspaper rival, the *Jamaica Gleaner*, carried information on events throughout the British Empire including Canada, South Africa, Australia, and India. But the focus was on the living conditions and aspirations of the black masses of Jamaica.

Another ardent well-informed Caribbean newspaper propagandist and political reformer was William Galwey Donovan from Grenada.[27] Donovan founded the *Federalist and Grenada People* in 1883 with the motto: "A naked freedman is a nobler object than a gorgeous slave." He was an early mentor of T.A. Marryshow, later regarded as the father of Caribbean federation. Donovan was not only a strong supporter of local self-government and the legal recognition of trade unions, but was also one of the first voices to call for a federation of the British Caribbean territories.

Perhaps no one distinguished himself more than T. Albert Maryshow in the cause of a West Indian federation.[28] Born Theophilus Maricheau in St George's, the capital city of Grenada, his parents were small cocoa farmers. His formal education ended with elementary school; at first apprenticed to a carpenter, he went to work for William Donovan's *Federalist and Grenada People* sometime around 1903. Within six years he was the senior editor of the newspaper as well as a columnist for another local paper, *The St. George's Chronicle*. In 1915 Marryshow founded *The West Indian* with the motto, "Educate, Agitate, Federate," and continued to be the publisher until he sold it in 1934. The first issue promised "an immediate and accurate chronicle of current events, an untrammeled advocate of popular rights, unhampered by chains of party prejudice, an unswerving educator of the people in their duties as subjects of the state and citizens of the world ... the day when our islands, together in an administrative and fiscal union, the West Indian Dominion, will take its place, small though it may be, in the glorious Empire."[29] Marryshow set up the Representative Government Association in 1918 in Grenada and was an elected member of the Legislative Council. His political agitation in 1937 contributed to the dispatch of the Moyne Commission to investigate the causes of British Caribbean unrest at the time.

While local economic considerations constituted an important dimension of the major impulse towards a West Indian federation in the mid-1940s, the political winds of change in the Caribbean were already blowing in that direction. The Second World War merely provided the spark and accelerated the impulse.[30] Moreover, Great Britain found itself destitute after the war and relinquishing its colonies was seen as one way to relieve the fiscal strain. The Montego Bay, Jamaica, conference, held in September 1947 under the chairmanship of Secretary of State for the Colonies Mr Creech Jones, resolved that a political federation of all the British Caribbean territories was urgently desirable and established a standing committee to develop plans for unified public services, a federal constitution, and a common currency. All the British territories except the Bahamas participated. Caribbean expatriate groups also attended and articulated their views on political change.[31] By 1949 the committee issued a lengthy, cautious report on the prospects as well as the problems of establishing a federation comprising all the British Caribbean territories. Although the committee indicated that Canada would be a major trading partner for the new entity – and Canada provided two merchant vessels for the new entity – the political model that appeared to be most influential in the report was Australia. The report anticipated all the obstacles that eventually caused the experiment, set in motion in 1958, to self-destruct prematurely in 1962 after only four years of existence.

The Caribbean federation began in 1958 with more than the proverbial three strikes against it. First, it was an instrument fashioned by a section of local elites in collaboration with the British government, and scant attention was paid to the majority of the population.

Second, the sovereignty of the new state was severely circumscribed by the power given to the governor general in a Council of State rather than to the prime minister. And third, the central government was weaker politically and economically than its component provinces. The federal budget was smaller than that of component divisions such as Jamaica or Trinidad and Tobago. Furthermore a number of issues such as freedom of movement and the imposition of tariffs remained unresolved. In the final analysis, federation was not seen locally as the best medium for attaining immediate political independence and so failed to attract the popular support needed for its eventual success. After floundering for three years, the federation saw its end arrive with the unexpected results of the Jamaica referendum in September 1961 that supported the exit from that entity.

Conclusion

The idea of a Caribbean confederation manifested itself during three different periods in the past four hundred years. Each time the impetus derived from a combination of different international circumstances but at no time was the example of Canada an important model.

The first discussions about federation took place in the later seventeenth century. At that time, the idea of federation was designed to provide a common protective cover for the fledgling settler colonies being established on the smaller islands of the Eastern Caribbean. Since Spain was no longer considered a major European power following the Peace of Westphalia in 1648 that ended the Thirty Years War, the principal threats in the Caribbean appeared to be from the French and Dutch. The rapid rise of English naval power and the development of the transatlantic slave trade diminished the immediacy of any threat or the urgency of local cooperation.

The second series of discussions took place during the later nineteenth century. Those discussions reflected the general ambivalence in Great Britain towards empire as well as the surreptitiously transformative influences of industrial capitalism. The general abolition of slavery between 1834 and 1838 and the implementation of a series of free trade measures between 1823 and 1860 reflected the pronounced expansion of British industrialization and the need to find international markets for the new industrial products. Free trade facilitated the movement not only of commodities but also of investment capital, an area in which Britain led the world until around 1914.[32]

The third series of discussions around the middle of the twentieth century were different from those of earlier periods. This time local Caribbean actors were as influential as the imperial bureaucrats. British post-war impoverishment and sophisticated advocacy from local Caribbean states coincided. Moreover, the creation of the United Nations gave implied support to colonized peoples by espousing the cause of political independence. As the world's largest imperialist power, Great Britain found it prudent to convert its Empire into a Commonwealth of Nations. In retrospect, the idea of a West Indian federation did not receive the careful attention it deserved, either from its local regional participants or from the British government. It was and remained a very weak structure that failed to realize the promises set forth by the participants.

NOTES

1 See C.A. Bayly, *The Birth of the Modern World, 1780–1914. Global Connections and Comparisons* (Malden, MA: Blackwell Publishing, 2004).
2 For the "age of revolutions," see R.R. Palmer, *The Age of Democratic Revolution: A Political History of Europe and America* (Princeton, NJ: Princeton University Press, 1960); Eric Hobsbawm, *The Age of Revolution: Europe 1789–1848* (London: Weidenfeld and Nicolson, 1962); David Armitage and Sanjay Subrahmanyan, eds., *The Age of Revolution in Global Context, c. 1760–1840* (Basingstoke: Palgrave and Macmillan, 2010). On the East India Company, see Philip Lawson, *The East India Company: A History* (London: Longman, 1993); John Keay, *The Honourable Company: A History of the English East India Company* (London: HarperCollins, 2010).
3 For a Caribbean perspective, see Franklin W. Knight, "The Caribbean in the Age of Enlightenment, 1788–1848," in *A Companion to Latin American Literature and Culture*, ed. Sara Castro-Klaren (Malden, MA: Blackwell Publishing, 2008), 228–46. See also, Arthur L. Stinchcombe, *Sugar Island Slavery in the Age of Enlightenment. The Political Economy of the Caribbean World* (Princeton, NJ: Princeton University Press, 1995).
4 See Jack P. Greene, *Peripheries and Center. Constitutional Development in the Extended Politics of the British Empire and the United States, 1607–1788* (Athens, GA: University of Georgia Press, 1986); Jack P. Greene, *Pursuits of Happiness: The Social Development of Early Modern British Colonies and the Formation of American Culture* (Chapel Hill: University of North Carolina Press, 1988).

5 Franklin W. Knight, "The State of Sovereignty and the Sovereignty of States," in *Americas; Interpretive Essays*, ed. Alfred Stepan (New York: Oxford University Press, 1992), 11–29.
6 William Woodruff, *The Impact of Western Man: A Study of Europe's Role in the World Economy, 1750–1960* (New York: St Martin's Press, 1967), 5–6.
7 Eric Hobsbawm, *The Age of Capital, 1848–1875* (New York: Random House, 1975).
8 And indeed, some colonial governors – like Sir John Peter Grant (1807–93), who served as governor of Jamaica from 1866 to 1874, and the Fabian Society member Sir Sidney Olivier (1859–1943), who served as colonial secretary for British Honduras, auditor general for the Leeward Islands, and several stints as acting governor and governor of Jamaica – were quite progressive and implemented important local social and economic reforms.
9 Carla Gardina Pestana, *The English Atlantic in an Age of Revolution, 1640–1661* (Cambridge, MA: Harvard University Press, 2004); Susan Dwyer Amussen, *Caribbean Exchanges: Slavery and the Transformation of English Society, 1640–1700* (Chapel Hill: University of North Carolina Press, 2007).
10 William Stapleton was the third son of Redmund Stapleton, whose family's Irish roots go back to the time of Henry II (1133–89). Stapleton arrived with Sir Tobias Bridge to Barbados in 1667, having been knighted the previous year. In 1668 he was appointed deputy governor of Montserrat and promoted to captain general of the Leeward Islands in 1671, the year in which he married the wealthy Anne Russell of Nevis and entered the sugar business. By 1686 Stapleton had acquired a number of highly productive sugar plantations on Montserrat, St Kitts, Antigua, and Nevis. "Context," Bangor University Stapleton-Cotton Manuscripts, Reference Code GB 0222 STAP. Available online at http://anws.llgc.org.uk. Accessed 08/04/2016.
  The capital of Barbados is named in honor of Bridge. Biographical details on the personal life of Bridge are scarce.
11 K.O. Laurence, ed., *The Long Nineteenth Century: Nineteenth Century Transformations*, vol. 4 of *UNESCO General History of the Caribbean* (London: UNESCO/Macmillan, 2011).
12 B.W. Higman, "The Sugar Revolution," *The Economic History Review* 52, no. 2 (May, 2000): 213–36; B.W. Higman, *A Concise History of the Caribbean* (Cambridge: Cambridge University Press, 2011), 97–140; Franklin W. Knight, *The Caribbean: The Genesis of a Fragmented Nationalism*, 3rd ed. (New York: Oxford University Press, 2012), 19–112.
13 Franklin W. Knight, ed., *The Slave Societies of the Caribbean*, vol. 3 of *UNESCO General History of the Caribbean* (London: UNESCO Publishing, 1997).

14 Bridget Brereton, *Law, Justice and Empire: The Colonial Career of John Gorrie, 1829–1892* (Kingston, JM: University of the West Indies Press, 1997).
15 Bernard Semmel, *Democracy versus Empire: The Jamaica Riots of 1865 and the Governor Eyre Controversy* (New York: Doubleday, 1969).
16 Hilary Beckles, *A History of Barbados: From Amerindian Settlement to Nation-State* (Cambridge: Cambridge University Press, 1990), 120–5.
17 Benjamin Pine served as lieutenant governor of Natal from 1850 to 1855, as governor of the Gold Coast between 1857 and 1858, and was appointed governor of Western Australia in 1868. Pine never went to Australia, selecting instead to take the position of governor of the Leeward Islands in 1869.
18 James Anthony Froude, *The English in the West Indies or, The Bow of Ulysses* (New York: Charles Scribner's Sons, 1888), 5–6.
19 Froude's book elicited a powerful response from a local Trinidadian intellectual, J.J. Thomas, *Froudacity: West Indian Fables Explained* (London: T. Fisher Urwin, 1889). In a biographical introduction to a new edition published by New Beacon Books in 1969, the historian Donald Wood wrote of Froude: "[It] was to arouse more anger than any other in the West Indies for its superficial and incorrect observations, its patronizing and contemptuous tone, and its insulting prophecies about their future if ever the English departed" (19).
20 David P. Geggus, ed., *The Impact of the Haitian Revolution in the Atlantic World* (Columbia: University of South Carolina Press, 2001).
21 Brian L. Moore and Michele A. Johnson, *Neither Led nor Driven: Contesting British Cultural Imperialism in Jamaica, 1865–1920* (Mona, JM: University of the West Indies Press, 2004); Brian L. Moore and Michele A. Johnson, *They Do as They Please: The Jamaican Struggle for Cultural Freedom after Morant Bay* (Mona, JM: University of the West Indies Press, 2011).
22 H.P., "Background to West Indian Federation," *The World Today* 6, no. 6 (June, 1950): 255–64.
23 H.P., "West Indian Federation," 257.
24 Ibid., 259.
25 Ibid., 260.
26 Biographical details for Robert Love are taken from Franklin W. Knight and Henry Louis Gates, Jr, eds., *Dictionary of Caribbean and Afro-Latin American Biography*, 6 vols. (New York: Oxford University Press, 2016), 4:130–2. Hereafter referred to as *DCALAB*.
27 *DCALAB*, 2:379–81.
28 *DCALAB*, 4:230–2. See also, Jill Sheppard, *Marryshow of Grenada: An Introduction* (Bridgetown, Barbados: Letchworth Press, 1987). It is unclear when Marryshow changed his surname.

29 "T.A. Marryshow," Caribbean Elections, http://www.caribbeanelections.com/knowledge/biography/bios/marryshow_theophilus.asp.
30 Bridget Brereton, ed., *The Caribbean in the Twentieth Century*, vol. 5 of *UNESCO General History of the Caribbean* (London: UNESCO/Macmillan, 2004).
31 W. Burghardt Turner and Joyce Turner, eds., *Richard B. Moore: Caribbean Militant in Harlem. Collected Writings, 1920–1972* (Bloomington: Indiana University Press, 1988); Joyce Moore Turner, *Caribbean Crusaders and the Harlem Renaissance* (Urbana: University of Illinois Press, 2005).
32 William Woodruff, *The Impact of Western Man: A Study of Europe's Role in the World Economy, 1750–1960* (New York: St Martin's Press, 1967); Niall Ferguson, *The World's Banker: The House of Rothschild* (London: Weidenfeld & Nicolson, 1998).

Contributors

Alban Bargain-Villéger is currently employed as a contract faculty member at York University. His academic interests include the study of communist, socialist, and anarchist ideologies, parties, and movements, and more recently, the concept of micro-insularity. His current research project involves a comparative study of Arran, Borkum, and Groix, three small islands off the coasts of Scotland, Germany, and France, from 1848 to 1940.

Edward Beasley is a historian of Great Britain, specializing in nineteenth century ideas about empire, race, and medicine. A professor at San Diego State University, he is the author of four books, the most recent of which is *The Chartist General: Charles James Napier, the Conquest of Sind, and Imperial Liberalism* (2017).

David R. Cameron, a Fellow of the Royal Society of Canada, is a professor of Political Science and Dean of the Faculty of Arts and Science at the University of Toronto. His professional career has been divided between public service – in Ottawa and Queen's Park, Ontario – and academic life. A long-time student of Canadian federalism, Quebec nationalism, and constitutional reform, in recent decades he has turned his attention to political change and constitution-making in conflict and post-conflict situations in Sri Lanka, Iraq, Somalia, the Western Sahara, and Jerusalem.

Ann Curthoys is an honorary professor of history at the University of Western Australia who has written widely on aspects of Australian history, especially the history of Aboriginal-settler relations. Her books include *Freedom Ride: A Freedom Rider Remembers* and (with John Docker) *Is History Fiction?*

Josep María Fradera is a professor of modern history at the Universitat Pompeu Fabra in Barcelona. He has been the sole author of the following publications: *La nación imperial. Derechos, representación y ciudadanía en los imperios de Gran Bretaña, Francia. España y los Estados Unidos (1750–1918)* (2015, 2.vols.); *La pàtria dels catalans (Història, política, cultura)* (2009); *Colonias para después de un imperio* (1995); and *Cultura nacional en una societat dividida (Patriotisme i cultura a Catalunya, 1838–1868)* (1992).

Benno Gammerl works at the Max Planck Institute for Human Development, Center for the History of Emotions, in Berlin. His research covers the history of homosexuality in Germany since the 1960s as well as the history of the British and the Habsburg Empires in the late nineteenth and early twentieth century.

William Jenkins is an associate professor in the Department of Geography at York University. His recent monograph, *Between Raid and Rebellion: The Irish in Buffalo and Toronto, 1867–1916* (2013), received awards from the American Conference for Irish Studies, the Geographical Society of Ireland, the Canadian Historical Association, and the Ontario Historical Society.

Franklin W. Knight is Leonard and Helen R. Stulman Professor Emeritus and Academy Professor at Johns Hopkins University in Baltimore. Knight's major publications include *Slave Society in Cuba during the Nineteenth Century* (1970); *The African Dimension of Latin American Societies* (1974); *The Caribbean: The Genesis of a Fragmented Nationalism* (1978; 3rd revised edition, 2012), and, with Henry Louis Gates, Jr., *Dictionary of Caribbean and Afro-Latin American Biography* (2016).

Jacqueline D. Krikorian is an associate professor in Political Science and Law & Society at York University. She undertakes research in constitutional politics, international law, and legal history. Her publications include *Roads to Confederation: The Making of Canada, 1867* (with David R. Cameron, Marcel Martel, Andrew W. McDougall and Robert C. Vipond, eds., forthcoming) and *International Trade Law and Domestic Policy: Canada, the United States and the WTO* (2012) She has been a Fellow at the Institute of International Economic Law at Georgetown

University Law Center and has held the Research Chair in U.S.-Canada Relations at the Woodrow Wilson Center for International Scholars (2014).

Marcel Martel is a professor and the holder of the Avie Bennett Historica Canada Chair in Canadian History at York University. He has published several journal articles and book chapters on public policy, minority rights, moral regulation, and identity. His most recent publications include *Roads to Confederation: The Making of Canada, 1867* (with Jacqueline D. Krikorian, David R. Cameron, Andrew W. McDougall, and Robert C. Vipond, eds., forthcoming), *Canada the Good? A Short History of Vice since 1500* (2014), and *Langue et politique au Canada et au Québec* (with Martin Pâquet, 2010), which was translated as *Speaking Up: A History of Language and Politics in Canada and Quebec.*

Thomas Mohr is a lecturer at the School of Law, University College, Dublin. He is Honorary Secretary of the Irish Legal History Society and Book Review Editor of the *Irish Jurist*, Ireland's oldest law journal.

Roberto Perin is a member of the History Department at Glendon College and he is known for his work on ethnicity, religion, and national identity. His new book, *The Many Rooms of This House: Diversity in Toronto's Places of Worship since 1840* (2017), looks at Toronto churches as markers of social and cultural change over the past century.

Carsten-Andreas Schulz is an assistant professor of International Relations at the Pontificia Universidad Católica de Chile and holds a DPhil from the University of Oxford. His research focuses on Latin American regionalism and the historical origins of international order.

Adrian Shubert is University Professor of History at York University. He has been a Guggenheim and a Killam Fellow; is a Fellow of the Royal Society of Canada; and was decorated by King Juan Carlos of Spain with the Order of Civil Merit. His major publications include *A Social History of Modern Spain* (1990; Spanish edition, 1991) and *Death and Money in the Afternoon: A History of Bullfighting* (1999; Spanish edition, 2002). His biography of Baldomero Espartero, *El Pacificador: Baldomero Espartero y la Formación de la España Contemporánea* (1793–1879) will be published in 2018.

Gabrielle Slowey is an associate professor in the Department of Political Science at York University, where she teaches courses in Canadian, Indigenous, and Arctic politics. Her research investigates the intersection between resource extraction, Indigenous peoples, governance, and the state in multiple regions (Northern Alberta, Northern Quebec, Yukon, NWT, Ontario, and New Zealand).

Timothy Stapleton is a professor in the Department of History and a senior research fellow at the Centre for Military, Security and Strategic Studies (CMSS) at the University of Calgary. A historian of war and society in Africa, his most recent books include a three volume *Military History of Africa* (2013), *Warfare and Tracking in Africa, 1952–90* (2015), and *A History of Genocide in Africa* (2017).

Kenton Storey is a freelance historical researcher working in the field of Indigenous law. He completed a PhD in comparative history at the University of Otago and has recently published his first monograph, *Settler Anxiety at the Outposts of Empire: Colonial Relations, Humanitarian Discourses, and the Imperial Press* (2016).

Index

Acadians, 115, 143
Act for the Better Government of Her Majesty's Australian Colonies, 1850, 197
Act of Union(s): Canada (1840), 145, 179, 181, 185; Ireland (1800), 69, 74, 179, 181, 184; South Africa (1909), 234–5. *See also* Durham Report; responsible government
Adams-Onís Treaty, 143
Afrikaner Nationalist Party, 236
Afrikaners, 19, 226–7, 229, 231–6
age of revolutions, 242
Alaskan purchase, 49–51, 72
Alfred, Taiaiake, 85–7
Algeria, 120
American Revolution (1776–83). *See* War of Independence, United States (1776–83)
Amery, L.S., 187
Anceau, Éric, 115
Anguilla, 246
Annand, William, 10–11
annexation: of British Kaffraria by the Cape, 228; of British North American colonies by the United States, 18, 29, 33, 37–40, 41, 47, 50–2, 56, 64, 70, 104, 111, 114, 166, 181, 200; Transvaal Boer resistance to, 231
Annexation Bill (US HR, 1866), 50–2
Annuaire des Deux Mondes, 15
anti-Catholicism: Canada, 64, 107; England, 100; United States, 101. *See also* Catholicism; Gavazzi, Alessandro; Know-Nothing movement
anti-democratic sentiments. *See* democracy
Antigua, 246, 249
Antilles, 147
Asch, Michael, 89–90
Atlantic Revolution, 28
Austen, Jane, 161
Australia, 17, 19, 62, 102, 120, 162, 165, 167, 183, 185, 194–209
Austria-Hungary, 11, 13, 18, 127–42
Austro-Hungarian compromise, 11, 128–31

Bahamas, 250–1
Baillargeon, Charles-François, 99–100, 104
Balfour Declaration, 35
Banks, Nathanial, 51–3

Barbados, 244–5
Barbuda, 246
Barkly, Henry, 230
Barnabò, Alessandro, 98–9, 101, 105
Basque provinces, 150, 155
Basutoland. *See* Lesotho
Battle of Isandlwana (1879), 231
Battle of Majuba Hill (1881), 231
Beach, Thomas, 74. *See also* Fenians
Beauchamp, Earl, 180
Bechuanaland. *See* Botswana
Bedini, Gaetano, 101–2
Belgium, 13–16, 20
Belich, James, 216
Belly, Félix, 119–20
Big Bear, 83
Blair, Fergusson, 13
Blake, Edward, 187
Blanchet, Joseph-Godéric, 14–15
Bleu (Party), 13, 16
Boers. *See* Afrikaners
Boer War. *See* South African War (1899–1902)
Bohemia, 130
Bolívar, Simón, 146
Bonaparte, Joseph, 28
Borrows, John, 87
Bosnia, 130
Botha, Louis, 235
Botswana, 235, 238–9
Bourget, Ignace, 99, 103–6
Bourinot, John George, 152
Bourne, Francis, 107
Boyle, Patrick, 64–74
Brazil, 28–9, 31, 33–9, 101, 119, 147
Bridge, Sir Tobias, 244
Bright, John, 39
British Columbia, 7, 49, 54, 80, 82, 110, 115, 144, 168, 181–5, 188–9, 195
British Kaffraria, 227–8

British North America Act, 1867, 7, 9, 30–1, 35, 48, 52–4, 83, 99, 107, 128, 130, 161–2, 166–7, 169, 174, 179, 181, 183–6, 188, 203–4, 230
British North American Association, 165
British South Africa Company, 235
British West Indies, 19, 242–56
Brown, George, 12, 73, 82
Browne, Thomas Gore, 215–16, 219
Brundage, David, 63,
Buckingham, Duke of, 203
buffalo, 80
Bulwer-Lytton, Edward, 170
Bury, Lord, 168, 173
Butt, Isaac, 182

Campobello affair, 65–6
Canada Club, 165
Canada East, 4, 7, 51, 112, 117, 119, 145, 163, 169, 178–9, 195, 201, 213
Canada West, 4, 7–8, 38, 51, 64, 66, 81, 145, 163, 167, 201
Canadian military threat to the United States, 54–5
Canary Islands, 150
canon law, 99, 105
Capalti, Annibale, 98
Cape Colony, 199, 218, 226–34, 237
Cardwell, Edward, 167, 170
Caribbean, 20, 51, 244–53
Caribbean territories, 242–56
Carlist Wars (1830s, 1870s), 150
Carlota of Mexico, Empress, 5
Carnarvon, Lord, 167, 170, 172, 174, 203, 229–32, 238
Cartier, George-Étienne, 7–8, 13, 99–100, 103–5, 114
Cass, Senator Lewis (Michigan), 101
Castello, John, 248

Catalonia, 149, 151, 153–4
Catholicism, 8–9, 17, 33, 64–5, 73, 82, 97–109, 111, 114, 118–19, 131, 133, 144, 184: College of Cardinals, 98, 101; *congregazioni generali*, 98–9; *congressi*, 98; Curia, 97, 100–1, 105; doctrine of papal infallibility, 98; Missionary Society of St Paul the Apostle, 102; Peter's Pence, 106; Pontifical Irish College, 100; Propaganda Fide (Congregation for the Propagation of the Faith), 98, 101, 106; *Scritture riferite in Congressi*, 98; Sulpician Seminary, 99; *Syllabus of Errors*, 105; Vatican Council, 98. *See also* anti-Catholicism; canon law; Civil Code (Quebec); divorce; education; Holy See; Papal States; *Roman Catholic Relief Act* (UK, 1829); ultramontanism
Cauchon, Joseph-Édouard, 16, 100
Cayuga, 80
Central African Federation (1953), 235–8
Chadwick, Owen, 98
Chamberlain, Governor Joshua, 55
Chamberlain, Joseph, 233
Chapman, Henry, 198
Charles II, 244
Charlottetown Conference (1864), 7, 10–11, 36, 110, 200, 211
Chauveau, Pierre-Olivier, 100
Childers, Erskine, 187
Chile, 28, 31, 36–7, 39, 146, 248
China, 203–4, 238
Chincha Islands War, 31
Chrétien, Jean, 86
Christie, William Dougal, 33
Cisleithania. *See* Austria-Hungary

Civil Code (Quebec), 105
Civil Rights Act (US, 1866), 48
civil war: Cape, 231; Latin America, 28, 40; New Grenada, 15; predictions of in Canada, 178; Spain, 150; US Civil War, 7, 11, 13, 15, 31, 38, 48–59, 51–2, 55–6, 61, 63–4, 66, 111, 120, 173, 199, 233
Clark, Andrew Inglis, 204–5
Coates, Ken, 79, 82–3, 85, 88
College of Cardinals. *See* Catholicism
Colley, George Pomeroy, 231
colonialism, 17, 79–93, 153, 195, 206, 237
Colonial Office (UK), 4, 104, 170, 173, 186, 197, 228, 230, 233, 245
Colonial Society, 167
Comerford, R.V., 62
Confederate Council of Trade, 32
Congo, 237
congregazioni generali. *See* Catholicism
Congress of the Confederate States (US), 49–50
Connolly, Thomas Louis, 3, 103–4
Constitution Act (New Zealand, 1846), 218–19
Constitution Act, 1982 (Canada): s. 35, 86
Constitutional Act (Canada, 1791), 145
Corntassel, Jeff, 85
Cortes: Portuguese, 28; Spain and colonial representation, 147–9
Coulthard, Glen, 85–7
Crawford, William Sharman, 178–9
Creighton, Donald G., 40, 81, 83, 88, 237
Crimean War (1853–6), 113, 199
Cuba, 11, 16, 18, 32, 51, 146–55, 245
Cullen, Paul, 100–1, 106
Curia. *See* Catholicism

264 Index

Davis, Thomas, 178
de Chateaubriand, François-René, 112–13
defence for British colonies, 7, 8, 12, 19, 37–8, 200–4, 216, 236, 244
democracy: Australian colonies, 198; British Empire and colonial administration, 120, 165; Catalonia, 153–4; Confederation and Canada, 8, 12, 15–16, 132, 169–74; Fenians and the United States, 67, 74; New Zealand, 211; Spain and Cuba, 150; United Kingdom, 162, 169–74; United States, 150
democratic deficit. *See* democracy
Democratic Sexennium, 153
Denmark, 11, 13, 51
denominational schools. *See* education
de San Martín, José, 146
de Villiers, John, 229
Devlin, Bernard, 182
Devlin, Charles Ramsay, 187
diamonds, 19, 226, 228
Dickens, Charles, 164, 168
Dilke, Sir Charles, 162–3
Disraeli, Benjamin, 168
divorce, 104–5, 205
doctrine of papal infallibility. *See* Catholicism
Doheny, Michael, 62
Dominica, 246
Donovan, William Galwey, 250
Dorion, Antoine-Aimé, 14–16
dualism (Austria-Hungary), 128–9
Duffy, Charles Gavan, 183–4, 186
Durham, Lord, 36, 161, 196. *See also* Durham Report
Durham Report, 36, 145, 179, 183, 195. *See also* Durham, Lord
Dussieux, L., 113

Earl of Derby. *See* Stanley, Edward Henry, Earl of Derby
Easter 1916 rising, 189
East India Company, 145, 242
Ecuador, 15
education, 8, 73, 82, 84, 88, 101, 103–7, 112, 131–3, 248–9
Edwards, Bevan, 203
Egypt, 146, 237
Elliot, T.F., 170–1
emigration: British, 165, 198–9, 201; Canadian, 70; Irish, 69, 78; Spanish, 150
Espartero, Baldomero, 146
Évanturel, François, 16
expansionism (US), 16, 37–9, 51

federal idea. *See* federalism
federalism, 10, 12, 14, 15–16, 19, 82–4, 104, 107, 115, 131, 150, 170, 172–3, 182–4, 188–9, 196–8, 203–5, 218–21, 226, 228–31, 234, 238–9, 244–52; Canada, Australia, and New Zealand as model for South Africa, 218, 233–5; Canada as model for Australia, 183–4, 194–5, 202–6, 218; Canada as model for Central African Federation (1953), 235–8; Canada as model for Ireland, 178–9, 183–9; in relation to an Imperial federation, 183; in relation to the United Kingdom, 183; New Zealand as model for Canada, 10, 16, 218; United States as model for Canada, 10. *See also British North America Act, 1867*; democracy; responsible government; self-government
Fenians, 5, 12, 17–20, 27, 32, 37–8, 51, 53, 56, 61–78, 111, 114, 128, 135–7,

166, 168, 179–82, 199, 202, 213, 221.
  See also Beach, Thomas
Ferdinand VII, 28, 146
First War of Independence (Cuba, 1878), 148, 154
fish, 54, 80, 144, 164
Florida, 143
Fortescue, Chichester, 180
France, 5, 11, 13–15, 18, 28, 30–1, 33, 36–7, 40, 55, 97, 100, 105–6, 110–26, 132–3, 143–6, 147, 149, 178, 203, 242, 252, 246
franchise. *See* voting
Franco-Americans, 55–6
Franco-British trade agreement (1860), 117
Franco-Prussian War, 11, 121
French Revolution (1789–1815), 105, 242
Frere, Governor Sir Bartle (Cape), 230–1
Froude, James Anthony, 246
fur, 80, 88, 163–4

Gavazzi, Alessandro, 101–2
Gcaleka Xhosa, 227. *See also* Xhosa people
George III, 82, 144, 210
German South West Africa. *See* Namibia
Germany, 11, 13, 106, 112, 115, 121, 132–3, 151, 203, 229, 233, 235
Gladstone, William Ewart, 166, 185–7, 196, 231
Glen Grey Act, 233
gold, 19, 72, 197, 226, 232, 234
Gordon, Arthur Hamilton, 166, 170
Gordon, George Hamilton, Earl of Aberdeen, 166
Gordon Riots (1782), 144

Govín, Antonio, 152
Grattan, Henry, 184
Gray, John Hamilton, 7
Great Exhibition (1851), 163–4
Great Law of Peace, 80
Greece, 14–15, 121, 173
Greer, Kirsten, 34
Grenada, 246, 250–1
Grey, George (Cape Colony and New Zealand), 218–19, 227–9, 232
Grey, Henry George, 196–7, 218–19
Guatemala, 15
Gun War (1880–1), 231
Guyana, 147, 249

Habsburg monarchy. *See* Austria-Hungary
Haiti, 28, 149, 151, 242, 247, 250
Haitian Revolution (1789–1804), 242
Hamilton, Alexander, 250
Hanseatic League, 151
Haudenosaunee Confederacy, 80
Hofmeyr, Jan Hendrik, 229
Holland, 13–14, 98, 147
Holy See, 97–109. *See also* Catholicism
home rule (Ireland), 74, 135, 151, 182–3, 185–9
Home Rule Party. *See* Irish Parliamentary Party
Honduras, 15
Horan, Bishop Edward John, 103–5
Howe, Joseph, 66
Hudson's Bay Company, 10, 82, 120, 144–5
Hungary, 127–31. *See also* Austria-Hungary
Hyam, Ronald, 229

India, 98, 130, 145, 147, 197, 242, 250. *See also* East India Company
Indian Act (Canada), 9–10, 84–6
Indian Rebellion (First War of Independence, 1857), 199, 221, 242
Indigenous peoples, 4, 5, 6, 8, 9–10, 17, 20, 41, 79–93, 98, 112–14, 127, 132, 143, 165, 194–5, 198, 205–6, 210, 219. *See also* Cayuga; Indigenous-settler relations; Maori; Métis; Mi'kmaq; Mohawk; Mpondomise people; Oneida; Onondaga; Seneca; Thembu people; Tuscarora; Xhosa people
Indigenous-settler relations, 79, 81, 83, 87–90, 168, 195, 205, 210, 215, 219, 228
Innis, Harold, 88
Ireland, 19, 61–78, 100–2, 106, 130–1, 144, 178–93, 231. *See also* emigration; Fenians; home rule (Ireland); Irish Free State; Irish Parliamentary Party; Irish Republican Brotherhood; unionists (Ireland)
Irish Free State, 63, 189
Irish Parliamentary Party, 182–4, 187–9
Irish Republican Brotherhood, 62–3, 69, 73
Irving, Helen, 205
Isabel II, 150
Italy, 11, 13, 17, 97, 100, 112, 121, 163, 229

Jamaica, 247–52
Jameson Raid, 232–3
John VI, 28
Johnson, J.K., 83
Johnson, President Andrew (US), 48, 53–4

Joly de Lotbinière, Henri-Gustave, 14–15
Jones, Creech, 251
Juárez, Benito, 33
Judicial Committee of the Privy Council, 186

Kearns, Gerry, 73
Kendle, John, 185
Kenya, 237
King, William Lyon Mackenzie, 183
Kingitanga, 215
Know-Nothing movement, 101
Knox, Bruce A., 218
Koffman, David, 8
Kruger, President Paul (South African Republic), 232–3

Labouchere, Henry, 197
Ladner, Kiera, 80, 82, 87, 89, 90
Laflèche, Louis-François, 104
Lancaster House negotiations (1979), 238
Lang, John Dunmore, 197
Langevin, Hector Louis, 99, 104
Larocque, Charles, 105
Latin America, 16–17, 27–41
Le Caron, Henri. *See* Beach, Thomas
Leeward Islands, 244, 246
Leslie, John, 80, 83, 85–6
Lesotho, 227–8, 231, 235, 238
Lightfoot, Sheryl, 89–90
Lincoln, Abraham, 48, 53–4
Little, Jack, 14
London Conference (1866), 99, 104, 179, 183–4
London Convention (1884), 231
Louisiana: sale of, 143
Love, Robert, 250
Lowe, Robert, 196

Lower Canada. *See* Canada East
Loyalists, 28, 73
Lynch, John Joseph, 103–4
Lynch, Timothy G., 66

Macdonald, John A., 7–8, 65, 69, 73, 81, 83, 90, 114, 189
Mackenzie, Alexander, 15–16
MacMullen, John, 9
Maine, 54–5
Malawi, 236–7, 239
manifest destiny (US), 37, 47. *See also* expansionism (US)
Manitoba, 7, 115
Maori, 210, 215–16, 218–19
Marryshow, Theophilus Albert, 250
Martin, Chester, 4
Martin, Ged, 4, 30, 222
Maura, Antonio, 152
Maximilian I of Mexico, 11, 18, 31, 118, 128, 135–6. *See also* Carlota of Mexico, Empress
McCulloch, Hugh, 50
McGee, Thomas D'Arcy, 14, 61, 65, 70–4, 99, 179–80, 182, 184
McKay, Ian, 111
Meehan, Patrick J., 67–9
Merivale, Herman, 196
Métis, 80, 86, 120, 145
Mexican-American War (1846–8), 33
Mexico, 5, 11, 15, 18, 31–3, 38–40, 55, 106, 114, 118, 121, 128, 135–6, 144, 146
Michie, Archibald, 196
Mi'kmaq, 80, 90
Mill, John Stuart, 198
Miller, J.R., 85
Mills, Arthur, 173
Missionary Society of St Paul the Apostle. *See* Catholicism

Mohawk, 80
Molteno, John C., 230
Monck, Lord, 73, 113
Monckton Commission (UK, 1963), 237
Montserrat, 246
Moore, Christopher, 68
Morant Bay Rebellion, 145
Moravia, 132
Moret, Segismundo, 152
Mozambique, 230
Mpondomise people, 231
Mugabe, Robert, 238–9
Murphy, Michael, 64

Namibia, 233, 235
Napoleon, 28, 146–7
Napoleon III, 11, 13, 18, 111, 115, 118, 154, 168
Natal, 227–34
nationalism, 51, 100: Afrikaner, 235; American, 67; Canadian, 130, 135; Fenians, 135; in relation to empire, 129; Irish, 62, 67, 74, 182; Irish-Canadian, 64; Spanish, 151, 154
nation-state, 127, 135, 150
Netherlands, 15. *See also* Holland
Nevis, 246
New Brunswick, 4, 6, 7, 9, 10–12, 32, 47–8, 51, 54, 65–6, 81, 103–4, 119, 163, 166, 170, 196
Newfoundland, 7, 48, 164
New France, 143
New Grenada, 15
Newman, John Henry, 102
New South Wales, 120, 195–8, 201, 203–5
New Zealand, 10, 16, 120, 165, 199, 203, 210–25, 228, 234, 248
New Zealand Wars, 215–18

Nicaragua, 15
Northern Rhodesia. *See* Zambia
Northwest Territories, 10, 14, 181
Nova Scotia, 3–4, 6–7, 10–12, 32, 37, 48, 51, 66, 81, 119, 163, 166, 168, 181–2, 196, 213
Nyasaland. *See* Malawi

O'Connell, Daniel, 144, 179
Ogelsby, J.C.M., 32, 34
Oka crisis, 87
Oneida, 80
Onondaga, 80–7
Ontario, 8, 66, 80, 82, 99, 104, 106, 115, 144, 187–8. *See also* Canada West
Orange Free State, 227–9, 231, 233
Orangeism, 73
Ottoman Empire, 29, 38

Palmerston, Lord, 170
Panama, 3
Papal States, 11, 17, 18, 101, 105–6, 118–19
Papineau, Louis-Joseph, 64
Paraguay, 31, 33
Parkes, Henry, 204
Paterson, John, 229
Peace of Westphalia (1648), 252
Pedi Kingdom, 230–1
Pedro I, 28
Pedro II, 34
Peel, Robert, 144
Peru, 31, 146
Peter's Pence. *See* Catholicism
Philippines, 18, 146–7
Pichette, Robert, 115
Piedmont, 11, 97–8, 115
Pius IX, 11, 98, 100–2, 105-6
Poland, 13

Pontifical Irish College. *See* Catholicism
Porter, Andrew, 161
potato famine, 102
Poundmaker, 10, 83
Pretoria Convention (1881), 231
Prince Alfred, 199
Prince Edward Island, 7, 10–12, 32, 48, 81
Prince of Wales, 199
Propaganda Fide (Congregation for the Propagation of the Faith). *See* Catholicism
Provisional Government (Ireland, 1867), 69
Prussia, 11, 15, 115, 119, 121
Puerto Rico, 18, 146–7, 245

Quebec, 7–8, 13, 16, 48, 74, 80, 98–100, 103–7, 110–26, 132, 144, 164–5, 184, 187–9. *See also* Canada East
Quebec Act (1774), 144
Quebec Conference (1864), 7, 10–11, 81
Queensland, 197
Queen Victoria, 61, 136, 152, 161, 164

race, 243–4: in relation to establishment of Canada, 82, 88; in relation to governance, 131–3, 184
Rameau de Saint-Père, François-Edme, 116
Rebellions of 1837–8 (Canada), 32, 36, 112, 145, 147, 150, 195
Reciprocity Treaty (1854), 32, 38, 49–50
reconciliation, 10, 17, 79, 85–90
Reconstruction (US), 48, 55, 67
Redmond, John, 184–5
Red River Rebellion, 120
Reeve, Henry, 171

Reform Act of 1867, 30
Report of the Commissioners from British North America Appointed to Inquire into the Trade of the West Indies, Mexico & Brazil, 32–4
Report of the Royal Commission on Aboriginal Peoples, 84, 87
representation by population, 38, 68, 104
Representation of the People Act, 1867 (UK), 169–70, 174
residential schools, 9–10, 84–5
responsible government, 28–9, 36–7, 68, 149, 168, 171–3, 185–8, 195–8, 205, 218–19, 227, 229, 233–5, 237: Canada as a model for Ireland, 178–9
Rhodes, Cecil, 232–3, 235, 238
Rhodesian Front, 237
Riel, Louis, 83, 145
Riker, William, 203
Roberts, William R., 64–5, 67
Rogers, Norman McL., 32
Roman Catholic Relief Act (UK, 1829), 100, 144
Romania, 121
Rouges (Party), 14, 64,
Royal Commission on Aboriginal Peoples. See *Report of the Royal Commission on Aboriginal Peoples*
Royal Proclamation of 1763, 82, 143
Royal tour to Canada (1860), 199
Russell, John, 36
Russell, Odo, 100
Russia, 5, 13, 49, 51, 72, 199, 201

Sagasta, Práxedes Mateo, 152
Saint-Domingue, 143, 146
Saint-Domingue crisis, 143
Sanfilippo, Matteo, 101

San Salvador, 15
Santo Domingo, 51
Savard, Pierre, 114
Scotland, 62, 120, 183
Scott, Duncan Campbell, 84–6
Scritture riferite in Congressi. See Catholicism
Second Anglo-Boer War. See South African War (1899–1902)
Second Reform Bill (UK). See *Representation of the People Act, 1867* (UK)
Second War of Independence (Cuba, 1895), 153
Selborne, Lord, 233
self-determination, 53, 111
self-government, 9, 28, 32, 128, 130, 149, 151–2, 178, 196–8, 234–7, 249–50
Seneca, 80
Seven Years War (1756–63), 143, 242, 245–6
Seward, William H., 49, 53–4
Sexton, Thomas, 188
Shepstone, Theophilus, 230
Sherman, General William T., 52
Silver, A.I., 112
Sinclair, Justice Murray, 89–90
slavery, 5, 18, 20, 48, 144–5, 147–8, 150, 152–3, 155, 199, 243, 245, 252
Smith, Andrew, 34, 165
Smith, Donald B., 81, 83
Smith, Ian, 237–8
Smuts, Jan, 235
South Africa, 5, 19, 167, 218, 226–41, 250
South African Act (1877), 230
South African League, 233
South African War (1899–1902), 19, 234–6, 238

270　Index

South Australia, 197–9, 202
Southern Rhodesia. *See* Zimbabwe
sovereignty, 151: Australia, 206; British West Indies, 243, 252; Indigneous peoples and North America, 80, 82, 90; Irish, 188; Maori, 215; monarchical (Canada), 145; Spanish, 152; Spanish-Americans, 146; Transvaal, 231
Spain, 11, 14, 18, 28, 31, 33, 143–57, 252
Spanish-American War (1898), 149, 242
Spanish Revolution (1868), 153
Stacey, C.P., 4, 37, 66, 168
St Albans raid, 49, 55
Stanley, Edward Henry, Earl of Derby, 128–9
Stanley, Frederick, 129
Stapleton, William, 244
Statham, Francis (1881), 231
Statute of Westminster, 1931, 29, 35
Stephens, James, 62–3
St Kitts, 246
St Patrick's Society of Montreal, 182
St Vincent, 246
suffrage. *See* voting
sugar, 18, 144, 155, 244–9
Sulpician Seminary. *See* Catholicism
Sumner, Senator Charles (US), 56
Swaziland, 235, 238–9
Sweeny, Bishop John (Saint John), 104, 107
Switzerland, 14–15, 115
Syllabus of Errors. See Catholicism

Tanzania, 238
Taranaki, 215–16, 219
Tasmania, 195–7, 204
terra nullius, 90
Texas, 33
Thembu people, 231

Thirty Years War, 252
Tilley, Samuel Leonard, 7
timber, 164
tobacco, 18, 147, 245
Tobago, 246, 252
Tone, Theobald Wolfe, 62
Transvaal, 226–34
treaty-making: with Indigenous peoples in British North America, 80–2, 86; with Mpondomise and Thembu people in South Africa, 231
Treaty of Paris, 144
Treaty of Vereeniging (1902), 234
Trudeau, Pierre E., 86
Truth and Reconciliation Commission, 79, 89–90
Tupper, Charles, 7–8
Tuscarora, 80

ultramontanism, 100, 118
Union Bill (Canada, 1822), 145
unionists (Ireland), 180, 183–9
Union of South Africa, 234, 236
United Irishmen rebellion (1798), 61
United Nations, 253
United Nations Declaration on the Rights of Indigenous Peoples (UNDRIP), 89
Upper Canada. *See* Canada West
US military threat to Canada (1860s), 4, 7–8, 12, 16, 17, 29, 37–8, 50, 53, 55, 56, 111, 130, 200, 202–4, 213. *See also* Canadian military threat to the United States; Fenians

Van Diemen's Land. *See* Tasmania
Vatican Council. *See* Catholicism
Venezuela, 15
Verne, Jules, 115–16

Victor Emmanuel II, 97
Victoria (Australia), 183–4, 197–8, 200–1, 205
Vidal, Alexander, 15
Voltaire, 112
von Apponyi, Count Rudolph, 128–9
von Bismarck, Otto, 112, 168
voting, 9, 12, 64, 68, 81, 132, 169, 172–4, 198, 232–5. *See also* democracy

Waikato, 215
Waite, Peter B., 4, 66
Wales, 120, 183
War of 1812 (Anglo-American), 47, 63–4, 80
War of Independence, Greece (1821–32), 242
War of Independence, Spain (1808–14), 154
War of Independence, United States (1776–83), 47, 54, 111
Wars of Independence, Spanish-American (1810–30), 242

Wellesley, Lord Lieutenant Richard, 144
Wentworth, W.C., 197
Western Australia, 197, 205
Westgarth, William, 198
Whitaker, Reginald, 67
White Paper (Canada, 1969), 86
Wilberforce, Robert, 102
Wiseman, Nicholas, 102
Wodehouse, Governor Philip (Cape), 229
Woodruff, William, 243
Wright, Donald, 40, 81, 83–4, 88

Xhosa people, 227–8, 230

Young, Sir John, 164
Young Ireland, 62, 69: exiles, 64; rebellion (1848), 62. *See also* Fenians; Ireland

Zambia, 236–7, 239
Zanjón Pact (1878), 148
Zimbabwe, 235–9
Zulu Kingdom, 227, 230–1

www.ingramcontent.com/pod-product-compliance
Lightning Source LLC
Chambersburg PA
CBHW030310080526
44584CB00012B/509